UNSTUCK

MOVING BEYOND DEFEAT

AMY HERNANDEZ

ECS

MINISTRIES

The Word to the World

Many ECS publications are also available in eBook formats.
For more information, visit our website www.ecsministries.org.

UnStuck: Moving Beyond Defeat

Amy Hernandez

Published by:
ECS Ministries
PO Box 1028
Dubuque, IA 52004-1028
phone: (563) 585-2070
email: ecsorders@ecsministries.org
website: www.ecsministries.org

First Edition 2015
Revised Edition 2016
Reprinted 2017

ISBN 978-1-59387-232-8

Code: B-UNSTUCK

Copyright © 2015, 2016 ECS Ministries

Edited by Helen Wieger

Printed in the United States of America

Contents

————————◆————————

Introduction

◆

Maybe you have wanted to work on your spiritual life for a variety of reasons, but whatever your motivation, eventually you grow discouraged. Why is it so hard? Why doesn't it stick? Why do you always end up back where you started? You've made progress before, but something keeps pulling you back as if you were bungee walking. Is this normal? Will you always find yourself back at the beginning again?

That's not quite what you were looking for, is it? You were hoping to be free from sin, pain, struggle, and doubts. You were hoping to arrive with the other spiritual giants and never be criticized or judged. You were hoping never to feel bad about yourself again.

Have you ever watched other believers, comparing your progress to theirs, as though they were spiritual competitors? Have you ever let your eyes gaze on those who seem far ahead, who seem never to struggle, and wondered, "What's wrong with me, why can't I stay strong like that?"

In his letter to the Galatians, Paul tells us that the desires of the flesh and the desires of the Spirit are in opposition. From this, I conclude that the Spirit and the flesh constantly work against each other, constantly oppose one another. Most of us don't like opposition, even when it is good for us. When my daughter tells me, "Mom, you really don't want to eat that donut; you know it won't help you lose weight," suddenly I want to eat that donut more than ever just because someone told me I shouldn't.

Opposition is exhausting. We instinctively avoid it, but in the spiritual life, opposition is good. If the Spirit is gaining control, the flesh will resist, and if the flesh is insisting on fulfilling its desires, the Spirit will tug against the natural self-satisfaction of your flesh. Either way, the struggle is healthy. It is better than giving in or giving up.

———————◆———————

Ever since Eve ate the fruit in the garden, Satan has been deceiving us, but hasn't been the only one. Our flesh blinds us, and misleads us. Our flesh creates clever counterparts so that, even though we have the Spirit and all the power that comes with Him, we find ourselves stuck in a loop repeating the same mistakes over and over again.

The apostle Paul wrote,

> *"If we live by the Spirit, let us also walk by the Spirit."*
> –Galatians 5:25

How does this work? Do you walk by the Spirit first and thus achieve death of the flesh? Or do you put the flesh to death and thus achieve walking by the Spirit? How can you know if you are walking by the Spirit or if you are putting confidence in your flesh? Can you be certain that your effort is completely powered by the Spirit? Does it count if it is half and half?

As a missionary in Mexico, I encountered a young woman whose struggles with sin resembled mine. Though I believed with all my heart that Christianity offered her the answer, I realized that I personally had not experienced enough victory in my own life to help her. All I could do was share her frustration and constant struggle. I felt like a child pretending to be a grown-up. That discovery must have signaled something in heaven, because the Lord put me in a trial that turned up the heat, put me in the press, squeezed the juice right out of me. The Lord and I got really honest in that trial where He showed me the ugly truth about my flesh and how I was keeping it alive, feeding it so that it would be my strength instead of Him.

I have written this book in three parts to help you expose the flesh and the many ways it is lurking about—all for the goal of crucifying it.

> **Prepare the Flesh for Death**

The first step is tackling the opposition, ie. the flesh. Because Satan can pinpoint your flesh tendencies with sharp accuracy, you need to be aware of them as well. You must know where your flesh is most vulnerable. You must know your flesh's weaknesses better than your enemy does.

> **Die to Self Daily**

Once identified, your flesh must be crucified. That's where you take up your cross every day. We will examine in Scripture four tools God uses to help us put the flesh to death. We will also explore how the flesh distorts the God-given purpose of those tools.

> **Walk Empowered by the Spirit**

Finally, by examining the role of the Spirit in our lives, we will learn why we must walk in complete dependence on the Spirit for truth, love, gifts, and prayer. We will also learn to recognize signs that the flesh is digging trenches that trap us and keep us stuck.

My prayer is that you will want to follow Christ by taking up your cross daily, by living every day with a death sentence. Dying to self is key to becoming unstuck, to becoming free to walk by the Spirit.

> **❝**
> *Dying to self is key to becoming unstuck.*
> **❞**

◆

Only the blind can see. Only the dead can live.

When Jesus healed a blind man on the Sabbath, the religious leaders couldn't see past their perceived broken law to the obvious: that only God could do such a miracle. Explaining the problem of their spiritual blindness, Jesus said to them, "For judgment I came into this world, that those who do not see may see, and that those who see may become blind." The religious leaders who heard this said, "We are not blind too, are we?" And Jesus said, "If you were blind, you would have no sin, but since you say, 'we see,' your sin remains" (John 9:39-41).

Admitting you are blind is the first step to seeing.

Admitting you are dead is the first step to living. Sounds counter-intuitive, doesn't it? Get used to it! Welcome to a walk of dying, where paradox is the norm, and where everything seems upside down.

Part 1

♦

Preparing the Flesh for Death

Chapter

1

Our Obsession

Identity Theft

Pendulum: a "mass hung from a fixed support so that it is able to swing freely under the influence of gravity."[1]

A pendulum has swing. Once a little movement is begun, gravity pulls the pendulum down. Kinetic energy keeps it swinging up again in the other direction. For a second it hits the heights, and then comes back down for another swing in the opposite direction. A pendulum has swing.

Our identity can act like a pendulum, can feel, for example, as if it is on a park swing. As believers in Jesus Christ, we say that our identity is in Him, but we don't always feel that way.

Imagine you are the "mass" of the pendulum sitting on a park swing and Jesus Christ is your fixed support. You look up, see Him, and think "my identity is in Christ; He defines who I am." But you are swinging, swinging back and forth from being good to being bad, from success to failure, from loved to ignored, from important to worthless. You are living life on a pendulum, on a swing, because your identity hangs on a chain, each link something that makes you feel good about yourself.

Someone ignored you. Bump. Your swing just got a little push from behind. Feeling a little irked, you begin to wonder why you aren't worthy of his notice. It is a tiny thought at first, but it stings just enough to make you feel bad about yourself. "What's wrong with me?" you think. "Why wouldn't he acknowledge my existence?"

What should you do?

If you are anything like me, you won't do the smart thing. Instead, you'll dwell on how bad it feels to be undervalued, lean back on thinking about how wrong he is to misjudge you, lean forward, feet tucked under, trying to understand why you're not worth his attention.

Back and forth, in full swing, the argument in your head intensifies. Negative thoughts about yourself pull you down to a darker place where you encounter anger, accusation and blame. You become consumed with convincing those around that you are worthy of their attention, with convincing yourself that you do matter. Success may come, but it will never last. You are swinging, and what goes up always comes down.

Where is Christ in this?

So engrossed in the swing, you've forgotten the support that is holding you, forgotten that Christ is your center! You are content to simply swing by Him, waving and shouting with each pass of the swing, "Hey Jesus, good seeing you. Glad you're still there. Catch you on the way back."

You've entered the pendulum effect where your value is constantly swinging, constantly fluctuating. You may think your identity is in Christ alone, but if you've got chains, you've got swing, and no matter how determined you are to be centered in Christ, you can't maintain that security. Seeking your identity in Christ when you feel bad about yourself is only half of the swing. What happens when you feel good about yourself? What happens when others make you feel loved, make you feel valuable? That value swings your identity in the other direction. It feels so good to be up high, free from those nagging doubts. Wouldn't it be great to always stay up here? But you can't because you are swinging and remember, what goes up must come down. What's going to happen when the swing drops? Will it stop in the center; will it return you to your identity in Christ? No it won't! You are going to swing right back to that awful side you hate to go to. Values you find in yourself apart from Christ are links in the chain that hold your swing. The longer the chain, the farther you will swing away from your center in Christ.

> *Your true value in Christ does not fluctuate.*

Our Obsession ◆ 13

But your true value in Christ exists on its own. It does not fluctuate, does not swing.

The Self-Worth Tank

As a child I desperately wanted to be liked. In the middle of my first grade year, we moved from Virginia to Tennessee. I discovered a loneliness I had never known before. The rest of the school year not a single student talked to me. Then that summer my family moved to another city and I entered a new school, this time dragging insecurity with me like a shadow. Inexplicably, the cutest, most popular girl in class befriended me. Through that experience, I learned the importance of being included by the right person, the value gained from being with the cool kid.

When we moved to Louisiana before my 7th grade year, my new best friend was not only the prettiest, most popular girl in the class, she was also the smartest. Again, I gained a sense of value and security through my friendship, but I could not trust that it would last. By this age, the conviction that everyone would eventually reject me was deeply rooted. I sought friendships because they were my biggest source of self-worth, but they were also my biggest threat of rejection. Quite unconsciously, I sought out people to make me feel more valuable, and it worked.

I was reading through Jeremiah and came to chapter 2, verse 13, when the words suddenly seemed to point directly at me, as if the Lord was saying, "You, Amy, have committed two evils, you have forsaken Me, the fountain of living waters, and hewn out cisterns for yourself, broken cisterns that can hold no water."

How ironic! I was so absorbed in fearing rejection, so busy seeking fulfillment through things or people outside of Christ, that I never considered that I was rejecting Him. I instinctively looked to others to infuse value into my

> **The "self-worth" tank is full of cracks.**

insecure little being. I was constantly building cisterns that couldn't hold water, and then feeling sorry for myself because I could never keep them full.

There is a flaw in this "self-worth" tank: it is full of cracks. You know this by experience. No matter how high the level of worth rises in your tank, it never stays there. That's because self-worth can't exist on its own. It needs the constant re-affirmation of others.

I lived like a self-worth junkie going through the highs and withdrawals of an addict, all the while entertaining the delusion that I found my value in Christ alone!

What a farce!

This obsession with our own value isn't just irony, or folly, or even insanity. It is evil!

> **"**
> *Obsession with your own value isn't just folly; it's evil!*
> **"**

Our Value System

One afternoon, when I was in college, I returned to my room and was shocked to find my roommate's bed buried in 3 feet of clothing! It looked as if her closet had blown up. She was the most recent victim of the "I can't find anything to wear" syndrome.

You know what we really mean when we say, "I have nothing to wear." We mean there is nothing to wear that makes us feel good.

Your value system is like a closet. On any given day, you open it to see what you could put on to make yourself feel better. "Hmmm," you say to yourself, "maybe I'll try this," and you pull out "being needed." "No," you think, "I need something better today." So you start looking through the closet, moving the hangers one by one, "looking beautiful," "attention from the opposite sex," "something I own," "the best grade," "popularity," "being useful," "recognition," etc.

What's in your values closet? What do you pull out to make yourself feel good? Are any of these in your closet?

➢ beauty
➢ body image
➢ abilities
➢ the admiration of important people
➢ being appreciated

➢ getting praise
➢ being treated fairly
➢ seeing justice done
➢ attention from men
➢ getting a boyfriend or girlfriend
➢ marriage
➢ having a father who loves you
➢ being a [good] parent
➢ having a family
➢ the best possessions
➢ a good education
➢ a high paying job
➢ involvement in ministries
➢ spiritual gifts
➢ a position of importance
➢ good behavior
➢ being right
➢ keeping a standard of perfection
➢ not disappointing others
➢ others' good opinion of you
➢ receiving approval
➢ making friends
➢ being preferred by your friends
➢ being popular
➢ having lots of money
➢ accomplishments

Are any of these good substitutes for your value in Christ? Do any of them make you content? Is there anything hanging in your "closet" that you should keep?

The Irony of It All

There is an ironic side to this value system.

I started noticing a correlation between what I valued and what I feared. Since I wanted people to like me, my biggest fear was rejection. Being useful made me feel valuable. Consequently, I feared not being needed. Because giving my opinion made me feel significant, not being consulted brought out my fear that I was insignificant. I liked being the one others confided in, so when I wasn't first to hear the news, I felt insecure.

Here's the irony of it all.

Usually, we assume that to avoid loss we must accumulate more, but have you ever considered that the more you gain the more you have to lose. Hence, rather than solving the problem of loss by amassing possessions, we magnify it. We can never fully achieve, never fully have all those things that make us feel good about ourselves. If anything increases our sense of worth, then the loss of even the tiniest amount of that thing can decrease it.

Were you hoping to gain confidence, to be more secure? I'm guessing that's not working out well for you.

Look back in your value closet and see the fear tucked behind each item.

➢ With beauty comes the fear of whatever makes you feel ugly.
➢ With a body image comes the fear of looking fat, having pimples, or experiencing a bad hair day.
➢ With your abilities comes the fear of someone being better than you.
➢ With the admiration of important people comes the fear of what others say about you.
➢ With others showing you appreciation comes the fear of being overlooked.
➢ With getting praise comes the fear of criticism.
➢ With fair treatment comes the fear of injustice.
➢ With attention from the opposite sex comes the fear of abandonment or of never getting married.

➢ With having a family comes the fear of being barren, of criticism of your children, of the death of a child.

➢ With making lots of money comes the fear of being poor.

➢ With involvement in ministries comes the fear of your ministry being taken away.

➢ With a position of importance comes the fear of not being consulted.

➢ With being right comes the fear of being wrong.

➢ With being perfect comes the fear of being less than perfect.

➢ With not disappointing others comes the fear of making mistakes.

➢ With others' good opinion comes the fear of what others think.

➢ With receiving approval comes the fear of disapproval.

➢ With making friends comes the fear of rejection.

➢ With being preferred comes the fear of being excluded.

➢ With being popular comes the fear of being mocked.

➢ With accomplishments comes the fear of failures.

With each item that gives you value, a fear is included. Can you ever get enough significance, build up enough value, to block all fears?

Fears are tricky. We often push them away to some dark corner where we never have to see them again and pretend they don't exist, but then, at the tiniest mention of them, tears well up in our eyes. Why do fears have such influence on us? Why do they control us?

Staring Down the Dog

My husband and I often find ourselves embroiled in a fierce argument, only to conclude that we are actually in agreement. Since I'm the argumentative one and most likely at fault for keeping the argument going, I feel quite silly realizing, at last, that we agree.

When you try to prove that a lie is not the truth, you are caught in a silly argument. Think about that for a moment. A lie, by its very definition, can't be the truth. A lie is a lie; it doesn't need to be proven false. You could spend countless hours and immense energy on a pointless attempt to prove a lie false!

Don't try to conquer a fear by arguing with it!

Look at your fear!

Stare it down and call it what it is: a big fat lie!

When you live guided by fears, you live by lies, which continue to feed your fears and eventually lead you to sin. I'll demonstrate with a few of my old lies.

------------------◆------------------

LIE #1: I must be perfect.

Being perfect makes me acceptable. Mistakes are unacceptable. I can be perfect.

RESULT: I fear failure. I fear being less than perfect. I respond with outbursts of anger and self-pity when others point out my imperfections.

LIE #2: I deserve to be treated fairly.

I can judge what is just and fair. Injustice is unacceptable. I deserve better.

RESULT: I am argumentative and defensive. I lash out at others. I feel war going on inside me.

LIE #3: If people really knew me, they would reject me.

Eventually everyone rejects me. I need to fix myself so people will like me. I'm worthless.

RESULT: I fear rejection. I am jealous. I view people as threats.

LIE #4: Guilt and remorse are the same as repentance.

Feeling bad about myself and feeling sorry for my sin are the same. I ought to feel bad about myself.

RESULT: I don't confess my sin. I don't live by grace. I don't show grace to others. I'm unforgiving.

Am I Good Enough?

Once upon a time there was a little pig that lived in the barn and played in the mud every day. She was happy and content, free to wander and roll in her favorite mud ponds.

One day, however, she spied a little pig playing outside with the children. This other little pig lived in the house and had such beautiful pink skin. She was loved and cherished and pampered. The children hugged her and called her sweet names. She got to spend all day with them. They fed her special treats and gave her little gifts.

The little barnyard pig looked on, thinking "I'm not much different from that little pig. I wonder why no one treats me like that." The little pig's happy contentment vanished, and in its place came an intense longing to be just like the house pig. Then she noticed that, unlike the clean, pretty pink pig, she was covered in mud. Of course, she concluded, clean, pink skin would make me worthy of living in the house. The little pig went in search of water where she could wash off the mud and find happiness.

Suddenly an awful thought stopped her. What if underneath the mud she was not pink? What if, after washing, she discovered she was not as beautiful as the other pig, not worthy of being chosen? Fear wrapped around her little heart and paralyzed her. "It's not the mud that makes me unworthy," she thought with horror, "I'm just not good enough." More than anything, she wanted to have pink skin, to be loved like the other little pig. Without that love she could never be happy.

Soon the fear of discovering that she was unlovable grew greater than her desire to be loved. That fear drove her back to the mud pit. Her only refuge was to put on more mud and hide behind a thicker layer. She couldn't stray far from the mud. It was her one place of security. As long as she stayed there, she wouldn't have to face that awful fear again.

At times she felt trapped and longed to be free, but at the slightest hint that she was losing a layer of mud, she resigned herself to her fate. She lived as she always had, only now the mud, instead of making her happy and content, reminded her that she would never, ever be good enough to be loved.

—————————◆—————————

Like that little pig, we can resign ourselves to eternal wallowing. We add layer upon layer to hide the ugliness we fear. We find security in building walls to keep in what little love we think we have. Our walls might be fat, depression, anger, rebellion, self-harm, alcohol, drugs, or obnoxious behavior. Our walls keep others away and distract us from the real pain, the real fear. We provide others with an excuse to reject us. That way we can't be rejected for the feared unworthiness that we've worked hard to hide. But no matter how deep we bury our fears, we remain desperately unhappy, afraid of being seen for who we are. We wish someone would know and love us anyway, but we are confident no one will, because we don't deserve love.

But what is the awful fear? How do we know if it is true?

Deep down, all of us have feared that we don't matter, that we are not worthy of love. In response, we may have become obsessed with our own worthiness, with feeling good about ourselves. It should not surprise us that the world is also obsessed with worth. We are drawn to seek our own self-worth and find our own significance because we want to be valued, wanted and, ultimately, loved.

The truth is that in Christ we are loved far beyond anything we can imagine or deserve. Can anyone love us more than our Creator who died for us? The truth is that everything we have is given to us in grace. Why do we act as though we deserve more? The truth is that there is nothing good in us apart from Christ. Why are we distressed when people think we're bad? We aren't perfect. Why do we try to make others think we are? That's a lie!

The truth is that Christ has bought us with His precious blood and we are not our own. We have no more right to call ourselves worthless than to claim honor for ourselves. How we feel about ourselves today, whether good or bad, has no bearing on who we are in Christ.

In Christ, we find all that we are, all that we need, all that gives us value. He is the only Person who makes us significant. Our identity is in Him and He is our Rock, solid, unchanging, and secure.

Considering this value that we have in Christ, I have to ask the question: is self-worth worth having? Furthermore, is self-worth a product of the Spirit or of the flesh? By the flesh I mean anything we are or have apart from Christ.

The flesh prompts us to seek our worth outside of Christ; the flesh deceives us into believing that we need to be more valuable, need to find more love and acceptance, need more satisfaction. When we seek to add to our value, we are saying, essentially, that Christ's value is not enough. That is not living by the truth of who we are in Christ. Finding our identity in Christ means He is our only source of value and worth. It doesn't mean that He makes us valuable to others, or that He increases our value as if we had any to begin with. It doesn't mean that He makes us feel good about ourselves. That is what the flesh wants.

> "
> *This obsession with self-worth is a snare of lies and fear.*
> "

Paul wrote, "If by the Spirit you are putting to death the deeds of the body, you will live" (Rom. 8:13b). But instead of executing the flesh, we often pamper it. We keep it alive because we rely on it to feel good, to do the "good" that others can see, to build our confidence and sense of self-worth. This obsession is what trips us up, makes us feel that we aren't growing spiritually, and makes us tired of ourselves. This obsession with self-worth is the flesh's crowning triumph of deception. But for us it is a snare of lies and fear.

Chapter

2

Deadly Desire

The Flesh Desires

When my daughter was three years old, I was helping her memorize Psalm 23:1, "The Lord is my Shepherd I shall not want." Typically I taught her verses by repeating them throughout the day, and, after a few hours, asking her to repeat it back. This method usually worked, but this time she just looked at me and refused. "I don't like that," she said.

What?! What do you mean, you don't like that? This is the Bible so you can't say you don't like it. Besides, you just have to memorize it to recite verses for your prizes, not because you like it.

Even as a child, she taught me a lesson on integrity. If she couldn't mean it, she wouldn't say it, and she definitely could not say, "I shall not want." Of course, she didn't know that the older English meant "I shall not lack anything," or that the psalmist was saying the Lord is such a good supplier of his needs that he has no needs left. She thought it meant she would have to give up wanting things, and she didn't like that.

To be honest, I don't like it either. I am a big "want" machine. All day long I think about what I want. If something gets in the way of my getting what I want, I get angry.

I can see how the word "want" shifted from the original meaning "to lack", and take on today's meaning "to desire." When you don't have something, you desire it, right? Even today you have probably thought of at least one thing you lack and therefore want. Want is driven by those things we don't have. Lacking something, however, isn't the only trigger for desire. Have you noticed that you can have the best of everything and still desire more?

I'll tell myself that one bowl of ice cream is enough, but before I even finish the bowl, I'm already dreaming about getting more. Indulging desires does not bring contentment, nor does having needs met bring satisfaction.

When is the flesh truly satisfied? Where's the shut off valve when it gets full? I think mine is broken.

> **"**
> *Indulging desires does not bring contentment.*
> **"**

Consider Eve as an example of how we want more when we already have enough. Eve is living in the most beautiful, idyllic place ever encountered on earth. She gets her fruit right off the tree when it's ripest, full of delicious flavor. She can satisfy her hunger any time with a divine banquet of food. And if that wasn't enough, she has intimate evening walks with God Himself. Can you imagine that! She can ask Him anything and He can explain it to her. The best of everything is hers! She has it all, literally. What else could she want?

God had told Adam and Eve that they were free to eat from any tree in the garden except for one. If they did eat of that one tree, they would die (Gen. 2:16-17). Adam and Eve took this so seriously that they wouldn't even touch the fruit on that tree. You'd think that Eve would be content enough to leave it alone. You'd think Satan would not have had a chance of deceiving her when all her needs were already satisfied. So what in the world made Eve want to eat the fruit? Certainly not need. The deadly became desirable.

> *"When the woman saw that the tree was good for food, and that it was a delight to the eyes, and that the tree was desirable to make one wise, she took from its fruit and ate; and she gave also to her husband with her, and he ate."*
>
> –Genesis 3:6

How did something poisonous appear good and pleasant? Why did Eve have a strong desire to taste what would bring death? What had changed? Was the fruit different?

No, the fruit had not changed, nor had God's command. The difference was in Eve's perception. She saw that the fruit was "good and delightful and desirable." Her eyes looked on what she couldn't have, her desire was triggered and she longed to satisfy that desire with what was bad for her. Eve had lifted the lid to take a peek at sin and had fallen in.

We don't have to look far to find sin and deceit. In fact, we don't have to look any further than ourselves. As Scripture says,

> *"For from within, out of the heart of men, proceed the evil thoughts, fornications, thefts, murders, adulteries, deeds of coveting, and wickedness, as well as deceit, sensuality, envy, slander, pride, and foolishness. All these evil things proceed from within and defile the man."*
>
> –Mark 7:21-23

> *"You lay aside the old self, which is being corrupted in accordance with the lusts of deceit."*
>
> –Ephesians 4:22

> *"The heart is more deceitful than all else and is desperately sick; Who can understand it? I, the Lord, search the heart, I test the mind."*
>
> –Jeremiah 17:9-10a

> *"But encourage one another day after day, as long as it is still called 'Today,' so that none of you will be hardened by the deceitfulness of sin "*
>
> –Hebrews 3:13

Can you believe that you are susceptible to being deceived by your flesh? I don't mean that the flesh is playing an innocent little trick on you. I'm saying that the flesh deceives you with deadly desire.

Like Eve's, our eyes deceive us. Our old self is corrupted by deceitful lusts. Our heart deceives us and is hardened by the deceitfulness of sin; it is a fountain of evil. What hope do we have of outsmarting it, of fixing it, or of even improving it?

None!

The Flesh Appeals

Achin couldn't resist the appeal of the flesh.

When the Lord broke down the walls of Jericho before the people of Israel, God commanded the people not to take anything from the city. But Achin did. He later explained,

> *"When I saw among the spoil a beautiful cloak from Shinar, and 200 shekels of silver, and a bar of gold weighing 50 shekels, then I coveted them and took them."*
>
> –Joshua 7:21, ESV

His eye spotted that beautiful cloak and he was hooked. He gave in to the cravings of his flesh. His lust eventually led to a disastrous defeat for the whole nation.

In her book "When God Weeps," Joni Eareckson Tada writes, "You'll never catch me lingering in the lingerie department where they display tall, elegant mannequins wearing beautiful, silk negligees."[1] "Why not? What's wrong with that?" you ask. Joni is paralyzed from the neck down. Mannequins can do something that she can't: they can stand and look attractive in those flowing gowns.

Choosing to gaze on what you don't have or can't do arouses lustful passions. Often we are drawn to look at the very things that make us feel bad about ourselves. Too often, we let ourselves stare. You see someone with that relationship you've always wanted, someone getting more praise or more laughs, someone smarter, prettier, skinnier, more popular, or more loved. Suddenly you feel unsure. You've been hooked by your flesh, and it won't be long before you sink (or swing) into that "I feel so bad about myself" place. All your focus is on making yourself feel better.

> **"**
> *Choosing to gaze on what you don't have arouses lustful passions.*
> **"**

Adam sees Eve holding the forbidden fruit towards him, inviting him to eat with her. What is going through his mind? Has he thought through the implications of what she has done? She's eaten the fruit and death has separated them. Now he has a choice. He can choose to not eat the fruit and have eternity with God, separated from Eve, or he can take the fruit, eat it, and be restored to Eve, but separated from God. He chooses separation from God. I wonder what was more appealing to Adam: the fruit or Eve.

The Flesh Enslaves

Flesh has a driving passion to be considered better, to make life better for itself. It also has a strong instinct for self-preservation. We, in the flesh, trust ourselves to know what is good for us; we believe our desires will bring us freedom and doubt the goodness of God's desires for us. Do not be deceived: the flesh does not desire our good. The flesh desires slavery.

"That's absurd!" you say, "Who in their right mind would desire slavery? The flesh could not want to enslave me!"

Remember how God came to Moses with a plan to take the Israelites out of Egypt?

> *"I have surely seen the affliction of My people who are in Egypt, and have given heed to their cry because of their taskmasters, for I am aware of their sufferings."*
> –Exodus 3:7

> *"The cry of the sons of Israel have come to Me, furthermore, I have seen the oppression with which the Egyptians are oppressing them."*
> –Exodus 3:9

The Israelites' life in Egypt had been slavery. God miraculously led an entire nation of 2 million people out of slavery in one of the most powerful countries of the time. They danced the dance of freedom— until they got trapped between the Red Sea and Pharaoh's army.

Then they said (you won't believe this!),

> *"Is it because there were no graves in Egypt that you have taken us away to die in the wilderness? Why have you dealt with us in this way, bringing us out of Egypt? Is this not the word that we spoke to you in*

> *Egypt, saying, 'leave us alone that we may serve the*
> *Egyptians'? For it would have been better for us to*
> *serve the Egyptians than to die in the wilderness."*
>
> –Exodus 14:11-12

They feared death and thought slavery would be better.

But then God revealed His incredible power to save them, once again, by leading, may I remind you, a nation of 2 million people between two walls of water and then drowning Pharaoh's army in that same water. In all of this, not a single Israelite died and not a single battle was fought. This was cause for great rejoicing, for shaking the tambourines, and for more dancing, until a month later.

Then this is what they had to say,

> *"Would that we had died by the Lord's hand in the land*
> *of Egypt, when we sat by the pots of meat, when we ate*
> *bread to the full; for you have brought us out into this*
> *wilderness to kill this whole assembly with hunger."*
>
> –Exodus 16:3

They preferred being slaves with full stomachs, over death in the wilderness. They would rather be slaves with pots of meat than worship the one true God in the wilderness. The Lord graciously fed them with bread from heaven.

At Rephidim, there was no water, and the people said,

> *"Why, now, have you brought us up from Egypt, to kill*
> *us and our children and our livestock with thirst?"*
>
> –Exodus 17:3

They feared dying of thirst, so the Lord gave them water from a rock.

At Mt. Sinai, Moses brought the people to the foot of the mountain to meet God, and God revealed Himself in trumpets blasting and thunder, in a mountain engulfed by fire, smoke and lightning, and in a violent earthquake. This was their God who brought them out of Egypt and they were terrified.

A year later they left Mt Sinai. Three days into their journey, the grumbling started again.

> *"We remember the fish which we used to eat free in*
> *Egypt, the cucumbers and the melons and the leeks and*
> *the onions and the garlic, but now our appetite is gone.*
> *There is nothing at all to look at except this manna."*
> –Numbers 11:5-6

Unbelievable isn't it? They longed to be back in Egypt so that they could eat all the fish, cucumbers, melons, leeks, onions and garlic that they wanted! God had promised them a land flowing with milk and honey, freedom to live in their own country and freedom to worship Him. They wanted something else, something they thought was better, easier. So when the Israelites finally reached that land, they were too afraid to enter because they feared that the people of the land were too strong to fight in battle.

> *"And all the sons of Israel grumbled against Moses and*
> *Aaron; and the whole congregation said to them, 'Would*
> *that we had died in the land of Egypt!"*
> –Numbers 14:2

Oh no, not Egypt again!

> *"Or would that we had died in the wilderness!"*
> –Numbers 14:2

So now they think the wilderness is a better place to die.

> *"Why is the Lord bringing us into this land, to fall by*
> *the sword? Our wives and our little ones will become*
> *plunder; would it not be better for us to return to*
> *Egypt?"*
> –Numbers 14:3

Right, the Lord went through all that trouble to bring them out of the land of Egypt just so they could be killed and their wives and children be made slaves again. Well, now they get their wish. They will die in the wilderness.

Could these Israelites possibly have more complaining to do?

> *"Why then have you (Moses) brought the Lord's*
> *assembly into this wilderness, for us and our beasts to*
> *die here? Why have you made us come up from Egypt,*
> *to bring us in to this wretched place? It is not a place*

> *of grain or figs or vines or pomegranates, nor is there*
> *water to drink."*
>
> –Numbers 20:4-5

Only three days after walking between walls of sea, three days after seeing the Lord's awesome power destroy the whole Egyptian army, they lust after Egypt. Three days of hardship and they want slavery again. Only three days of journeying from the mountain where they heard God's voice and all they can remember are the leeks, garlic, and onions of Egypt. They exaggerate the situation, misrepresent the Lord, and twist the truth to make the past seem better. Are we much different?

Like the Israelites, our flesh hates to suffer and will always choose to please itself, even if that means being enslaved.

> *Your flesh hates to suffer and will always choose to please itself.*

Flesh desires slavery.

◆

Moses had a different attitude.

> *"By faith Moses, when he had grown up, refused to be*
> *called the son of Pharaoh's daughter; choosing rather*
> *to endure ill-treatment with the people of God, than*
> *to enjoy the passing pleasures of sin; considering the*
> *reproach of Christ greater riches than the treasures of*
> *Egypt; for he was looking to the reward."*
>
> –Hebrews 11:24-26

The flesh wants you to go back to "Egypt," back to slavery in sin, but that isn't who you are in Christ.

> *"Therefore there is now no condemnation for those*
> *who are in Christ Jesus. For the law of the Spirit of*
> *life in Christ Jesus has set you free from the law of sin*
> *and of death. For what the Law could not do, weak as*
> *it was through the flesh, God did: sending His own Son*
> *in the likeness of sinful flesh and as an offering for sin,*
> *He condemned sin in the flesh, so that the requirement*
> *of the Law might be fulfilled in us, who do not walk*
> *according to the flesh, but according to the Spirit."*
>
> –Romans 8:1-4

Do you assume that your flesh wants what is best for you? Do you trust your flesh to make the best choice?

In Christ we have the best that exists, but we are tempted to prefer what we can do for ourselves, what this world offers, even though it fails miserably and leaves us craving more. We can't shake that nagging feeling that if we could just do this or have that, our lives would be better.

Just the other day the thought breezed into my mind: "If I was just thin, I'd be happy." Bunk and hogwash! Why does the grass always look greener on the other side? If I have Christ and He is all I need, why do I continue to feel that I'm not good enough, that I need more to be happy?

The flesh enslaves us to sin, to the fulfillment of selfish desires. The flesh compels us to look inward to satisfy our needs, but the flesh is never satisfied.

The Flesh Deceives

In Mexico, kids line up to be blindfolded and handed a stick to swing wildly, hoping to hit a piñata full of candy. The rest of us stand around and make sport of them. We shout directions: higher, lower, to your right, to your left. Some directions are good, but most are misleading. How do the kids know who to trust, which voice is telling the truth?

I have heard that when a pilot flies through a storm, his senses tell him something totally different from what the instrument panel says. He has to fight against what his senses tell him to do and follow something else. His senses are untrustworthy.

When we find ourselves blinded and lost in an emotional storm, we are easily confused and unsure of which voice to follow. The flesh calls out directions. Will any of them lead us out of the torment? Are any trustworthy?

Many times my head and heart have felt like a swirling mass of dark clouds and confusion. I have entered emotional fogs where I couldn't see, but I could feel with such intensity that I wanted to cry. I have known the desperate desire to get out of the fog before it turned into a black cloud.

Are you familiar with that swirling turmoil of thoughts that leave you feeling lost and confused? Have you ever felt desperate to escape, but hopeless to find a way? The fruit of the Spirit is peace, not turmoil and confusion. This black fog is a product of the flesh.

Feelings are voices of the flesh that give terrible directions. Follow them and, more often than not, you'll find yourself circling deeper into the storm. Argue and reason with them and you'll do no better.

Let's get something clear: the flesh will never guide you into the truth!

The flesh will deceive and mislead you. The Spirit is your only guide to the truth and the only Person who can lead you out into the sunshine. Ask Him to show you the truth. If you follow His directions and are still in the fog, you probably got distracted by something the flesh threw at you.

Imagine playing tennis by yourself. If you keep returning the ball, the game will never stop. Engaging with the flesh is like that. The flesh will throw things at you that will draw your attention away from the Spirit's directions. These might be things like getting defensive, anger at unjust treatment, or feeling offended. If you want the Spirit to guide you out of the fog, you have to stop returning the flesh's balls. Don't agree when the flesh tells you that you are right to justify yourself. Don't get distracted by how much you've been hurt. Don't play the game with the flesh by affirming your feelings. Don't throw up your hands and say that prayer doesn't work. And definitely don't try to find your way out by reversing your steps. Trying to work your way out by reasoning how you got there or by arguing with yourself will not only waste time, it will dig you a deeper hole.

The flesh has lured you into this storm. It isn't going to lead you back out. What's worse, it isn't just calling out misleading directions, it's also appealing to the cravings of the flesh. The flesh entices us to take pleasure in sick things. The flesh will make it appealing to feel hurt, will make self-pity attractive, and will lure you with feelings of guilt. The flesh will even make self-condemnation seem appealing.

Maybe it isn't so surprising that the Israelites wanted to go back to Egypt.

This is your opposition. Expose it!

Chapter

3

The Opposition

I remember the first time I realized that my jealousy was sin.

For six years I had wanted to be pregnant. Funny how we think of that in years when, in reality, the hope of pregnancy rises and falls monthly. For 72 months I had hoped that this was the month when my dream of having a baby would come true. So when a close friend announced that she was expecting, after trying for only one month, I was devastated. Back and forth I went with God about my pain, round and round in bitterness and anger, always asking "why me?" I hated feeling hurt, but I didn't want to let go of the pain either.

I have found that feeling hurt is a distracting detour sign pointing me away from dealing with my own sin. When I follow the signs of my hurt, I avoid the signs the Spirit puts up to convict me of my sin. So, there I was, faithfully following the wrong signs, even though they kept bringing me back to the same place. And there I would be today if God, in His grace, had not gotten my attention with a sign of His own.

I was reading the Bible, clueless of its sword-like quality, when the Spirit showed me what was in my heart. There, on God's "billboard," in big ugly letters, was JEALOUSY. I was horrified to realize that, for as long as I could remember, I had given in to jealousy. I had carried that despicable thing around with me everywhere, but I had never given it a name, never acknowledged that it was sin.

As a young child, I had been convicted that I was a sinner. I believed that Jesus Christ's death on the cross was the only payment for my sin acceptable to God. But in the two decades since, I had never been broken like this, never wept over my sin, never confessed my jealousy as an offense to God.

What an amazing relief I felt after I confessed my jealousy! It was as though I had been cleaned up and made beautiful inside. It felt good to know that the Lord had done this and that I would be a better tool in His hands. Now that I had felt the dagger of conviction, I wasn't about to give in to that sin again.

Wrong! I grossly underestimated my flesh. It wasn't long before I was struggling with jealousy again. Okay, I was back in the sin, but at least now I was able to catch it before it got out of hand, right?

No, not right! Instead, I would continue in jealousy until I was knee deep in the muck of my sin. As painful as my disappointment was with myself, I wouldn't step out of the muck. I just sat down and wallowed in it. Dreadfully tired of myself, I thought the Lord must be also.

Muck: moist farmyard dung; manure. Also known as guck, mire, mud, ooze, slime, slop.

In a 1909 issue of Popular Mechanics, Henry Haven Windsor writes, "Mud holds an anchor best of all, as it allows the anchor to dig deep down and not only holds firm by hooking onto the mud, but by the suction as well. Some people cannot understand how mud bottom forms a good anchorage; but if these will take off their shoes and stockings some day and walk through shallow water and mud where they sink six inches or so into that mud, the principle will be satisfactorily explained."[1]

If you drop something in the mud, not only does it sink in, it gets sucked in. Sin is like mud. The longer you stand in it, the deeper you sink and the stronger the suction becomes. Do you find yourself repeatedly stepping into the same muck of sin? Do you wonder at times if you have grown spiritually at all? When we think we are strong enough to resist temptation, we fail to take into account the suction created by the muck of our sin.

We have a natural inclination in us to sin; it is called "the flesh" or "the natural man." We are born with this tendency to put ourselves first, to satisfy our needs, to be selfish. Our sin stains us, bringing spiritual death. The only cure is the blood of Jesus Christ. Yet we, who have put our faith in Jesus and been spiritually reborn, continue to struggle with sin, baffled by the weakness that keeps us repeating defeat. Why is it so hard to be spiritual?

In Galatians, Paul tells us

> *"The desires of the flesh are against the Spirit, and the desires of the Spirit are against the flesh, for these are opposed to each other, to keep you from doing the things you want to do."*
>
> –Galatians 5:17, ESV

I read the words "to keep you from doing the things you want to do," and I think to myself, "What is it that I want to do?" I have a vision of myself wanting to do good and trying to be godly. But then I complain that it is too hard and take the easy way out. Why must it be so difficult to love others? It is much easier to exclude them, to avoid them, or to hate them. But that easy way always lands me right back in the muck. Again!

There are things appealing to the flesh that we reach out and grab without thinking. We do what is natural, without a thought about whether it is right or wrong. That's what I believe it means to carry out the desires of the flesh. Each time we default to doing what is natural to us, we are choosing not to live by the Spirit.

> **"**
> *Living by what comes naturally is like living in muck.*
> **"**

The flesh is always lurking about and most of the time we don't see it, not even when we fall into sin. Flesh is behind the desire to feel good about ourselves. Flesh has an insatiable appetite so that even when it is fed, it demands more. Flesh always puts ME first, asking "how does this affect me?" When we feel threatened, hurt or rejected, that's flesh. When we want others to notice us and be impressed with what we're doing, that's flesh. When we refuse to suffer, that's flesh. Flesh surfaces in the guilt that follows confession, in anger and rage, in jealousy and fear, in self-love, self-hate, self-pity, self-sufficiency, revenge, insecurity, conflict, gluttony, lust, deception, hate, hurt, discouragement, comparing, complaining, rebellion, and rivalry, to name just a few.

These are so common in our existence, so natural in our lives, that we almost forget they are there. We've grown to tolerate them, even telling ourselves that we have a right to pursue them. Living by what comes naturally is like living in muck. It is living by the flesh and it is what keeps us stuck, what makes us feel that we aren't growing spiritually, what makes us so tired of ourselves.

Spiritual Hearing Aids

That day the Spirit convicted me, I was reading in Galatians. Preparing to be the M.C. for a conference on the fruit of the Spirit, I wanted to sound as though I knew what I was introducing. Context in the Bible is everything, so I read the verses leading up to the fruit.

> *"Now the deeds of the flesh are evident, which are: immorality, impurity, sensuality, idolatry, sorcery, enmities, strife, jealousy, outbursts of anger, disputes, dissensions, factions, envying, drunkenness, carousing, and things like these."*
>
> –Galatians 5:19-21a

There it was, "jealousy." That was the first time I recognized that I had a major problem with this sin. It wasn't the first time I had read this verse. Why had I easily ignored it, I wondered? Why had God's Word not pierced through my spiritual complacency and stubbornness before? Did I really think I could live the Christian life while tolerating so much fleshly behavior? Had I grown immune to the words of Scripture, 'tone deaf' to their power to correct me? If I could live 20 years as a child of God without grieving my sin, something was seriously wrong. If I had grown deaf, I needed some spiritual 'hearing aids'. The reality of my failure scared me, and I was afraid of repeating it.

> **❝**
>
> *Your job is to crucify the flesh, leaving the Spirit to produce fruit from a supernatural seed.*
>
> **❞**

Does the thought of spiritual failure scare you? Scrutiny of our flesh is uncomfortable, so we prefer to skip ahead and search ourselves for evidence of the Spirit's fruit. If we can't find any, we quickly grow some of our own and make it pretty. We don't want to spend a lot of time rooting out what is ugly.

Our job is not to produce spiritual fruit to cover the flesh. Our job is to crucify the flesh, leaving the Spirit to produce fruit from a supernatural seed. You can only walk by the Spirit once your flesh has been put to death. And for that sinful, natural side of your flesh to die, it must be exposed.

The identity of the flesh is . . .

- self-satisfaction
- selfish sexual pleasure: fantasy, pornography, masturbation
- looking sexy
- exerting power over others
- independence from God
- ME-first attitude
- fame
- celebrity status
- depression
- anxiety
- panic
- control
- complaining
- pride
- jealousy
- envy
- anger
- rage
- venting
- temper tantrums
- outburst of anger

- drunkenness
- gambling
- adultery
- binge eating
- pity parties
- gossip fests
- lying
- deceitfulness
- hostility
- suspicion
- quarreling
- controversy
- conspiracy
- scandal
- being offended
- holding grudges
- finding fault
- dividing friends
- making enemies
- taking pleasure in pitting people against each other
- influencing people to join your side
- insisting on your way
- refusing to accept humble positions
- needing to be right
- trying to "out-do" someone else
- pleasure in inflicting pain on others or on self
- self-hate

Since the flesh is always in opposition to the Spirit, it manifests itself as opposite to the fruit as well. These too are evidence of the flesh.

➤ selfishness	➤ self-absorption
➤ hate	➤ unreliability
➤ disdain	➤ inconsistency
➤ discontentment	➤ negligence
➤ bitterness	➤ giving up easily
➤ not forgiving	➤ harshness
➤ conflict	➤ a critical spirit
➤ threats	➤ roughness
➤ fear	➤ rudeness
➤ revenge	➤ indulgence
➤ irritation	➤ impulsivity
➤ cruelty	➤ gluttony
➤ meanness	➤ laziness
➤ stinginess	➤ lack of discipline

Don't just examine yourself for the fruit of the Spirit; also watch yourself for the fruit of the flesh. The flesh is the one hindrance to the Spirit's work in your spiritual life, but seeing it alive and kicking can seem too disheartening, even too disgusting. The temptation to give up on identifying your flesh when what you see dismays you is exactly what the flesh would have you do.

All the Good I Do

Because the flesh is good at keeping out of sight, keeping you blissfully unaware of its tactics, the majority of this book is devoted to exposing flesh's tricks.

> "The Searchlight of the Spirit exposes us to ourselves, and such a discovery leaves us appalled. How can even He who is the God of all patience have patience with us? Like Job we abhor ourselves and repent in dust and ashes. But the light is not turned upon us to rob us of our hope. There is a lifting up.

If only we desire to be purged from self with its entangling nets, its subtleties, its disguises."

–Amy Carmichael, *If* [2]

Honestly, when you finished reading the detailed list of the flesh, did you feel a little discouraged with a growing discomfort of ugliness? You might be tempted to walk, or even run, away from this exercise of identifying your flesh. You probably feel a strong desire to either pamper yourself or to fix what seems wrong. Please do nothing! To act at this point would likely be responding to your flesh's pull to feel good again. I know because I spent years doing just that. Sometimes I would distract myself in front of the television. Other times I would lose myself in a good romance book. I would indulge in comfort food or go shopping for clothes. I would focus on my ministries, try to impress others with my abilities, or dream up more public ministries to increase my significance. I would put off doing things I wasn't good at or that I found boring. I would try to make friends because I was desperate to feel loved and accepted.

We've been looking at the ugly side of our flesh, at those lusts that deceive us, but what about the confidence we put in the flesh, the side of our flesh that gives us strength and makes us feel capable, the side that we want people to see? The flesh, your flesh, is concerned with looking good, concerned with the appearance of doing good. We expect the flesh to look bad, so if we manage to look good we conclude that we have conquered the flesh. But looking good is itself a trick of the flesh.

If I think I look good, I feel good. Conversely, if I think I look bad, I feel bad. When my flesh looks bad, I feel bad, but when my flesh looks good, I suddenly feel confident. Does that confidence mean it has stopped being my flesh?

According to Galatians 5:22-23, the fruit produced by the Spirit is love, joy, peace, patience, kindness, goodness, faithfulness, gentleness and self-control. We often have trouble finding evidence of these good things in our lives, and strive to produce them ourselves. Whenever I do this, my fruit always rots. The problem is that my flesh is the first to volunteer to attempt the fruit of the Spirit, producing a counterfeit spirituality that will inevitably fail.

Just because what I do seems good to me doesn't mean the Spirit produced the fruit. No amount of "good" fruit I produce can start me on a walk in the Spirit. If I look to the flesh to feel good about myself, then I have not left flesh to walk by the Spirit. It's a neat little trick that keeps me stuck. Flesh lives boldly on to keep tempting me, to keep causing me to stumble.

> **If you look to the flesh to feel good about yourself, then you have not left flesh to walk by the Spirit.**

The Bobsled Analogy

Two men, using all the strength in their legs, push their sled along 50 meters of an icy track to gain as much speed as possible before jumping into the sled and steering down a winding, perilous runway.

Sometimes we treat the Christian life as if it were a bobsled race. Using our own strength, we try to give ourselves a good push to godly living and assume that, at some point, we can just jump onto the Holy Spirit and He'll pick up the pace, continuing in the same direction.

You might argue, "Since you put it that way, it sounds bad, but is it really that bad to try hard? Is it wrong to make an effort? Doesn't Paul, in his letters to Timothy, tell him to "pursue righteousness," "fight the good fight" (1 Tim. 6:11-12), "be diligent to present yourself approved to God" (2 Tim. 3:15)? Doesn't God expect me to do my part first?"

> **What you do in the flesh will not be picked up and carried on by the Spirit.**

I am not advocating spiritual laziness, but neither will I promote a flesh and Spirit collaboration. I am saying that what I do in the flesh, even though it seems full of good effort, will not be picked up and carried on by the Spirit. Remember, the flesh and the Spirit are constantly opposed to each other. They do not, at any time, work together towards the same goal. They cannot share the same path.

Look at the path that each is taking.

➢ The flesh desires to glorify me, and seeks self-satisfaction.

➢ The Spirit desires to glorify God, and seeks self-sacrifice.

How certain are you that your good efforts are in the Spirit?

A Shaky Foundation

As a child, I wanted to be heard and I hated being ignored, so I developed a habit of talking. This habit included repeating myself, talking louder than those around me, and interrupting people who were already talking. When you talk that way, people tune you out, or avoid you altogether. Unfortunately, I didn't get that memo, but I did begin to sense that people didn't want to be around me. Being ignored just made me desperate, which, in turn, made me more annoying. My behavior drove away the very people from whom I was seeking affirmation.

Eventually, being heard was not satisfying enough; I needed others to agree with me. Knowing someone disagreed with me was not okay. That was equivalent to being wrong! What tactic did I use if I couldn't get someone to agree? I simply repeated myself over and over again, as if repetition would convince another that I was right.

My need to be heard, coupled with my annoying behavior, created quite the dilemma. Victimized by my own voice, I became my own worst enemy. To this day, I stiffen at being told that I am too loud or being asked to stop talking. I can still feel desperate when overlooked or slighted. It takes me right back to shaky ground and I instinctively reach out for my flesh to regain my confidence.

When your confidence is shaken, what do you instinctively reach out for? How do you ensure that you feel good about yourself? What do you do in order to be loved?

There's a boardwalk on the Jersey shore. I've walked it while juggling my chair, towel, cooler and umbrella. It's an awkward load, but manageable as long as I am walking on the boards. If I step off the boardwalk and onto the sand, however, it all falls apart. Little grains of shifting sand do not a firm foundation make.

A firm foundation provides sure footing, a sense of security and confidence. Without a firm foundation, you will lose your balance and reach out for something to steady yourself, something to grab on to. As a believer in Jesus Christ, my head tells me that Jesus is my foundation, my confidence, my Rock. After all, that is what God's Word tells me. But I don't always live as though that is true. Insecurity threatens me almost daily. I feel the ground shake underneath my feet. I lose my balance, and when I do, I reach out and grab without thinking. I'm hoping to restore my confidence, to feel strong again.

What makes you stand tall, feel "okay," feel good about yourself? These things have probably formed the foundation of your confidence, your sense of value. Unfortunately, this foundation consists of little grains of sand. Those little grains of sand continually shift.

Since childhood, most of us have unconsciously been accumulating a record of what has made us feel valuable or loveable. While this data has shaped us, it has also taunted us with a shaky sense of confidence because, no matter how many times we pull ourselves back up, our foundation is never firm.

On Christ I stand firm. He is solid Rock beneath my feet; anything other than Him is sand. My head tells me that I am standing on that Rock, Jesus Christ, so why do my feet tell me the ground is shifting, why do my legs feel wobbly?

Rescue Me

One summer, when we were at a camp in the Sierra Nevada Mountains, an earthquake shook southern California. I was awakened in the middle of the night by the feeling that our cabin was rocking. The tremors of a minor earthquake can be very disorienting. The brain senses the movement and, unable to identify the cause, registers it as confusion. In my groggy state, I reasoned a solution and drifted back to sleep. I woke up the next morning eager to talk about the bear that had shaken our cabin during the night.

When the foundation of my self-worth shakes as if trembling in an earthquake, I become disoriented and confused, wondering what is wrong. My automatic assumption is that the shaking of my worth comes from outside me. My instinct is to grab something solid, something strong, something that restores my sense of balance.

In comes Flesh to the rescue.

It's not the weak, ugly, bad side that comes. Ugly flesh just makes me feel worse. No, only a strong, confident, powerful me is welcome at a time like this. And shouldn't it be that way? Shouldn't I counter a drop in self-esteem by remembering all that is good in me, all that is positive? I am in Christ after all. It's not right to think bad thoughts about myself. Right?

When there is a tremor in your self-confidence, when you feel insecure about who you are, what thoughts come to mind?

Do you ever think . . .

➢ "I could have done that better."
➢ "Can't they see how good I am? I'm just as good as so and so."
➢ "I don't want anyone to think I'm not perfect."
➢ "I can't stand someone not thinking well of me."
➢ "Why doesn't anyone recognize my abilities?"
➢ "I deserve to be treated better than that."
➢ "I'm not such a terrible person."

When we look to ourselves for confidence, we are actually welcoming the flesh to tell us who we are, even who we are in Christ. Does that sound right? Can that work?

Do the thoughts listed above make your doubts disappear, or do you bounce between confident thoughts and thoughts such as these . . . ?

➢ "Something is wrong with me."
➢ "I'm not good enough."
➢ "I'll never be good enough."
➢ "I'm too stupid."
➢ "I'm ugly."
➢ "I can't do anything right."
➢ "No one could ever love me."

> ➢ "I'm bad."
> ➢ "I always screw everything up."
> ➢ "I'm just a big failure."
> ➢ "I'm worthless."

Wait! This isn't right, either. We shouldn't believe these things. Like a hamster on a wheel, we keep spinning these thoughts, wondering why the wheel won't stop.

What happened to our confidence in Christ? Who has stolen it? Was it Satan, our spouse, a co-worker, someone from church, our "best friend," that gorgeous, popular, always evangelizing, perfect person, our boyfriend or girlfriend, our roommate, our boss, our dad, our mom, our in-laws?

If it wasn't for them, we think, we could feel confident all the time, be more secure in who we are. We wouldn't have to feel as if we aren't good enough, as if we aren't doing enough. We wouldn't have to feel so ugly, worthless, or undeserving of love.

Will someone please make the ground stop shaking!

————————◆————————

I caught the look of despair in a young man's eyes on Sunday. The next day he sat across from me at my dining room table. He had done it again, he explained. He had repeated the same bad choice, ended up in the same rotten failure. Only this time it had cost him more than he had been prepared to pay and the regret refused to slide off. More than anything, he wished for a do over, wished for a chance to undo the negative effects, wished for a chance to restore the good opinion of others. "I am an idiot, yes," he says, "but there is still good in me. I know it's there; I just have to prove it to those around me, make them see all that is worthwhile in me." That is what he thinks when he is at the top of the roller coaster, the top of the swing, but in the lows of his plunging, swinging emotions, he despairs of ever being better. "I am a repeat offender; stupid choices are my pattern. What hope do I have of avoiding the mistakes next time? Maybe I'm not cut out for this Christian life. Maybe following Christ is a hoax. Where is this power to live a godly life? Why doesn't being a Christian make any difference?" The urge to quit, to strike out on his own, to be free to do as he pleases is strong. It would set him free from this burden of guilt and disillusionment.

Have you ever been grateful to God for using your failures to make you into a better servant for Him, only to find yourself the next day in despair over having failed to be better? Does your mood ever turn gray with bad feelings about yourself? Discontent with your situation, do you focus on feeling good about yourself, on looking good in front of others?

Gratitude to God is the Spirit's fruit, fretting over feeling bad is from the flesh. The transition from one to the other is so subtle that the switch goes undetected. Imagine you are following a car to your destination, but in a moment of distraction you take your eyes off the car. When you look back, you assume the car in front of you is the one taking you where you planned to go. What if it isn't? What if the distraction was timed perfectly to confuse you? What if a switch was done to deceive you? What would be the outcome?

> **Gratitude is the Spirit's fruit, fretting over feeling bad is from the flesh.**

We pursue feeling good about ourselves as if we were still following Christ, when in truth, that pursuit is a leading of the flesh. Christ did not come to earth and pay the price for our sin to boost our sense of worth, to make us feel good about ourselves. Using our identity in Christ to bolster a positive image of ourselves is a delusion of the flesh.

> **You cannot pursue feeling good about yourself and follow Christ at the same time.**

The flesh is only concerned with promoting me. In the flesh, I am drawn to think about me, worry about me, satisfy me, elevate and protect me. When I try to increase my value through self-promotion, I am being led by the desires of the flesh.

The flesh does not desire victory over sin, does not desire identity in Christ, does not desire to carry a cross.

Bury Me

The hour for the Son of Man to be glorified had come, and Jesus said, "unless a grain of wheat falls into the earth and dies, it remains by itself alone, but if it dies, it bears much fruit. He who loves his life loses it; and he who hates his life in this world shall keep it to life eternal. If anyone serves Me, let him follow Me; and where I am, there shall My servant also be; if anyone serves Me the Father will honor him" (John 12:24-26).

For Jesus Christ, that hour of glorification was death on a cross and resurrection from the grave three days later. In His day, death by crucifixion wasn't just the most painful method of execution, it was also the most humiliating. The criminal was required to carry his own crossbeam to his death. He was then hung as a spectacle, often stripped naked. This form of execution was reserved for the worst of the criminals. And this was how Jesus bore the punishment for our sin. But before He carried that crossbeam, Jesus said, "If anyone wishes to come after Me, he must deny himself, and take up his cross daily, and follow Me" (Luke 9:23).

In his book *50 Reasons Why Jesus Came to Die*, John Piper titles one chapter, "To Create a Band of Crucified Followers." He writes "when Christ went to the cross, His aim was to call a great band of believers after Him. The reason for this was not that Jesus must die again today, but that we must. When He bids us take up His cross, He means come and die."[3]

Before you can begin to crucify the flesh, you must be willing to abandon finding any significance by it.

The hour for a decision has come. What will you do with your flesh? To walk in the Spirit, we must crucify the flesh. In Christ, we are freed from slavery to our flesh. But this freedom doesn't come automatically. It requires a walk of dying.

Before you can begin crucifying the flesh, you must see your flesh lose its value. You must be willing to abandon finding any significance in your flesh. Up to this point, I have been exposing your flesh in its deceptive, alluring power. It is the flesh that opposes the Spirit living within you and hinders you from walking by Him. My purpose has been to lead you to this fork in the road where you must make a decision.

Will you accept a walk of dying to self in order to walk by the Spirit?

Chapter

4

Dead Man Walking

We all have a natural tendency to hide or fix the things we don't like about ourselves, and to promote the things we do like. While the positive parades on stage for everyone to see, the negative hides safely behind the curtain. At least that is what we think; but in the end, whether in front of or behind the curtain, our actions are natural and fleshly. Like the filthy rags of our righteous deeds, eventually our impressive acts are revealed as what they are: dull, stained, tarnished, rotting, selfish, and worthy of the dung heap.

Doing what comes naturally is our default setting.

By "naturally" I mean what is of our human, physical self as distinct from the Spirit that dwells in the believer. I mean our human nature, our sin nature, our personality, our emotions, our hormones, our skills, talents, good or bad traits, passions, and desires. I am not implying that all that is natural is bad, but that our natural capacity is not on par with God's divine power and is not to be relied upon for walking by the Spirit.

For example, hormones are part of our natural selves. God created them to keep us alive. But they are natural and will never produce a spiritual reaction. Every human being has a God-designed personality. Some are pleasant, others are not. If reacting according to our personality is judged as good by others, that does not mean that we have acted in the Spirit. Personality, pleasant or not, is natural. We should neither excuse nor commend ourselves based on our personality.

It is natural for me to rely on myself. It is natural for me to complain, natural to be irritable, natural to be influenced by hormones. When I go with my natural inclination, I will most likely whine, yell, or pout. That's my reality. Natural is what I revert to when I'm tired. Natural is how I react when I'm not exercising self-control. Natural comes quite naturally to me. I never wake up and tell myself, "today I need to work on being irritable." I don't have to talk myself into "being willing to be right." I caught on to those things quite naturally. It is natural for me to get angry, be impatient, give up, plot revenge, show off, flirt, indulge appetites, gossip, demand my rights, put my own needs first, defend myself, assume I'm right, want to look good, compare myself with others, be jealous, ridicule, divide, compete, take the easy way out, avoid suffering, be self-righteous, pervert justice, and deny mercy. Without thinking I do what is natural to me, and when I do that, I am not walking by the Spirit.

> *"But a natural man does not accept the things of the Spirit of God; for they are foolishness to him, and he cannot understand them, because they are spiritually appraised."*
>
> –1 Corinthians 2:14

Do we mistakenly infuse the natural with spiritual value? Is there virtue in being gifted in music, in being at ease talking to a big crowd, in being a people-pleaser, in being soft spoken, in being attractive or good at making friends? Do any of these things make us spiritually mature?

Paul tells us that the foolishness of God is wiser than any wisdom man thinks he has, and that the weakness of God is stronger than any strength man can muster up. When God wanted to put to shame the wise of the world, He chose to do that through the foolish of the world. When He wanted to shame the strong of the world, He chose to use the weak of the world. He has chosen what is despised, what is nothing, in order to cancel the things that exist (1 Cor. 1:25-28).

Does this make sense to our natural way of thinking?

Paul explains that God uses such bizarre methods so that no man will boast before Him (v. 29).

I like the idea of being important. I often find myself wanting to impress others. Even when I'm doing something for the Lord, there is always this side of me that wants to get credit for what I do. I admit it: I want to hear praises, and when I do, I easily lose sight of other motivations.

Humans are obsessed with assigning value to themselves, to things, and to others. The more we value something, the more effort we spend preserving, protecting, and pampering it. The more effort we devote to something, the more likely we are to feel pain over its loss or damage. Mistreatment is unthinkable! It reduces the value we have assigned to a person or object below what we think it should be. This value, however, has a serious flaw: we are never secure with our estimation of our own value, never confident that we are valued the way we think we deserve. More concerned with what man sees than with what God thinks, we calculate and time everything we do to bring honor and praise to ourselves.

Jars of Clay and Fluffy Towels

> *"But we have this treasure in jars of clay, to show that the surpassing power belongs to God and not from us."*
> –2 Corinthians 4:7, ESV

Jars of clay.

I love the way that sounds. I picture the jars, brown and earthy, made of dirt, fragile, common, expendable. Not much excitement over them, unless they are found in an archaeological dig. But Paul wasn't thinking of archeology when he wrote these words.

The jar of clay is NOT the treasure; rather, the treasure is in the jar of clay. What does that mean? It means that God is our source of the greatest, most incredible, limitless power there is and we are, well, weak. That treasure is "the light of the knowledge of the glory of God in the face of Jesus Christ" (2 Cor. 4:6b, ESV). The jar of clay is our mortal flesh, our decaying bodies.

What is the value of clay? How much should we invest in the conservation and beautification of our clay jars? Will the time we've spent focused on making life better for our jars of clay balance with its true value?

———————————◆———————————

The realization of the extent of the priority I placed on this jar of clay came to a climax in one ridiculously stupid event.

We were crossing the border into Mexico at Ciudad Juarez. I found crossing the border to be a nerve-racking experience. It was especially nerve-racking this time because I was unfamiliar with the city. My tension kept rising, and by the time we got to the hotel for the night, I was deep into "pamper Amy" zone, the land where Amy's needs come first, where anxiety is balanced with self-delighting.

Now, here is where it got stupid.

I claimed the fluffiest towel in the bathroom for myself. In my own mind I labeled it mine. After a difficult day, I felt entitled to some comforts. So when my daughter happened to use "my" towel, I vomited the filth of selfishness. I didn't realize why I was angry or even how selfish my actions were; I just felt that having that fluffy towel taken away was the end of the world.

Looking back now I can say, "unbelievable!" Was I actually upset about not getting the fluffy towel? No! My outrage was over what it represented: an assault on the value I had attributed to myself. I inflate my importance, and then, when I am taken advantage of, I get angry. Instead of groaning for the reason Paul gives, "longing to be clothed with our dwelling from heaven" (2 Cor. 5:2), I groan because my body feels a little pinch of discomfort. I live under the impression that I have the right to be happy, am entitled to more, deserve better treatment.

Reality check.

Jars of clay are not placed in silk lined boxes; they're not given the "fluffy towel" treatment.

Anyway, fluffy towels are an illusion, not worth the effort. All I've ever got from making myself a priority is misery and fear.

Paul wants us to live differently. He tells us we have this treasure in jars of clay, and that truth changes everything! Because . . .

> *"We are afflicted in every way, but not crushed;*
> *perplexed, but not despairing; persecuted, but not*
> *forsaken; struck down, but not destroyed."*
> –2 Corinthians 4:8-9

How can I be attacked by affliction from all sides, but never be crushed? How can I be plagued by severe doubt, but not despair? How can persecution not leave me feeling forsaken, abandoned by God? How can I know that I won't be destroyed no matter how hard I am beaten?

This jar of clay has no value apart from Christ. I am a dead and a dying man, made alive only by the treasure of the light of the gospel of the glory of Christ in me. That treasure cannot be crushed, it cannot be destroyed, and it is the only thing that matters. What happens to this jar shouldn't make any difference.

Fools for Christ

Paul had heard that the church in Corinth was divided and quarreling. There was a competition among the believers; they had made following men a source of division.

But "is Christ divided" Paul asks (1 Cor. 1:13).

Apparently the church was divided over who had the greatest wisdom, or who had the best delivery, or even the best message (some things haven't changed). The Corinthian believers were elevating their teachers, and, in so doing, were indirectly elevating their own status.

> *"And I, brethren, could not speak to you as to spiritual men, but as to men of flesh, as to infants in Christ. I gave you milk to drink, not solid food; for you were not yet able to receive it. Indeed, even now you are not yet able, for you are still fleshly. For since there is jealousy and strife among you, are you not fleshly, and are you not walking like mere men?"*
> —1 Corinthians 3:1-3

They were walking like natural men and not in the Spirit. They thought they were wise, but their wisdom had the features of the wisdom James warned us about.

> *"But if you have bitter jealousy and selfish ambition in your heart, do not be arrogant and so lie against the truth. This wisdom is not that which comes down from above, but is earthly, natural, demonic. For where*

*jealousy and selfish ambition exist, there is disorder and
every evil thing."*

–James 3:14-16

So Paul asks the church at Corinth point blank,

"For who regards you as superior?"

–1 Corinthians 4:7a

That is, based on whose opinion are you better than another?

"What do you have that you did not receive?"

–1 Corinthians 4:7b

Paul elaborates,

". . . and if it was given to you, why do you presume to boast about
it as if you could take credit for it? Oh, you are such full, rich kings
now, and that, of course, would imply that we, your teachers, are kings
too. Do you imagine yourselves walking into the amphitheater, or better
yet, riding in on a glorious chariot with all eyes on you? Can you touch
the awe in the air; hear the roar of the crowd shouting your name? Good
for you! You are finally known for how great you are, finally full of the
honor you have wanted, and you would put us up there right beside you."
(I believe Paul meant that sarcastically) "But," Paul continues—and
this is a huge "but"—God has chosen a completely opposite and an
absolutely more inferior way for us. He has placed us at the end of the
line. We are those who arrive last to the amphitheater as the prisoners,
a spectacle of death to all those who see us, to be jeered and taunted"
(1 Cor. 4:8-9, paraphrase).

*"We have become a spectacle to the world, both to
angels and to men. We are fools for Christ's sake, but
you are prudent in Christ; we are weak, but you are
strong; you are distinguished, but we are without honor.
To this present hour we are both hungry and thirsty,
and are poorly clothed, and are roughly treated, and
are homeless; and we toil, working with our own hands;
when we are reviled, we bless; when we are persecuted,
we endure; when we are slandered, we try to conciliate;
we have become as the scum of the world, the dregs of
all things, even until now."*

–1 Corinthians 4:9b-13

Scum of the world? Dregs of all things? What are you saying, Paul?

A couple years ago, a massive rain fall resulted in a foot of sewage water in our basement. I was traveling, so my husband and daughter had to clean up the mess. A few weeks later, we noticed that there was still a smell in the basement. A plugged drain had been overlooked, and when the grate was lifted . . .! I will not attempt to describe the nauseating scum. Some things are just too disgusting!

Paul's word is not flattering or polite.

The Greeks had a special use for this word translated "scum." It's what they called the criminals who were kept to be offered as sacrifices to the gods whenever a calamity occurred. Could Paul have had this meaning in mind when he described himself as scum? Was he saying that our lives are simply a sacrifice to God?

Is that really what you think, Paul, because that just isn't natural!

I never consider myself as a sacrifice, but I often fear that others do. Maybe that is what Paul was saying. He could have been moaning about the mistreatment he'd got from the world, protesting that others had treated him like scum. That seems more logical, less absurd, more natural, more like me.

But if Paul was describing how the world viewed him, why did he say it was God who had put him in the theater for public exhibition as a man condemned to death? He knew that God had not set him up as wise, honored and the strong of this world, but as a fool for Christ sake, full of dishonor and weakness.

Paul described himself as a spectacle, as scum, to make a point to Corinthian believers, who thought that men should seek significance and elevate their status among one another.

Living to Die or Dying to Live

Paul said his earnest hope was,

> ". . . that with all boldness, Christ will even now, as always, be exalted in my body, whether by life or by death. For to me, to live is Christ, and to die is gain. But if I am to live on in the flesh, this will mean fruitful labor

*for me; and I don't know which to choose. But I am
hard-pressed from both directions, having the desire to
depart and be with Christ, for that is very much better;
yet to remain on in the flesh is more necessary for your
sake. Convinced of this, I know that I will remain and
continue with you all for your progress and joy in the
faith."*

–Philippians 1:20-25

Think about what Paul is writing here. He is in prison and he doesn't know which to choose, to live or to die. How difficult of a choice is that? Wouldn't it be natural for us to prefer to live? But then, if I were in prison, I probably would rather die. I, of course, would choose based on what was best for me. Not Paul! His primary desire is not for his own good, which for him would mean to die and be with Christ, but for the good of others and for the preaching of the Gospel.

> **To live by the Spirit requires a mindset that is "upside down" to your natural self.**

To live by the Spirit requires a mindset that is "upside down" to our natural selves. Obeying Jesus's teachings will go against everything that is natural to us. It is unnatural for us to ask for help, to admit we are wrong, to turn the other cheek, to love our enemies, to do good to them, to submit to others, to give thanks in all things, to suffer, to be weak, to surrender our rights, to love mercy, to be faithful, to pray, to be humble, to be content, to seek unity, or to accept slavery.

———————————◆———————————

Paul instructs us to,

*"Put on the Lord Jesus Christ and make no provision for
the flesh in regard to its lusts."*

–Romans 13:14

What does it mean to "put on the Lord Jesus Christ"? Do I wear what He wore, do what He did, act as He acted? How do I walk His walk?

In the past, when a prison warden took a man on death row down a corridor, he would shout "dead man walking," as if to say this man was considered already dead.

Jesus said,

> *"If anyone wishes to come after Me, he must deny himself, and take up his cross daily, and follow Me."*
>
> –Luke 9:23

The criminal condemned to die by crucifixion had to carry his own cross, demonstrating that he was going to his death. He was a dead man walking. Jesus wants those who follow Him to walk in the Spirit with a cross on their back.

Is this how I am to "put on the Lord Jesus Christ"?

> *"Even so consider yourselves to be dead to sin, but alive to God in Christ Jesus."*
>
> –Romans 6:11

> *"For we who live are constantly being delivered over to death for Jesus's sake, so that the life of Jesus also may be manifested in our mortal flesh."*
>
> –2 Corinthians 4:11

Some of what is natural in us requires death to deal with it. Some of it requires a good haul to the trash dump. All of it needs to come under the control of the Spirit.

Paul says that death has already occurred in the believer,

> *"Knowing this, that our old self was crucified with Him,"*
>
> –Romans 6:6a

and

> *"Those who belong to Christ Jesus have crucified the flesh with its passions and desires."*
>
> –Galatians 5:24

He also says that we have an active role in putting to death whatever belongs to our earthly nature, replacing it with compassion, kindness, humility, gentleness, meekness, patience, tolerance, and forgiveness, and, above all love, the glue that holds us all together in harmony. We must also rid ourselves of such things as anger, rage, malice, slander, filthy language, and lying (Col. 3:5-14).

Paul understood that to walk by the Spirit, the natural man has to die. He lived taking up the cross of Jesus every day, and willing to play the fool in the world's eyes to do so. If our goal is to walk by the Spirit and die daily, we would do well to learn from Paul.

But this can be a hard pill to swallow. Paul's method seems harsh and excessive. Surely God does not mean for us to live like this; surely our cross doesn't have to be so severe.

By now, if you have been considering dying to self, not holding on to this life, not valuing your life above Christ in you, you have probably met some resistance, some thoughts that begin with "but."

Dead Men Don't Get Paid

Have you ever thought, or do you think, that life owes you something, or even that, in some way, God owes you (though you may be reluctant to say that out loud)?

Do you expect or hope for a return on life's hardships? Have all the sacrifices you've made in life been free, or have they been made with an unconscious expectation of payback?

> **"**
> *Have all the sacrifices you've made in this life been free, or are you clinging to what life owes you?*
> **"**

Maybe you thought you were denying yourself, when actually you've been investing in a savings account that is earning interest. Your life has been unfair and you've been slipping credit slips into your Bank of Just Return in the city of Fairplay. Eventually you hope to make a withdrawal or cash in your investment. You know there is a reward in heaven, but you've got a major investment here too, one that has been accruing interest and that you aren't willing to give up yet. That expectation of payback, of reward for your sacrifice, makes it unthinkable for you to die to self.

Owing or being owed is bondage. Christ did not come to place you in that bondage. In fact, He gave His life to pay your debt, so that you can live freely in Him. What gain can you get from this life that compares to that? There is nothing this world offers that can satisfy as Christ Jesus can.

Are you clinging to what life owes you? Are you holding out because you need to get some reward first? Death to self requires sacrificing debt, because a dead man doesn't get paid.

Living Is Not Surviving

If you are coming to this walk of dying with a well-established habit of ignoring your needs because you don't think you matter, you may be trying to redefine your old pattern of survival as dying to self. They are not the same. Your old patterns have been the flesh's way of protecting itself. Those patterns must be crucified as well.

> **"**
> *Unless you are sure of the life you have in Jesus, you cannot die to self.*
> **"**

Do your attempts at dying leave you feeling crushed, hopeless, discouraged? If so, you may be trying this backwards, attempting "spiritual suicide" to gain acceptance or make restitution. Unless you are sure of the life you have in Jesus, you cannot die to self. Only the life of Jesus in you has the capacity to sacrifice, expecting nothing in return. Only the life of Jesus in you transforms dying to self into victorious living.

> *"Always carrying about in the body the dying of Jesus, so that the life of Jesus also may be manifested in our body. For we who live are constantly being delivered over to death for Jesus's sake, so that the life of Jesus also may be manifested in our mortal flesh."*
> –2 Corinthians 4:10-11

I can't explain it, can't understand it, can't grasp it; I only know that there is nothing more true than this: two opposite realities co-exist in me, both the dying and the life of Jesus at the same time. That should radically change the way I live. For Jesus's sake, for His purpose, for His glory, for His name, I live to be constantly handed over for death. I carry in this body the dying of Jesus, so that His life will be seen in me. I live to die so that the real living is Jesus in me.

That's the truth that I see in Paul's life.

That's the treasure worth living and dying for.

From Woo-hooing to Wallowing

I must warn you: there is a slippery slope to this dying.

I'll illustrate with the example of my struggle with jealousy of pregnant women. How do you suppose I felt when I saw a pregnant woman, or heard that exciting announcement, "we're having a baby"? It was dreadfully hard to resist my flesh, but I didn't want to live in that jealousy anymore. I would fight back, saying to myself, "NO! Don't go there, Amy! Drop it and back away."

Did I hesitate, or did I back away?

Well, sometimes I felt powerless to resist the pull; the temptation was stronger than my desire to back away. Sometimes I felt that jealousy had its claws in me and wouldn't let go. And sometimes there was victory! Woo-hoo! I would back away from my flesh, blown away by the realization that it was all in God's power and not in my own. Unfortunately, I often backed into a slippery slope that led to a pit of self-pity.

How do you define self-pity? I think of it as compassion turned inward. Feeling sorry for myself is comforting, in an oddly warm and sticky way. Besides, we all need a little compassion, don't we? What's wrong with making sure we get some?

Self-pity is a way of avoiding the death sentence. It is our reaction to not being good enough when we want to be wanted. It is our reaction to suffering when we want to be comfortable. It is our reaction to disappointment when things don't go our way. This slippery slope is just more of flesh's deception that guarantees its desires and lusts will live on.

Oswald Chambers said, "No sin is worse than the sin of self-pity, because it removes God from the throne of our lives, replacing Him with our own self-interests. It causes us to open our mouths only to complain, and we simply become spiritual sponges—always absorbing, never giving, and never being satisfied. And there is nothing lovely or generous about our lives."[1]

Where does self-pity come from? Is it born out of those things you hate about myself? Or is it the other way around: self-pity leads to self-loathing?

If you were to sit down and jot a list of what you dislike most about yourself, of what you wish was different, of what makes you angry, sad, or discouraged about yourself, how quickly could you write it? How long would the list be? There's a lot of hate directed at you, isn't there?

Is hating yourself the same as dying to self?

Jesus said,

> *"If anyone comes to Me, and does not hate his own father and mother and wife and children and brothers and sisters, yes, and even his own life, he cannot be My disciple. Whoever does not carry his own cross and come after Me cannot be My disciple."*
>
> –Luke 14:26-27

On the surface, this appears to answer "yes" to the question above: self-hatred is a mark of the disciple who carries his own cross. To this I would agree wholeheartedly, if I thought, for one moment, that my self-hate has led to self-denial or death to self.

The same content is put differently in Matthew 10:37, "He who loves father or mother more than Me is not worthy of Me." That flips the perspective on this meaning of hate. My love for Jesus should make the love I have for others, or for myself, look like hate. Well then, if by hating myself, I gained even an ounce of love for Jesus, I might agree that self-hate has spiritual benefit. Sadly, the self-hate born of self-pity is just a twisted form of self-love.

In fact—and you know this is true—no amount of hating yourself can ever produce love for another. That's because the focus of self-hatred is ME! I don't really want to die to self. I want to remake me, fix me, be proud of me; and when that doesn't happen, I'm back to poor, pitiful me. I enjoy it here, so don't make me move!

Which do you think comes first, self-pity or self-hatred?

Answer: neither one.

The root of both is pride. Pride makes me feel sorry for myself, makes me feel discouraged about myself. In pride, I cling to my sin, to my desires, to my guilt. In pride, I love myself more than I love God.

Do you want to hate something? Hate your pride; nail it to that cross you carry as you follow Jesus.

Weight of the Beam

> **"**
> *Every day you wake up with a death sentence; every day you are a dead man walking.*
> **"**

Each year, I grow more and more convinced that, to live by the Spirit, I must crucify the flesh. I've tried to avoid it and find another way, but each time I find myself defeated yet again. The only solution is to constantly be dying to self. I must daily consider my flesh dead, daily carry around the death of Christ in my body. Every day I wake up with a death sentence; I am a dead man walking. The more I pamper the flesh and try to keep it alive, the harder it is to face the firing squad.

I've never known a more persistent and proud foe than my own flesh. It wants nothing to do with death. It kicks and screams its way to the executioner. And just when I think I've slain the beast, it rises again.

My flesh doesn't want to be crucified, doesn't want to carry a cross. I don't like skipping a meal, wouldn't think of subjecting my body to cold showers, have zero tolerance for discomfort, and am insulted if ridiculed, misunderstood, or betrayed. I don't want to give up my rights, my liberties, or my life. Why would I? I won't as long as I am asking what's in it for me.

> **"**
> *Your death sentence carries with it the certainty of life.*
> **"**

Crucifying the flesh is not natural! Without the Spirit, we cannot begin to choose to die to self today, and tomorrow, and the day after that. The good news is that, unlike the man who has been sentenced to death, who walks the hall to his execution, who has no hope, we have hope. Our death sentence carries the certainty of life. We are dead to sin, but alive in Christ.

Every day that I write I am tested. This Scripture I read, these thoughts I contemplate, reverberate in my head. At first I react with "I can't do this!" Then I tell myself, "No, Amy, this is it: this is your chance to die, this is your chance to feel the weight of the beam on your shoulders."

Frequently I'm asked, "How do I die to self?" The question always catches me off guard. I search for an answer, tempted to come up with three simple steps. Instead I stare blankly at the person who asked. I feel stupid; I'm writing a book on this and I can't answer the most basic question. Here is my mistake: I keep thinking that dying to self is something I do.

That's the wrong approach. God hasn't left us in charge of the dying process. In His word, we learn of four effective methods that He has designed and put in place. The answer to the question, "How do I die to self?" is not found in what we do, but in surrendering to God's use of those methods.

The next section describes in detail God's four step method to dying to self: weakness, suffering, humility, and repentance.

Part 2

◆

Accepting the Tools God Uses

Chapter

5

Embracing Weakness

Normally, when I feel weak, something inside me screams, "resist, resist, resist." My thoughts grow desperate, "fight it," "you're stronger than this," "you don't have time for it," "you are expected to be strong." The more I resist, the more I turn inward; the more I turn inward, the more I sink into a black hole of discouragement. I feel like Gollum in *the Hobbit*,[1] muttering snarly remarks and slapping his head against a rock. I whine. I pout. I feel sorry for myself. I look pitiful. But, hey, I'm dealing with it, right?

Resist weakness. That sounds spiritual, sounds strong. But who is making the call? Is it of the Spirit? Or is it the flesh? Where does weakness start? Have you considered who is giving you directions on handling weakness? How do you know if it's the flesh or the Spirit? What does each look like? Which do you prefer to work with? Do you even care, as long as the weakness is dealt with quickly and you feel strong again?

There is a trickery of words, a slight of the hands. The flesh will blur the lines between weakness and temptation, making it hard for us to discern the difference. What advantage does this sneaky trick give the flesh?

Well, if you can be distracted into resisting weakness, how likely are you to be distracted from resisting temptation?

Have you noticed how we speak of some weaknesses with fondness rather than hate? For example, we say we have a weakness for chocolate, or donuts, or as Mr. Darcy would say, "a pair of fine eyes in the face of a pretty woman."[2] We are nonchalant about being too weak to resist flirting, kissing, gossiping, complaining, sleeping, drinking, binge eating. What's the big deal? It's harmless; it doesn't hurt anyone; you can't help it. "Fight your weaknesses," flesh tells us, "unless it makes you feel good; then make excuses."

Flesh subtly deceives us into resisting the wrong thing. As a result, we drop our guard against temptations. We become self-absorbed in our disappointment with our weaknesses, too distracted to watch and pray.

Still confused? Let me clarify. On the one hand, we have weaknesses that makes us feel inadequate, that sap our strength. Those are the ones we don't like; they hurt our pride. On the other hand, we have weaknesses for pleasure, sin, and indulgences (which are, in reality, temptations). Those are the ones we tolerate and find hard to resist. So when we find that we have succumbed to our weaknesses to sin, we are despondent over our failure to be as strong as we thought we were, and the flesh has won the battle either way.

> **The flesh will use weakness to make you miserable; God will use it to teach you to die to self.**

Can you spot the trick? Can you see the difference well enough to take a big ole' permanent marker and write in bold lines?

Make it clear: Resist Temptation; Embrace Weakness.

Let's get something straight: weakness is God's tool! The flesh will use weakness to make us miserable, but God uses it to teach us to die to self.

A dead man has no strength. A dead man never says, "I should have been able to do that."

Optimistic Delusion

I am a dismal failure at skiing.

In spite of that, I used to tell myself that I ought to be able to ski. I only had to try harder. That's how I found myself riding a ski lift in the Sierra Nevada Mountains one Christmas. Why would I ever think that I couldn't ski? It shouldn't matter that I don't have the strength in my legs to stop, or that I fear heights, or that I hate going fast. Why should those things stop me?

Optimistic delusion.

I couldn't even get off the ski lift without falling. That's when I began to doubt my resolve. What was I thinking? After a few more falls and the terrifying sensation of gaining speed, I was crumpling as well as I could crumple while wearing ridiculously long, heavy, floppy poles on my feet.

"I can't do this!" kept screaming in my head.

"Why can't you do this?" the argument in my head yelled back.

"I don't know! Because I'm too weak! Because I'm a pitiful failure!"

"Oh great," I said to myself, "now you're going to melt into a mass of tears." Perfect! Would somebody just shoot me? I'm about die here anyway.

I can't understand it. Millions of people can ski. Why can't I? I should be able to do this! I should be strong enough to pull myself together, to stand up on those blasted skis and sail down this steep and slick mountainside. Instead, I am staring into my husband's face while he slowly brings me down the mountain one step at a time, stopping my skis with his own. Ugh!

I hate being pitiful. I hate being weak. I want to believe that I can do anything.

My working premise is that I should be strong enough, that I should be able to cancel weakness with determination. Does this work? Not usually, but I keep thinking it will.

> **Every time you hope to find strength in yourself, you miss the true power of weakness.**

Do you do this too? Do you tell yourself, "I should be strong enough to do this"?

The problem isn't that we think we are strong. Most of us know we're not. The problem is that we think we should be strong.

Are we too optimistic, too deluded? Does that delusion keep us stuck, trip us up when we try to walk by the Spirit? Every single time! Keeping this delusion of strength alive prevents us from learning God's purpose for weakness. Telling ourselves that we can be strong, that we should be strong, gives us just enough strength to keep from dying to self. Every time we hope to find strength in ourselves, we miss the true power of weakness.

Weakness Is Good?

I think of weakness as a place we go to unintentionally. When we arrive at Weakness, not only are we disappointed that we didn't arrive where we wanted to, we're also frustrated because we were trying to avoid this place. "Why am I here again? I don't want to be here!" we exclaim. We feel angry, afraid, trapped, and hopeless. There is something suffocating about weakness that makes us feel desperate. We're embarrassed at having come to Weakness despite our efforts to avoid it. Nothing is going the way we want, and we can't make sense of our failure to do anything about it. We refuse to accept our failure to be strong, disturbed by the thought that others will think we're weak and get the wrong impression of us. We hate being reminded that we are weak when others correct us, when our failures, mistakes and bad choices make our weaknesses public.

Yet there are so many things that make us feel weak.

Being wrong, being afraid, being emotional, losing, apologizing, failure, vulnerability, and loneliness all feel weak, and feeling weak feels just plain wrong.

So we conclude that anything that makes us feel weak is bad and must be avoided.

What if weakness was entirely different? What if weakness was a condition, a permanent condition that needs no cure? What if weakness was good? What if it was better than strength?

But . . .

I can't stop thinking of weakness as bad, can't stop thinking of all that I dislike about weakness.

Weakness forces me to acknowledge my neediness, and that word feels like a stomach punch to my pride. I remember reading David's words describing himself, "As for me, I am poor and needy" (Ps. 70:5, NLT), and being struck by how hard I work at not having to say that about myself. I like to think I'm strong and self-sufficient. Being needed is alright, but being needy is altogether different. Being needed tells me that I am valuable. If, however, I appear weak and needy, my pride is insulted.

Although we are born needing everything done for us, before we are a year old, we rebel against such dependence. Why? What makes us work so hard to be independent? Are we better off when we don't need anyone? Are we stronger?

> **"**
> *When weakness morphs into "not being good enough," it is swallowed up and defined by the flesh.*
> **"**

None of us are good at everything, but we would like to think we can be. Ashamed when others discover our inadequacies, we cover our weaknesses. We work hard at appearing strong, at hiding our emotions, at building walls.

When weakness morphs into "not being good enough," it is swallowed up and defined by the flesh. Weakness becomes an accuser, a nagging doubter of our sufficiency. Stuck in this cycle, we see the friends we depend on for strength as reminders of our failure. Our attempts to hide weakness and imitate strength leave us destitute, angry, and full of self-pity. We've lost control of the flesh, and it has gained control of us. How did we get here? We try to fling weakness away, but it slams right back. Like a magnet, it attracts every negative thought possible. Convinced we are worthless, we withdraw in misery and anger, afraid that others will discover our terrible secret: we are weak!

> **"**
> *When the flesh takes charge of weakness, it makes us forget that we are dead men walking.*
> **"**

When the flesh takes charge of weakness, it makes us forget that we are dead men walking. The flesh insists that we are too strong to die, even when we feel drained of all strength.

When the Spirit takes over our weakness, something amazing happens. God comes in and accomplishes things we never dreamed were possible. We are awed by His greatness and humbled by our smallness. Not once are we dismayed by our inadequacy. Not once do we compare ourselves to God and resent Him for his strength. Instead, we are grateful for our limitations, realizing that without them we could never know God's creative power in our lives.

Describing himself and his coworkers, Paul wrote,

> *"We were so utterly burdened beyond our strength that we despaired of life itself. Indeed, we felt that we had received the sentence of death. But that was to make us rely not on ourselves but on God, who raises the dead."*
> –2 Corinthians 1:8b-9, ESV

It is insane that we rely on ourselves when we could depend on the power that raises the dead!

Weakness doesn't belong in the hands of the flesh. We don't have to prove we're strong. The flesh has no right to slap us in the face with our weakness.

Weakness says power from God. Embrace it!

The Subtle Defeat

Is defeat an inevitable consequence of weakness? If offered the choice of enduring weakness or acting defeated, which would you choose? Which do you normally choose? The flesh prefers defeat, and I'm not talking about the magnificent defeat that God produces when He breaks us; I'm talking about the sickly, pitiful, whiney defeat that is common to our natural selves. Defeat is the flesh protecting itself, refusing to be broken by God. Defeat is the proud choice of your flesh when it faces its own weakness and refuses to accept it.

Accepting defeat is easier than accepting weakness, and the easy way is always more appealing to the flesh. The flesh would have us believe that weakness is bad, would have us resist weakness until we feel defeated. The flesh would have us believe that we can't endure weakness, that we are better off discouraged.

The flesh would have us believe that hope disappointed us, but conveniently ignore that it was hope in ourselves that failed us, not hope in God. The flesh would offer us an anemic imitation to dying to self, allowing us to mope about in misery rather than experience victory. The flesh would have us believe that our only choice is to wallow. That's the deceitfulness of the flesh, the subtle allure of defeat.

We are dead men walking, starting every day with a death sentence. Weakness is a tool God uses to accomplish that death. Until we accept that truth, weakness will just as easily be used by the flesh.

> **Weakness is your strength! It says power from God.**

How often I have delayed the Lord's blessings because I chose to remain disappointed in myself, rather than admit my weakness and rely on Him!

Remember Hannah's prayer,

> *"The bows of the mighty are broken, but the feeble bind on strength."*
>
> –1 Samuel 2:4, ESV

Weakness is your strength!

Strap it on, and stop acting defeated!

Brag About Weakness

> *"If I have to boast, I will boast of what pertains to my weakness."*
>
> –2 Corinthians 11:30

What was this weakness Paul was talking about? Whatever it was, he repeatedly prayed for God to remove it, without getting the result he wanted.

Been there, done that.

I've been in that place many times, asking God, pleading with Him, to relieve me of what makes me feel weak, especially before anyone else notices it.

For Paul, God did not remove the weakness, and people noticed. He was often criticized for not being as good as other preachers. Was it that criticism that prompted him to beg God to remove his weakness? Did he, at some point, think the critics were right, that he needed to be fixed?

That's what I would be thinking.

"Fix me, God, make me better; or, more accurately, make me as good as others."

In the end, Paul realized that his weakness was meant to keep him humble. He discovered, through experience, that his greatest strength came through his weakness.

It would be logical to conclude that if we want strength and power (and I mean the authentic stuff), we should seek weakness. After all, if we were willing to embrace weakness, we would have access to super power.

But we aren't willing, are we? We aren't willing to appear weak because our goal isn't true strength, but the appearance of strength. And that, my friends, is our pride taking charge, our flesh exerting dominance.

If we were living by the Spirit, we would say with Paul, "if I have to brag, then I will brag about everything that makes me look weak."

Sound ridiculous? Seem backwards? Yep, but we should be used to that. Nothing about walking in the Spirit makes sense to our natural selves. In the flesh, we're too proud to be weak. In the Spirit, we will talk about our weaknesses as if we were proud of them, not to bring glory to ourselves, but to bring glory to God.

Paul's 180° approach to weakness, however, must dramatically change how we see and react to weakness. To boast in our weaknesses means we are no longer ashamed of them, no longer frustrated, angered, or discouraged by them. It means that we no longer hate what makes us feel weak. To boast in our weaknesses is to stop taking pride in our strengths, and, instead, to take pride in our weaknesses.

Think about the things you want others to see you doing, the things you secretly hope will gain you a reputation of brilliance, the things that make you feel superior, the great things you've accomplished. If you could, you would brag about them a little. Maybe you do.

Now think about your weaknesses in the same way. Rather than making you inferior, your weaknesses commend you to greatness in the Lord. Rather than causing shame, they glorify God. Don't hate them; rejoice in them.

(If I had fuses in my brain, they'd be blowing.)

Boasting in our weaknesses saps power from the flesh, causing it to die a little more, taking us one step closer to living by the Spirit.

Paul's Paradox

A paradox is the joining of two concepts to say something that seems absurd. Paul's paradox seems absurd.

> *"For when I am weak, then I am strong."*
> –2 Corinthians 12:10b

It started with Paul's desperate pleas to be rid of his thorn in the flesh and this reply from the Lord: "My grace is sufficient for you, for my power is made perfect in weakness" (2 Cor. 12:9, ESV).

I wonder how long it took for those words to take root and flourish in Paul's heart. He couldn't have reached his "coup de grace" to weakness overnight, couldn't have reached this following statement in a matter of hours:

> *"Therefore, I will boast all the more gladly of my weaknesses, so that the power of Christ may rest upon me. For the sake of Christ, then, I am content with weaknesses, insults, hardships, persecutions, and calamities. For when I am weak, then I am strong."*
> –2 Corinthians 12:9b-10, ESV

The decisive blow the Lord's words had on Paul's thorn in the flesh couldn't have come quickly and easily, for though the words threaten all my norms regarding strength and weakness, they never seem to crush them altogether.

Will they ever, I wonder? Why do I doubt that they can?

Paul didn't doubt. He pushed his paradox beyond all that is natural in us. Take, for example, this crazy conclusion at the end of his letter to the Corinthians.

"For we are glad when we are weak and you are strong.
Your restoration is what we pray for."
–2 Corinthians 13:9, ESV

Glad when we are weak! I've never thought of weakness and joy in the same room, much less cozying up on a couch together.

I frequently get deeply discouraged, angry at myself, frustrated with my weakness, but I'm rarely (okay, never) glad about it. Maybe, just maybe, I might find weakness tolerable in the company of other weaklings, but if others look stronger than me, then I get temperamental. Appearing weak sends my mind into a tailspin of self-torturing thoughts. I certainly have never conjured up happy thoughts at those times, never wished others to be stronger.

That the apostle Paul could say that he will, with all gladness, take pride in his weaknesses seems ludicrous. He says he is well-pleased, content with weaknesses, insults, distresses, persecutions, and calamities!

Hold on! Weaknesses, insults, distresses, persecutions, calamities.

Hello! That is an exact copy of my list of things to avoid! I thought it looked familiar.

What could make Paul be happy with this? Well, apparently, the Lord's words inspired him. Let's take another look at a paraphrase of what He said.

MY grace is enough to satisfy, to make you content,

Do you live as if His grace is enough, always and in every situation?

MY miraculous power and deeds are fulfilled in the weakness that keeps you from being able to accomplish what you want.

Are you willing to exchange pride in your own fulfillment for joy in His?

The flesh cannot take pleasure in weakness because its only desire is self-fulfillment. If we keep walking in the flesh and looking at weakness from our perspective, we will only see what keeps us from being independent, from being able to do what we want, from being good enough.

In the Spirit, weakness is where God takes what we can't do to do what only He can. When we are pleased in our weaknesses, He is most glorified and we are most satisfied.

> **"**
> *God is most glorified when you are pleased in your weaknesses.*
> **"**

Crazy Joy

Against all odds, against three crafty enemies, against fear of death, sleepless nights, threat of bodily harm, tricks, and lies, Nehemiah can talk about joy!

His book reads like a journal, a detailed account of how the Lord led him to rebuild the wall around Jerusalem, and of the trials and resistance he encountered throughout the 52 days of building.

Nehemiah faced three nasty and persistent opponents: Sanballat the Horonite, Tobiah the Ammonite, and Geshem the Arab. These three openly mocked and ridiculed Nehemiah for his plan to rebuild the wall. His enemies were as determined to stop him as he was to finish the job. Their taunts were sharp, their threats frightening, their lies and tricks intimidating. Nehemiah didn't whine about the unfairness, didn't run and hide, didn't give up, or mope. Instead, he led the people by example, made plans for their protection, kept the workers going, cared for their needs, and continually prayed to God. These weren't long prayers, just a short "God, make me strong," and back to work he went.

When the wall around Jerusalem was complete, the people gathered at the Water Gate. Ezra stood above them on a wooden platform and read the law to them from early morning until noon. Many were hearing the words of God for the first time, and a tremendous revival spread through the crowd. People were weeping in response to what they were understanding, when Nehemiah calls for it to stop. Stop hurting, stop feeling sorry, stop crying, stop being sad!

"Excuse me! Are you minimizing my pain?"

No, that's not what the people said, but that is what I say when I feel that someone is cutting off my expression of pain and sadness. When I feel bad or feel sorry for myself, I think that I have to feel sad. Isn't that how it works? When I hurt, I want others to affirm that pain, to tell me I'm right to be sad. It's an insult to be told to get over my sadness before I'm ready. Do they think I can turn on the happy faucet anytime I want to? That's the problem. I don't want to! I want to keep the right to hurt, because it says my pain is legitimate. Besides, if I stop showing how sad I am, no one will feel sorry for me.

For Nehemiah and the people there would be plenty of weeping and confessing in twenty-three days, but they were not to weep this day. This was the day to enjoy lots of rich food and sweet drinks, and to make sure everyone else had enough food for a feast. This day was holy, set apart for the Lord.

When Nehemiah commanded them to stop crying and start rejoicing, did he intend them to wait until they felt happy? Did their feelings change instantly? Probably not. So why do we think that we have to feel happy before we can be happy?

◆

When I was severely depressed, I felt no joy. Many mornings I stood in the shower sobbing, water mixing with tears, but no matter how much water washed over me, I couldn't wash the sadness away. We had a waterproof CD player for the shower. One morning, as I was leaning my head against the wall sobbing silently, a song broke through and I heard,

> "We are all as happy as we make up our minds to be,
> I have just decided that nothing's gonna take this joy from me.
> It's a good day
> even if things aren't going my way.
> Jesus is Lord and I am saved!
> It's a good day!"[3]

What a concept! I could decide that joy would stay in my day because Jesus was Lord! I didn't have to wait for all my sadness to go away, didn't have to look for something to bring joy into my life. I was saved, and that was reason enough to rejoice. Something changed, and for the first time, I had a new plan to choose joy each day, no matter what.

The story of Nehemiah tells me that, not only can we choose to be glad even when our feelings are sad, we should choose to do so. It's crazy, I know, but it works.

On that day Nehemiah told the people about a crazy joy, that is,

"The joy of the LORD is your strength."

—Nehemiah 8:10

"Oh," you say, "is that all?" That's all because it is that simple. This joy is not of ourselves, but of Yahweh, the highest name of God. What's more, the strength of this joy does not refer to human strength, but refers to a fortress, a refuge, a stronghold, or a safe place. The joy of Yahweh is your fortress. The joy of Yahweh builds walls of protection around you.

> **"**
>
> *The joy of Yahweh builds walls of protection around you.*
>
> **"**

Does that sound like the joy you feel, like the joy you can find inside yourself? That doesn't sound like any joy I know! If you want strength in weakness, you will want this Crazy Joy, and you can have it.

◆

Habakkuk, an Old Testament prophet, wanted God to fix the wickedness of Israel that seemed to surround him, so he complained, or, as I prefer to call it, he stated his opinion. The Lord replies, "Look around, be amazed, you won't believe what I'm planning" (Hab. 1:5, paraphrase).

Okay, you've got my attention, what is it? The Lord says, "I am going to raise up the dreaded Chaldeans to invade and destroy" (v. 6, paraphrase). How's that for punishing wickedness?

Habakkuk may be wondering if his complaint has backfired. He questions the Lord, "Do you really think it's right that such an evil people should destroy one that is more righteous" (v. 13, paraphrase)? The thought of being invaded by the Chaldeans caused him to shake with fear. He described his response in this song.

> *"I hear, and my body trembles; my lips quiver at the sound; rottenness enters into my bones; my legs tremble beneath me. Yet I will quietly wait for the day of trouble to come upon people who invade us. Though the fig tree should not blossom, nor fruit be on the vines, the produce of the olive fail and the fields yield no food, the flock be cut off from the fold and there be no herd in the*

stalls, yet I will rejoice in the LORD; *I will take joy in the God of my salvation.* GOD, *the Lord, is my strength; He makes my feet like the deer's; He makes me tread on my high places."*

–Habakkuk 3:16-19, ESV

Fear has made Habakkuk weak, but, somehow, even in that frightened and weakened condition, he manages to accept the circumstances. Though neither the instrument God uses, nor the removal of blessing will be pleasant, Habakkuk declares that he will wait quietly.

How can he do this?

He chooses joy, even though all he feels is fear. He doesn't wait until circumstances change or he feels differently. He claims his joy because his God saves, is in total control, is right in all that He does. And what does joy in the Lord give him? It gives him strength. It gives him feet like a deer.

Trials are hard! They seem to drag on forever, make us feel weak and afraid. Crazy Joy is easily obtained, lasts forever, makes you strong, and makes you secure. Unlike the human joy we usually seek, crazy joy is never just a feeling, never a fake; it is always a reality in the Lord. Joy like a fortress! Does that not shout stability and safety to you?

Broken and Crushed

Perhaps no show of weakness is more bitter than when you were expecting yourself to show great strength.

———————◆———————

Conversation in the Upper Room

Jesus: You will all fall away, because it is written, 'I will strike down the shepherd, and the sheep will be scattered.'

Peter: Oh, not me, even if all these others run away, I won't.

(disciples turn and glare at Peter)

Jesus: Simon, Simon, (sighing deeply) Satan has demanded permission to sift you like wheat, but I have prayed for you, that your faith may not fail; and you, when once you have been restored, strengthen your brothers.

Peter: Lord, I am ready to go to prison or death with You!

Jesus: No, Peter, actually this very night, before the cock crows, you will have denied me three times.

Peter: Not so. I will die first before denying You.[4]

When I read this, I think, "You are not as strong as you think you are, Peter. Sure, you sliced off an ear in the name of defending the Lord, but you couldn't even stay awake to pray for Him or acknowledge you knew Him." Then again, I shouldn't be too quick to accuse him, since I am just as prone to miscalculating my own strength.

How could Peter have been so far off from reality? Jesus, who knows all hearts, hears Peter's bravado and sees right through him. He knows that His impetuous follower is actually weak and will crumple under fear. Why is Jesus not dismayed by this? How can He keep putting up with Peter?

I'm not sure what shocks me more: that Satan demanded permission to put Peter through the wringer, or that the Lord gave Satan permission. I feel indignant at what seems to be setting Peter up to appear weak. "Why not let him be strong, Lord? Why expose him to this humiliation?"

Few things get me more riled up than feeling that I've been set up to fail. I don't like having my weaknesses forced into the open, put on parade for others to judge.

Jesus does, however, show compassion, reassuring Peter, promising to pray that his faith won't fail. Do you suppose He does that for us too? "If you do, Lord, do you think you might be able to change it up a little to pray that I won't fail, because I hate failing?"

What does failure say about me? Why does my weakness discourage me? Why does it discourage me more than Peter's weakness discourages the Lord?

Jesus promises that something good will come out of Peter's failure. Peter will strengthen his brothers. Failure, it appears, is not the final verdict, not the 'end of it all', as I often perceive it.

The Master Creator and Designer has a beautiful vision for our failures! Failures are like blank canvases. We can choose to pick up the brush and try to paint something by number, or we can choose to hand the brush to the Master Painter who will cover our failure with vibrant colors and designs.

When I was first writing this, I thought "what was the point of crushing Peter?" My answer came while celebrating the Lord's Supper. I was reminded of Isaiah 53:5, "He was crushed for our iniquities." Ashamed, I realized that I wasn't standing up for Peter; I was standing up for myself, protesting God's methods of breaking me.

Am I that egotistical? Could I ever have weakness thrust upon me that would come anywhere close to the weakness that Jesus faced the night of his betrayal? My Savior held back His strength, allowing Himself to be beaten, tortured and mocked, to be falsely accused, and sentenced to death by crucifixion. He didn't have to do that.

One of my sweetest childhood memories of my dad is hearing him belt out

"He could have called ten thousand angels
To destroy the world and set Him free,
He could have called ten thousand angels,
But He died alone for you and me." [5]

Turns out, it was closer to a hundred thousand angel army according to Matthew 26:53! Uh-huh, that's right, Peter; He didn't need you! In the greatest paradox of all, what appeared to be defeat was victory!

God . . .

> *"Having forgiven us all our trespasses, by canceling the record of debt that stood against us with its legal demands. This He set aside, nailing it to the cross. He disarmed the rulers and authorities and put them to open shame, by triumphing over them in Him."*
> —Colossians 2:13b-15, ESV

The tears flow. I feel very small, and that seems right. Then it hits me. Perhaps, the greatest display of strength isn't in appearing strong, but in restraining strength and allowing one's self to be weak.

Chapter

6

Enduring Weakness

Endurance: The ability to hold out for the duration, while going through hardship, pain, and stress.

Sounds dreadful! Sounds scary! Endurance is not my thing. I'm not good at it. It seems too risky to face something I know might drag on for a long time. Doubts of whether I can endure weigh me down and make me want to throw up my hands and say, "I can't do it anymore." Maybe I'm afraid I won't be able to endure; maybe I'm lazy and just don't want to work hard. Either way, I prefer that my endurance not be tested. I want everyone, including God, to make life easy for me. That's one reason I don't like weakness hanging around. Weakness tests my endurance, therefore, weakness scares me.

I'm not into jogging. The idea doesn't appeal to me. Never done a marathon, and probably never will. That is, I've never ran in a marathon. Now, if we are talking about a marathon of Jane Austen movies? That I can do.

There is a big difference.

When I settle down with my coffee and knitting to embark on hours of movie watching, I don't have a single doubt regarding my ability to make it to the end.

When I approach running, however, doubt of whether I can make it is the only thought in my mind. From the second I start, all I can think about is when I can quit. Every inch of my body tells me this is not a good idea, and my brain agrees. I'm afraid I'll feel pain, afraid I won't be able to make it, afraid I'll embarrass myself.

I can conjure up no image that could make me want to do this.

Perhaps the thought of endurance and weakness scares you. Perhaps you are in a trial that has you feeling so weak that you doubt whether you can endure.

➢ How does a woman who thought she was pregnant and has just been told that the expected baby is actually a cancerous growth endure the wait to learn if the tumor is malignant?

➢ How does any woman endure the hours of labor to deliver a stillborn child?

➢ How does anyone endure a future without holding the child she had loved and kissed whether for 5 months or for 2 years?

➢ How does one endure a lifetime of being trapped in a useless body, a future of constant pain?

➢ How does one endure the news of cancer, and then endure a treatment worse than the disease?

➢ How does a son or daughter watch his or her mother slowly be drained of all strength, suffer, and die?

➢ How does anyone endure sexual abuse, betrayal, being dumped, or cheated?

➢ How does a woman endure shame, addiction, depression, the monthly reminder of no pregnancy, and delays in international adoption?

I can put a face with each of these scenarios, multiple faces with some. Yet, they are only a thin layer on the top of many stories I have heard, each making me ask, "How can anyone endure that?!" I'm not a merciful person, but even I find it impossible not to weep over the stories. My heart aches. How does anyone endure?

The author of Hebrews says, "run with endurance," but there are times we aren't sure if we can even crawl.

The Crowd of Witnesses

Let me introduce you to the people that the author of Hebrews told to run with endurance:

"Remember the former days, when, after being enlightened, you endured a great conflict of sufferings, partly by being made a public spectacle through reproaches and tribulations, and partly by becoming sharers with those who were so treated. For you showed sympathy to the prisoners, and accepted joyfully the seizure of your property, knowing that you have for yourselves a better possession and a lasting one. Therefore, do not throw away your confidence, which has a great reward."

–Hebrews 10:32-35

Remember!

Then the author walks us down the hall of faith for a walk of remembering.

"There's Abel," he says, pointing to the picture of a man offering a lamb sacrifice, and there is Enoch walking with God right next to him."

"There's Noah building the ark." He gestures to the other side of the hall, and takes you over for a closer look.

"Here are Abraham and Sarah standing outside their tent holding their baby son Isaac, even though they look old enough to be grandparents. Look," he says excitedly while dragging you back across the hall, "that's Moses in the basket, and Moses by the burning bush, and Moses telling Pharaoh to let God's people free, and Moses leading the people between great walls of water." The author stops with a sudden calmness that feels almost eerie by comparison to his excitement of just seconds before. Looking solemnly into your eyes he speaks as if this one act of faith stands out above the rest, "Moses chose to endure abuse rather than enjoy the limited pleasures of sin," he says slowly, almost reverently.

Then, just as suddenly, he returns to his former excitement, dragging you to the next display. "You'll like this," he says, "it's a YouTube clip of the walls of Jericho falling down. See that woman walking out unscathed? That's Rahab," he stops and turns, watching your face for a reaction, "she's a prostitute."

On and on it goes.

There were many more! Some mocked and beaten, some imprisoned and in chains.

> *"They were stoned, they were sawn in two, they were tempted, they were put to death with the sword; they went about in sheepskins, in goatskins, being destitute, afflicted, ill-treated (men of whom the world was not worthy), wandering in deserts and mountains and caves and holes in the ground."*
>
> –Hebrews 11:37-38

All these endured, but none of them got what was promised. Why? Because God had something better for us, and, without us, these could not be made perfect.

But they endured!

Hey, there they are! Can you see them, can you hear them? They're cheering you on, saying, "don't give up." And look, straight ahead. It's Jesus!

He has his hands out, saying, "You're not alone. I'll never leave you. Come, I'll give you everything you need to run this race. I've gone before you; I know every step, every pothole, every twisted ankle, and every sin that weighs you down."

You know those movie scenes where the hero fights against all odds to finish a race, and there, at the end, is a crowd cheering him on. Do you remember how you felt when you watched it? I am inspired when I watch someone endure to the end, but what I am most touched by is the cheering crowd gathered to help bring him home. Seeing that support gives me such a lift, I could almost swear I was floating.

Oh,

> *"SINCE WE HAVE SO GREAT A CLOUD OF WITNESSES SURROUNDING US, let us also lay aside every encumbrance, and the sin which so easily entangles us, and let us run with endurance the race that is set before us, fixing our eyes on Jesus, the author and perfecter of faith, who for the joy set before Him endured the cross, despising the shame, and has sat down at the right hand of the throne of God. For consider Him who*

has endured such hostility by sinners against Himself, so that you will not grow weary and lose heart."
—Hebrews 12:1-3

Imagine that! Now there's an image that motivates, that takes the weight off and makes us feel lighter, that makes us think maybe, just maybe, we can endure. No, not can! It makes us think maybe we will endure. Maybe, one day, we'll even be able to say that with no "maybes" attached. Amazing, isn't it, how that image can change everything we are feeling instantly. It's the image we need every day as we wake up with this death sentence.

The beauty of accepting God's use of weakness to bring about the dying of your flesh is the promise of the living of Jesus that accompanies it. In the living Jesus, we have all that we need to endure weakness. In the living Jesus, we have

> In the living Jesus, you have all that you need to endure weakness.

the most perfect One who understands all our weaknesses. In the living Jesus, we have the hope of an eternal reward.

The Fellowship of Jesus

"Now that we know what we have."
—Hebrews 4:14, The Message

When you know you have something, it changes things; sometimes it changes everything. Like knowing you have cancer. It changes your future, your choices, your thoughts, your hopes. Nothing around you has changed, but suddenly you see everything differently. A little while ago you wanted to bite someone's head off, now you can't even remember why. That morning's irritations become insignificant. Yesterday's quarrels and squabbles become irrelevant. You wonder how you could have worried about such mole hills. Living takes on a new focus because life has become fragile. Before you twiddled away time, now you treasure every minute.

Knowing that you are expecting a baby also changes your whole outlook on the future. Dreams and plans for his or her arrival consume your every thought. You never knew you could love this way. Now that you know what you have, life will never be the same.

The author of Hebrews is telling us that we have a Great High Priest. Knowing that should change everything!

Jesus became one of us so that He could be a merciful and faithful high priest. We're not used to having high priests these days. What does a high priest do?

> **Imagine if your only access to God were through one man. What would that man be worth to you?**

The High Priest was chosen by God to be the one representative of the people before Him. The high priest prayed for the people, and was the only man allowed to enter the Holy of Holies. Even then, he was allowed to enter only once a year to make atonement for the sins of the people. Once a year he went through the veil with a blood sacrifice.

Imagine if your only access to God were through one man. What would that man be worth to you?

---◆---

During the last meeting of the last day at a ladies retreat in the Sierra Nevada Mountains, someone announced, "Would you please go to the office, your husband needs to talk to you." As usual, I was talking and missed part of the announcement. Was that my name that had just been called? I glanced at my friend, and her worried look confirmed that it was. She insisted on walking with me to the office. Along the way we talked about what it could be. I couldn't imagine anything serious. Even though only emergency calls were allowed, I didn't want to believe it was bad news. I picked up the phone, aware of my friend staring anxiously at me. I stared back, barely able to get out two words, "it's bad," before I could only sob. I now knew that my dad had died of a massive heart attack, and everything changed. Steel bands gripped my heart and I thought I would never feel again. I thanked God for my friend and her merciful sympathy when I needed her. But I felt that something was missing, that I was waiting for something more.

We drove down the mountain toward home, and I was waiting. We got in the car and drove four hours to southern California; I was still waiting. We flew to North Carolina, rented a car, and drove three more hours to Roanoke. Still waiting.

Finally, after what seemed an eternity, we pulled up to my brother's house where my dad had last spoken, had held the last grandchild he would know, and I found what I had been waiting for. At the sight of my mom and my five siblings pouring out the door, I breathed again and those steel bands around my heart broke. As I felt my family's arms holding me together, I was more grateful than ever to have been blessed with such a large family. I knew that they knew how I felt, and the release I experienced was incredible. They were affected by my dad's leaving this world as much as I was. Their loss, their grief, was the same as mine. We didn't have to say it. We just felt it. We were of the same fellowship of feelers now.

> *"For we do not have a high priest who cannot sympathize with our weaknesses."*
>
> –Hebrews 4:15a

"*Sympathesai,*" the Greek word that describes what Jesus our High Priest does for us, means more than sympathize. It means that he fellow-feels with us. It means that he is affected by the same feelings that affect us.

Though I excel most at feeling sorry for myself, occasionally I feel sorry for someone else. That's usually what I think sympathize means: to feel sorry for someone. I can say I'm sorry for you, but to say I know how you feel would wound you more. Pity makes me feel compassionate, but it fails to reach the depth of another's pain, agony, or weakness.

What a difference it makes to talk to others who are able to feel what you feel! You can see it in their eyes, hear it in their voice, and you know that they know. You feel comforted, feel that you're not alone, feel that there is hope.

> **Our High Priest can say, "I know how you feel," and mean it!**

Jesus, Our High Priest, is full of compassion, understands all our weaknesses, and never loses His patience with us, even when we act like idiots. He loads us up with all the grace and mercy we could ever need, especially when we have nothing left. Our High Priest can say, "I know how you feel," and mean it!

Do you realize what this means? That person you've been longing for exists. You know the one I'm talking about, the one you thought couldn't exist because you have been let down, disappointed and disillusioned so many times that you are too afraid to trust again, too afraid to believe.

But believe you must!

Two Sisters and a Funeral

Enter Martha.

She muttered as she chopped the figs, the current target of her frustration. Was all that noisy "comforting" necessary? She couldn't see the joy in their coming, since it meant that she had to slave away in this hot kitchen. Someone poked their head in, "Did you hear? Jesus has been seen on the road!"

Martha dropped her hands and leaned on the table where she had been chopping figs. Her shoulders slumped as tension drained from her body. She was relieved he had finally come, definitely relieved, but she also felt bitter that he hadn't come sooner. Her lips tightened. If he had just come when she sent for him, Lazarus would still be alive, and she wouldn't have to worry about the future for her and her sister. She straightened her back. "What are you doing standing here," she scolded herself. "You know you'd much rather have him here, than that room full of mourners from Jerusalem." She hesitated for a moment, thinking of the disaster that could occur if she left the food cooking. "Let it burn," she thought, and dashed out the door to meet him.

She saw Him in the distance and her steps changed from a run to a march as she approached Jesus, ready to speak her thoughts. "If you had been here, Lord, my brother would not have died," she blurted out. Did she detect a little accusation in her voice? She hadn't meant for it to sound that way. "I know God gives you anything you ask for," she said, hoping to soften her tone.

"Your brother will rise again," Jesus said reassuringly.

"Yes I know that, and it is indeed a great comfort, knowing he will rise again on the last day," she replied.

But was it? She had heard this consolation many times, even believed it, but did it comfort her now? Did knowing about the resurrection change her feelings about losing her brother?

Jesus said, "I am the resurrection and the life. Believe in Me and you'll live; believe in Me and you'll never die. Do you believe Martha?"

"Yes Lord, I believe You are the Christ, the Son of God, the One we've been waiting for. I believe."

So why didn't she feel better? Was that all He had to offer her? She turned away, her steps less determined. "I guess it's enough, for now," she thought as she headed back to the kitchen.

Jesus watched her walk away, shaking his head slightly. She hadn't understood what He was offering.

Do you sometimes fear that all you will find, when you come to God in the midst of your pain, is doctrine and platitudes? Are you afraid that Christianity will disappoint you, that the Bible will leave you feeling empty? Do you wonder if you are missing something?

Doctrinal truth is exactly what some people need to hear, the perfect anchor in their storm. For others, knowing the truth doesn't calm the seas. They have no trouble believing, but their feelings refuse to follow. They may conclude that God is not in touch with how they feel, even wonder if He is real.

Feelings can never replace my faith; what I believe can never be born of how I feel. That's good, since my feelings are as unpredictable and changeable as the wind. Basing my faith on how I feel is scary. That would be similar to building a house on a swinging bridge or over a sinkhole.

But in driving a wedge between my faith and my feelings, what have I done with my feelings? Have I pushed them into a room I believe God doesn't want to enter? Have I settled for thinking that I can only relate to God through doctrine and concluded that He doesn't care about my feelings? Am I resigned to forever carrying the burden of my feelings on my own?

Does doctrine make a difference? Absolutely!

Do your feelings matter to God? Just as much!

Enter Mary.

Four days had passed since Lazarus had died, and still, she couldn't believe it. She missed him terribly, missed his voice, missed his strength. Looking around the room, she stored away in her mind each of the friends and family that had come to be here and grieve with her. Their tear streaked faces, their wailing voices made her feel better somehow, as though they were absorbing some of her grief. It was good not to be alone, if only . . . "No," she insisted, "Jesus would have come, if he could have. He loved Lazarus too. He still might come." She hoped he would. His presence would bring such comfort.

"Mary," someone tapped her shoulder, "your sister is asking for you."

My sister Martha, dear Martha, Mary thought. "Sometimes I wish that she could understand me, cry with me, but I'm glad, at least, that I don't have to go through this alone."

"The Teacher is here, he wants to see you," Martha whispered in her ear.

Joy swelled up within her. It was such a relief to know he had arrived. Tears blurred her vision as she ran. She longed to bring her pain and sadness to him, knew that he would know what was in her heart. He was like that, always seeing right through her, always knowing the right words to say.

She reached him and immediately clung to his feet. Smiling, she thought of the hours she had spent at those feet, and of the costly perfume she was keeping just for them. Then she remembered Lazarus, and she felt the knife in her chest again.

"Lord, if you had been here," she sobbed, "my brother would not have died." At first, her tears stuck in her throat, but then they broke through with loud, gut-wrenching cries. "When will this pain stop, when will I run out of tears?" she wondered.

Mary's grief moved Jesus deeply. "Where have you put him?" he managed to ask before weeping silent tears.

Why did Jesus respond so differently to these two sisters? Why did one get truth and the other get tears? Did He know what they each needed?

Mary got sympathy, and Martha, well, let's just say that she's about it get one more mouth to feed.[1]

Soul Anchor of Hope

Hope is powerful.

The tiniest thread of hope can keep us holding on against the craziest odds. Toss us the thinnest line, and we'll hold on to the hope that our mother will love us the way mothers should or that our dad will protect us as fathers ought to. Against all reason we hope that the boyfriend who left will come back, or that, this time, we really are pregnant, or that, for once, things will be different.

A tiny drop of hope is like super glue.

When I began writing on weakness, I planned to include something about our High Priest understanding our weaknesses, but I never expected to spend so much time in Hebrews. When I tried to pull that one strand out, I couldn't separate it from the rest of the letter.

Hebrews tells us that Jesus is a priest according to the Melchizedekian order. What does that mean? It means He is a priest forever, and it means that his priesthood came with an oath God swore by Himself, because He could swear by no one greater.

> *"The Lord has sworn and will not change His mind,*
> *'You are a priest forever.'"*
>
> –Hebrews 7:21

You may think, "that's nice; not sure why that is important to me."

It's like this: life has a way of tossing you about like a beach ball on the ocean. You need an anchor to keep you from being bounced about. This Melchizedekian priesthood comes with a hope the size and weight of an anchor, not at all like that thin, fragile hope that keeps us holding on to something or someone that isn't even good for us.

This anchor comes with a high priest that lives forever. Forever: that means everlasting, has no end, won't run out, never stops, never quits, goes on and on.

This anchor comes with a promise, an oath, from God that He will never leave you, never give up on you. And God doesn't lie or change his mind.

Read and decide for yourself.

> *"In the same way God, desiring even more to show to the heirs of the promise the unchangeableness of His purpose, interposed with an oath, so that by two unchangeable things, in which it is impossible for God to lie, we who have taken refuge would have strong encouragement to take hold of the hope set before us. This hope we have as an anchor of the soul, a hope both sure and steadfast and one which enters within the veil, where Jesus has entered as a forerunner for us, having become a high priest forever according to the order of Melchizedek."*
>
> –Hebrews 6:17-20

> *"Who has become such not on the basis of a law of physical requirement, but according to the power of an indestructible life."*
>
> –Hebrews 7:16

What's more, previous priests were always being replaced because they died, but Jesus,

> *"Because He continues forever, holds His priesthood permanently. Therefore He is able to save forever those who draw near to God through Him, since He always lives to make intercession for them."*
>
> –Hebrews 7:24-25

Teaching about our Great High Priest tends to be relegated to theological study. We hear the words "high priest" and think of an outdated position in an obsolete system of animal sacrifice, exciting for those who love to debate theology, but lacking practical encouragement.

Like Martha, we know what Christ has done for us in the past and we're certain of what He will do for us in the future, but we doubt that what He is doing for us now is what we need.

Jesus Christ, Our High Priest, gives us free and confident access to the presence of God, access He bought for us with His own blood, through the sacrifice of His own body. With Him, where He has gone right up to heaven, we have a hope so sure and trustworthy it is an anchor for our soul. How beautiful for a soul, caught in a raging storm, to find himself or herself secured to an anchor that will not budge! What soul, blinded and confused by insecurities, unreliable relationships, disappointments, illnesses, and lost jobs, doesn't long for such a hope!

Because Jesus lives forever, He saves forever. Because He lives, He intercedes for me, forever and always. His life is indestructible; therefore, my hope is indestructible!

The Lord designs trials to reveal our weaknesses, which in turn, builds our endurance. That cross on our back will make us wobbly, it will make us weak, it will feel like suffering, it will humble us. That is what we can expect when we walk by the Spirit.

If you haven't experienced this yet, you will, and, when you do, you will want an anchor. The hope of eternal life in Christ is your soul anchor.

To My Fellow Runners:

Things you need to know for this race:

1. In your fight against sin, you've barely begun to resist, so know that there is much more to come. Hang on, stay steady, don't collapse.

2. Remember your charge as sons, expect discipline; the Father disciplines his children. Discipline means He loves you; don't dismiss it and don't faint.

3. It is for discipline that you endure; it is for your good, for your sanctification.

4. No discipline ever seems joyful, so don't be surprised if it makes you sad.

5. Get up off the ground; strengthen your weak hands and feeble knees even when you feel like giving up.

6. Watch your path; choose a straight one by choosing to do the right thing. This allows injured parts to heal.

7. Do everything you can to be at peace with everyone. No fighting or bickering allowed in the race.

8. Be on the watch for stragglers, for those who have dropped off along the way.

9. Don't let bitterness grow roots in your heart; letting it do so is like breathing toxic fumes.

10. Don't indulge the flesh, no matter how much pampering it demands; indulging will always result in a loss of blessing.

–from *Hebrews 12 Manual for Runners*[2]

Finally, know this:

You will make it.

Jesus has passed through the Heavens and guarantees you a fantastic finish, provided you don't give up.

Chapter

7

Counterfeit Suffering

"**D**o you think you'll be suffering at the next place you go?" asked the young man sitting at my table, savoring real Mexican food. Arrian Zane had sworn he would be the first person to visit us in Mexico, and he was, arriving just one month after we had. His question made me laugh, but was he really joking? I had to agree that this was not suffering, and I felt that I was letting him down, disappointing him with such an easy life on the mission field. An unsettling thought popped into my head, "maybe I am not a legitimate missionary if I am not suffering."

Most of the time, we can emphatically say, "I don't want to suffer"! Sometimes, though, a little suffering makes us feel qualified, as if we had chosen an honorable way; but that is only a very little suffering. Our prayer is mostly "give us this day, Lord, suffering within reasonable limits, suffering that suits our plans. Never let us suffer without seeing a greater purpose in it. Or, if possible, never let us suffer at all."

Weakness was an easy topic for me to write about: I can admit that I have experienced weakness. As I consider suffering, however, I am hesitant to say that I have suffered. Even though I think I suffer, I'm embarrassed to make that claim; it seems like an insult to those who have truly suffered. How can I claim to be a sufferer when I can always find someone who has suffered more than I have?

This is my dilemma, my quandary, the source of my reluctance to write about suffering. Suffering is a difficult subject.

"For to you it has been granted for Christ's sake, not only to believe in Him, but also to suffer for His sake."
–Philippians 1:29

While grieving his wife's death, C.S. Lewis wrote, "We were promised sufferings. They were part of the program. We were even told, 'Blessed are they that mourn,' and I accept it. I've got nothing that I hadn't bargained for. Of course it is different when the thing happens to oneself, not to others, and in reality, not imagination."[1]

Did you know that you were getting the package deal, that suffering is always part of the Christian life?

God intends for us to suffer, but that doesn't make me like the pain. When I was clinically depressed, I felt locked in a room of pain and suffering. All I wanted was to be out of there as fast as possible. I thought suffering was wrong, thought I had done something wrong to deserve it. These thoughts made me sink deeper into hopelessness. Again and again I begged God to take away the suffering. I hated the pain, absolutely hated it! I felt miserable, blamed others, and whined enough for three lifetimes. "Why is God picking on me?" I thought. Self-pity oozed from every pore. It was gross! In what seemed a never ending suffering, I became obsessed with making the pain stop. I wish I could tell you that one of the benefits of walking in the Spirit is freedom from pain, but I cannot. I can, however, tell you that the flesh will tempt you to avoid pain.

> **"**
> *Did you know that suffering is always part of the Christian life?*
> **"**

When the flesh offers us ways to numb pain, we jump at the chance. In the flesh, we find a wide array of numbing agents: food, drugs, alcohol, sex, or cutting. But, if we accept the offers of the flesh, we won't share Christ's sufferings. And if we walk according to the flesh, we will, to our horror, want those around us to suffer too. Our vindictive nature will suggest that, "If I have to suffer, then someone else is going down with me, preferably the one I see as the cause of my pain."

In his book "Simply Jesus," Joseph Stowell says, "The question is not are you willing to suffer? We have little choice about that. The question is, are you willing to meet Jesus there—right in the midst of your pain?" To walk in the Spirit is to meet Christ in pain. Suffering is a place of fellowship with Jesus, a place of His choosing, a place to die. Stowell encourages us to stay with Him there, "and as you feel His pain in yours, thank Him that He loved you enough to suffer like this for you."[2]

> **There is a deeper knowing, a deeper intimacy, in experiencing pain with Christ.**

There is a deeper knowing, a deeper intimacy, in experiencing pain with Christ.

Fellowship of Sufferers

"For just as the sufferings of Christ are ours in abundance, so also our comfort is abundant through Christ. But if we are afflicted, it is for your comfort and salvation; or if we are comforted, it is for your comfort, which is effective in the patient enduring of the same sufferings which we also suffer; and our hope for you is firmly grounded, knowing that as you are sharers of our sufferings, so also you are sharers of our comfort."
–2 Corinthians 1:5-7

God used Joseph's suffering for good, even for the good of those who caused his pain. In the midst of his suffering, Job acknowledged that he couldn't receive good from God without also being willing to receive the bad. Jesus learned obedience through His suffering, which He endured silently. And then there was Jonah. Just recently I discovered how much he suffered. My suffering looks much like Jonah's.

Jonah, after choosing to disobey God, finds himself caught in seaweed at the bottom of the sea, then "rescued" by a big fish that swallows him. He then has to live three days in a pool of stomach acid and decaying fish. Can you imagine floating around in a pitch black bag of acid, being jostled about with chunks of stinky food? That must have hurt, must have been unbearable. I imagine Jonah would have preferred to be anywhere but there. That is terrible suffering!

Eventually Jonah gets vomited onto a beach, but then life gets even worse for him. God denies him what he most wants: to see evil people get what they deserve. On top of that, God commands him to be the means of salvation for those evil people. Jonah is so upset by the unfairness, he wants to die. Not getting what you want—now that's suffering.

But then God showed kindness to Jonah. He caused the sweetest little plant to grow right next to him, just to give Jonah shade. Jonah rejoices over his little plant! Finally, something good has happened to him. It isn't much, but after the miserable time Jonah has endured, it is precious. By some cruel twist of fate, however, a worm attacks his plant. Jonah is forced to watch his precious, beautiful, shady plant wither away, right before his eyes! Such suffering for poor Jonah, such loss and discomfort he must endure! The scorching heat and oven-like winds are unbearable, even worse than before, because he had known the joy of his shade plant. Jonah despairs of life itself.

This may seem to be a sarcastic dramatization of Jonah, maybe even funny. Believe me, it's not meant to be! It's not funny that I didn't have to put any effort into imagining what Jonah might have felt. It's not funny that I only had to think like myself. Those words came from my heart. That's how my "suffering" has looked—my suffering in the flesh, that is. I have brought much suffering on myself by disobeying, by demanding fair treatment, by seeking my own happiness, by spitting on God's compassion.

Through the eyes of the flesh, we see suffering as the withdrawal of compassion. That angers us, makes us demand God's compassion for ourselves, makes us resent His compassion on others whom we see as less deserving. Suffering in the flesh wants compassion only for itself, and that is true self-pity.

Do we have a right to seek compassion for ourselves? Do we have a right to be angry? Like Jonah, we would answer "yes, we do," and, like Jonah, we would be wrong.

> **Compassion is God's right, suffering is ours.**

Compassion is God's right, suffering is ours.

Why do we feel wronged by suffering? Why does suffering hurt our pride and make us angry? Is it not good that God brings suffering into our lives to help us make the right turns, to help us along to that death, to help us feel the cross on our backs? Good thing, huh? Right. Are you shaking or nodding that head?

The root of our opposition to suffering, I believe, is that it challenges our value system, making our flesh feel undervalued. If we value something, how do we treat it? We care for it, pamper it, love it; we never inflict pain on it. That is why, when we view our suffering through the flesh, we find ourselves doubting God's love. If He loved us, we reason, He wouldn't hurt us. If He valued us, He wouldn't let us suffer.

When we side with the flesh in suffering, we are unwilling to care about God's purpose for suffering. In siding with flesh, we feel anger at having to suffer and resentment that we can't be rid of it instantly. Suffering terrifies us because it seems that it will never end.

The suffering with which we are most familiar is bitter suffering, the suffering of unmet expectations and unfulfilled longings, the suffering of unfair treatment and undeserved loss. But when we choose to reach for the cross, to crucify the flesh, three quarters of what we think of as suffering evaporates, and what's left is a beautiful countercultural suffering, suffering that brings joy.

To walk by the Spirit, we must put the flesh to death. God allows suffering in our lives to accomplish that death, but flesh is quick to substitute counterfeit suffering. That's why our "suffering" never produces the joy that the Lord promises it will. Flesh would have us believe that suffering attacks our basic human rights. Flesh wants us to believe that giving up our rights IS suffering. When we follow this reasoning, we wander into the realm of suffering that God did not prepare for us. There we are bogged down in self-pity over denied longings and unfair treatment.

Does our disillusionment and disappointment feel like suffering? Yep, it can feel like the end of the world, like agony, like the "depths of despair."[3] It makes us stare so intently at ourselves that, when we finally look up, our vision is blurred. The tune of suffering in the flesh contains the bitter notes of whining, pouting, anger, and self-pity. Something is off key. These tones are a long way from the rejoicing that Paul, Peter and Jesus say suffering should bring.

If you hope never to suffer, or want the "get it and be done with it" approach to suffering, I have bad news for you. Suffering is not a buffet dinner. You can't choose when you will suffer, how long you will suffer, what good, if any, will come of it, or what type of suffering you will endure.

Beware of thinking that you deserve a choice in the matter. When we try to dictate the terms of our suffering to the Lord, we are not learning to suffer in the Spirit. God is not going to get on board with our choices and check us off the list of suffering recipients. Besides, if we had the choice, I doubt we would ever choose God's way. Has anyone ever said, that, had he known about it beforehand, he would have chosen God's path of suffering? Would you have chosen that path?

Suffering is guaranteed; the choice before us is whether to suffer our way in the flesh, or to suffer God's way in the Spirit. Suffering is not optional. I repeat, it is not optional, no matter how much your flesh insists that it is. The first step to authentic suffering in the Spirit is surrendering the right to choose how we will suffer, and agreeing to the Lord's terms.

Counting the Cost

Imagine with me that we are part of the crowd following Jesus.

It was becoming a common experience. To go anywhere with Jesus was to be jostled and pushed by the huge crowd following him. This time he stopped and turned to face us, saying, "To follow me, you must hate your mother, father, wife, children, brothers and sisters, even hate your own self. To follow me, you must carry your own cross. Know what it will cost you and decide beforehand whether you are willing to make that sacrifice. Don't be

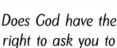

Does God have the right to ask you to give up everything?

like the builder who ran out of funds and had to abandon the project; he was the brunt of many jokes. Don't be like the king who miscalculated his forces and lost the battle. It would have been better for him to have asked for peace. Once you have put your hand to the plow, look straight ahead. If you keep glancing back, your furrows will be squiggly. So if you truly want to follow me, you have to give up everything that you have." (Luke 14:25-33, paraphrase).

Think about that. Does God have the right to ask you to give up everything? Are you willing to follow Him if it is that costly?

After living eight years as missionaries in Mexico, we returned to the United States. Everything we wanted to bring with us had to fit on a 4 x 8 flatbed trailer with a 1,000 pound limit. The most important items were the books, 40 boxes of them. There was no way that we could put those on the trailer; the weight alone made it impossible. We decided to mail them to our new home in Dubuque, but that had to be done from the US. Friends who were traveling to Texas agreed to take half the boxes and leave them in a warehouse at the border. My husband later made a trip with the other half, retrieved the other boxes from storage, and shipped them all. When he came home, he reported having successfully mailed 39 boxes. "Ummm, dear," I said, "there should have been 40 boxes."

I had to wait 2 months to figure out which box had been lost. It was torture to wait and trust the Lord. Oh, how my flesh wanted to start agonizing over what was probably gone forever! Finally, after beginning to unpack in Dubuque, I discovered that among the lost items were several journals that I had written while in Mexico. Not only were they irreplaceable, they also represented the most difficult trial of my spiritual life. I was saddened by losing something so personal, but consoled myself with thoughts of God's sovereign control. Surely He had a reason for taking them. Every now and then I thought about those journals, wondered where they ended up, wondered how the Lord used them to bless someone. Then one day, out of the blue, a new thought occurred to me. What if those priceless journals had ended up in a garbage dump, buried in gross decaying stuff? The thought pricked my pride. Those journals represented my life. I didn't like the idea of my life being tossed in some trash dump. And then it hit me: that is exactly what my life in the flesh is worth. Isn't that what Paul said?

> *"I count all things to be loss in view of the surpassing value of knowing Christ Jesus my Lord . . . and count them but rubbish so that I may gain Christ."*
> –Philippians 3:8

Why must I search for gain in the life I have lived? Why do I insist on seeing good in my suffering in order to endure it? Why do I find more value in my life than in the life Christ has given me? The reality is that my life, compared with who I am in Christ, is trash buried in a garbage dump.

———————————◆———————————

Imagine that you've been given a big warehouse to fill with all that you have and wish you had. This imaginary space can hold more than possessions; it can also store abilities, dreams, relationships, even body parts.

What would you store in your warehouse?

Here are some questions to help you take inventory:

➢ What do you have that you can't live without?

➢ What do you have that makes you happy?

➢ What do you have that you made sacrifices to get?

➢ What do you have that makes you feel lovable?

➢ What do you have that makes you feel useful to God?

➢ What do you have that makes you feel useful or valuable to others?

➢ What do you have that you are proud of?

➢ What do you have that is priceless?

➢ What do you hope to have in the future?

➢ What do you wish you had right now?

Now imagine that you are going to invite Jesus to walk around your warehouse and look at everything you have. As you walk with Him, you will offer Him the pick of anything He wants to take.

One more detail. In the corner of the warehouse is a locked room, and you have the key. In that room, you can store anything you want to keep, anything you don't want Jesus to take.

What would you put in there?

The things in that room are what rob you of contentment. The things in that room keep you trapped, make your life on earth seem worth holding on to. Because you value those things, you fear losing them.

Because they are a source of happiness, you complain when they fail to satisfy. Because they make you feel good about yourself, you compare them with what others have. Because you feel you have a right to keep them, you suffer when you lose them.

I'm not advocating that we load everything that we have on a truck and take it to the municipal dump. Jesus did not mean for us to do that when He said that no one can be His disciple unless he gives up all his possessions. He does, however, want us to change the way we value what we have. He wants us to be willing to let Him have all that is ours. If we value things properly, we won't mind losing anything. We will already consider it loss compared to having Christ.

> "There is no ongoing spiritual life without this process of letting go. At the precise point where we refuse, growth stops. If we hold tightly to anything given to us, unwilling to let it go when the time comes to let it go or unwilling to allow it to be used as the Giver means it to be used, we stunt the growth of the soul. It is easy to make a mistake here, "If God gave it to me," we say, "it's mine. I can do what I want with it." No. The truth is that it is ours to thank Him for and ours to offer back to Him, ours to relinquish, ours to lose, ours to let go of."[4]
> —Elisabeth Elliot

How much of what you consider suffering would be gone if you let go of all that you feel you have a right to have?

The Freedom of Surrender

As I consider whether I suffer, I wonder what qualifies as true suffering. Do cold showers or mornings without coffee count as suffering? Who decides how long, how deep, or how wide discomfort must be to be considered suffering?

> *How much of your suffering would be gone if you let go of all that you feel you are entitled to have?*

Webster's dictionary defines suffering as "being forced to endure pain, inconvenience or loss,"[5] all three of which are subjectively determined. Everyone has a different tolerance for pain. I think cold water for a shower is inconvenient; others find cold water more convenient than no water. And then there is loss. The feeling of loss is in the perception of the sufferer and depends heavily on what we feel we have a right to have. For example, the world says, "it's your right to be happy." Therefore, if your marriage makes you unhappy, you should leave it. Our constitution tells us we have a right to freedom? From what do we have a right to be free? Our politicians say we have a right to health care and to equal pay. Advertisements say we deserve the latest trends or newest electronics. Society tells us that we have a right to a bigger house and a more comfortable lifestyle. The flesh tells us that we have a right to achieve our dreams, to be treated well, to take revenge, to be satisfied, to do whatever makes us feel good.

Suffering in the flesh is being denied what we think is rightfully ours. It is subtle, but effective. For suffering in the Spirit to occur, this illusion of suffering, built around what we think we have a right to, must be exposed. Nancy Leigh DeMoss, in her book, "Lies Women Believe," lists lie #10 as "I have my rights."[6] Some of the things she says women wrongly believe they have a right to are . . .

➢ to be happy.
➢ to be understood.
➢ to be loved.
➢ to a good marriage.
➢ to companionship.
➢ to romance.
➢ to be treated with respect.
➢ to be valued and appreciated by your husband and children.
➢ to rest and time off.
➢ to a good night's sleep.
➢ to have help with the housework.

Do you live as though you have a right to those things? I do. And to Nancy's list, I add my own right . . .

➢ to be heard.
➢ to have my next meal within 5 hours.
➢ to always be comfortable.

➤ to not be asked to get up once I sit down.

➤ to never be betrayed.

➤ to be consulted about everything.

➤ to not have my plans changed.

This concept of rights creates a false sense of loss, which then creates an illusion of suffering.

Please read that sentence again.

Our basic right "to be happy" can, by itself, bring us into a place of suffering where we don't belong.

> **This concept of rights creates a false sense of loss, which then creates an illusion of suffering.**

Suffering, I remind you, is God's tool to crucify the flesh, but that crucifixion won't happen as long as we believe that sacrificing the things we have or wish we had, or living with unfulfilled longings, is true suffering. Suffering isn't optional. We can, however, choose to reduce unnecessary suffering by surrendering our rights. Flesh distracts us by creating an illusion around the choice of surrender, convincing us that surrender is the suffering to avoid. When we fall for that illusion, we are more trapped than ever, more miserable in our suffering. We are never satisfied, always focusing on what we don't have, comparing our situations with others, and concluding we have the short end of the stick. Life seems unfair, we blame God, and we stagnate.

Can you see how these "rights" compete with living the death sentence? Can you see how they keep the flesh alive and kicking, keep you in spiritual quagmire?

> "Along each step of this process, we will have to give up our claims to our rights to ourselves. Are we willing to surrender our grasp on all that we possess, our desires, and everything else in our lives? Are we ready to be identified with the death of Jesus Christ?"[7]
>
> –Oswald Chambers

Little Pools of Desire

Just as the loss of what we think we have a right to creates counterfeit suffering, so do unfulfilled longings. Do you long to be happy, to be accepted, to be successful, to be recognized, to be loved? Do you long for your life to mean something? Do you long for intimacy with someone you can trust?

Longings.

They are like little pools which are always draining dry, no matter how frantically we run around trying to keep full. We long for moms to care for us, for dads to be proud of us. We long to be understood, to be wanted, to be desirable, to feel safe. The world preaches that we shouldn't have to live with unfulfilled longings, and our flesh says amen to that. We raise fists in the air, shouting "I deserve to be happy!" as if sadness were a personal attack. Unfulfilled longings test our patience with God, make us question if following Him is worthwhile. When God's purposes don't allow us to satisfy those longings, we'll make a train wreck of our lives if, in doing so, we are free to pursue our own happiness.

Longings.

They control us and we let them. Is it crazy to think that they don't have to, that they shouldn't?

God has created us with needs and has given us all things to enjoy. But do we have to be driven to satisfy a longing the moment we have it? Why do we cling to satisfaction of our longings as our only means of joy? Why does our grip on earthly joys get tighter when we feel God prying our fingers open?

> **"**
>
> *Do you cling to the satisfaction of your longings as your only means of joy?*
>
> **"**

Here's a thought. Why not let your longings go unfulfilled?

What? "Why would I consider that?" you may ask. "What would be the purpose?"

If we are always rushing to fill up our longings, constantly checking the levels of our pools of longing, comparing the fullness of ours with those of our neighbors, always insisting on finding satisfaction here on earth, using others to make us feel better about our unfulfilled longings—if we are always doing that, will we ever give God a chance to satisfy us?

Unsatisfied longings often create a deep sinkhole where God seems to have abandoned us, where He can't hear us and we can't hear Him. Everything in you longs to fill that emptiness, but you are afraid. Hopelessness has set in and you believe joy is no longer available to you, believe you aren't worth the trouble. You want to believe that God cares, but the deep emptiness of your unfulfilled longings convinces you that He doesn't.

You'll trust Him when He fills them.

Could that dark pit be where you find God rather than be evidence that He doesn't care? Could that "valley of the shadow of death" hold comfort for you rather than fear? In "The Song of a Passionate Heart", David Roper imagines encountering the Lord in that dark place of the 23rd Psalm, where you learn to depend on the sound of His voice, learn childlike trust that reaches out and slips your hand into His, learn to know what His hand feels like.[8]

It can be the best place for you, because in that dark place where life seems to have no meaning, God's love becomes better than life itself: His presence becomes the very breath you breathe!

You won't learn to trust Him when there is light and you have confidence in yourself. You won't turn to Him when you are satisfied with what you can see and touch.

We run when we should stay, scream when we should listen, doubt when we should trust.

Darkened Doorways

We live as if our life has two doors, the first leading to the physical realm, the second to the spiritual, and we are left to choose between the two. Naturally we choose the physical. Our desires are quickly satisfied with touch, taste, and smell, with instant pleasure from what we see and feel. With so much earthly satisfaction, we find ourselves unmotivated to choose Door #2. We yearn for many things in this world, and then wonder why we don't yearn for the Lord.

Satisfaction in the physical realm fades. You would think that when Door #1 proves unsatisfactory, we would be drawn to what God offers in the spiritual realm. You would think that, but that doesn't usually happen. Instead, in our despair at not being fulfilled, we often conclude that God has let us down. If He won't provide for our physical needs, we think, how can we trust Him to meet our deeper spiritual needs? So we sit and stare into the emptiness behind the door to the physical world, fearing that, if we look behind the door to the spiritual realm, we will find greater emptiness.

> **We yearn for many things in this world, and wonder why we don't yearn for the Lord.**

Well, this isn't getting us anywhere, isn't helping us pull our gaze away from what we don't have. Can we ever move from this place?

◆

"For the enemy has persecuted my soul; he has crushed my life to the ground; he has made me dwell in dark places like those who have long been dead. Therefore my spirit is overwhelmed within me; my heart is appalled within me. I remember the days of old; I meditate on all Your doings; I muse on the work of Your hands. I stretch out my hands to You; my soul longs for You as a parched land."

–Psalm 143:3-6

David was in anguish. He had been anointed king, but instead of living in a palace, he was hiding in desert caves, hunted by enemies who wanted to kill him. David knew how it felt to be in a dry and weary land where there was no water, to live without fulfilling his most basic longing. Thirst creates the most intense longing your body can feel. David accepted everything he felt in his longing for water and through that longing, connected with his most intense longing for the Lord. That desperate need for water became the conduit to his soul where he longed for God more than his body longed for water.

David found the secret. Through his physical experience, he connected to his spiritual experience. He saw not two separate doors, but one door leading to the other. How did he make them connect? He borrowed the language of longing.

"My soul thirsts for you," he wrote, "my flesh faints for you, as in a dry and weary land where there is no water" (Ps. 63:1b).

Unable to touch the spiritual, we are drawn to the physical. But when that physical doesn't satisfy, it becomes, not a closed door, but an invitation to the spiritual. Through the physical, we connect to the spiritual. David let unfulfilled physical longings lead him to spiritual reality. He turned his longings to "God longings." Rather than separating us from God, our longings and sufferings are the means of connecting us to Him.

> **Rather than separating you from God, your longings and sufferings are the means of connecting you to Him.**

In boldly calling for an acceptance of suffering, I may give the impression of bravery. Don't be fooled. That future scares me as much as it scares you. I am the collapsing kind, but find comfort in these words by Oswald Chambers:

"Why shouldn't we experience heartbreak? Through those doorways God is opening up ways of fellowship with His Son. Most of us collapse at the first grip of pain. We sit down at the door of God's purpose and enter a slow death through self-pity. And all the so-called Christian sympathy of others helps us to our deathbed. But God will not. He comes with the grip of the pierced hand of His Son, as if to say, "Enter into fellowship with Me; arise and shine." If God can accomplish His purposes in this world through a broken heart, then why not thank Him for breaking yours?"[9]

By surrendering our rights and turning our longings to God longings, much of what we experience as suffering in the flesh will disappear, but there is more to this illusion of suffering.

The Illusion of Suffering

Have you noticed that no matter how hard you try to "get over" suffering, it always seems insurmountable? Have you noticed that suffering makes you feel alone? When suffering comes, do you sense that God has withdrawn? You look for Him, but He has disappeared. Just when you need Him most, He seems to be no more substantial than smoke.

In times of suffering, we squint to catch a glimpse of God, strain to touch Him. We might even question whether God exists. Suffering seems to steal the little confidence and joy we had in knowing Him. One moment, we believe that God will use this suffering in our lives, just as he did for Joseph, and the next moment that belief disappears.

Has God abandoned us to suffer alone? Has He disappeared, or is His absence an illusion? Was God ever with us or have we been deceived?

An illusion is a distortion of our perceptions. An illusionist tricks us by creating a distraction that draws our attention away so that we miss what he is doing. He appears to work magic, but what he is really doing is misleading us by making us see what he wants us to see. Our brains are tricked into thinking we didn't see what in fact happened right before our eyes.

Is God an illusionist?

I read these statements in the Bible, and, for a brief moment, I wonder if God is not creating an elaborate illusion.

> *"But to the degree that you share the sufferings of Christ, keep on rejoicing; so that also at the revelation of His glory, you may rejoice with exultation."*
> —1 Peter 4:13

> *"The Spirit Himself testifies with our spirit that we are children of God, and if children, heirs also, heirs of God and fellow heirs with Christ, if indeed we suffer with Him in order that we may also be glorified with Him. For I consider that the sufferings of this present*

time are not worthy to be compared with the glory that is to be revealed to us."

−Romans 8:16-18

"For this momentary light affliction is producing for us an eternal weight of glory far beyond all comparison."

−2 Corinthians 4:17

"Now I rejoice in my sufferings for your sake, and in my flesh I do my share on behalf of His body, which is the church, in filling up what is lacking in Christ's affliction."

−Colossians 1:24

Outrageous words such as these can make it difficult to believe God, to trust Him to be true to His word. Can joy and glory really be associated with suffering? It seems impossible to think about rejoicing in the midst of suffering, much less to experience joy. We're certain that our pain is not an illusion, but we can't imagine a reality where pain and rejoicing coexist.

It is hard enough to believe that a loving God allows suffering. Yet we are asked to accept that God is the source of suffering, and that suffering can be so . . . so . . . joyful and glorious! If this is true, what is wrong with us? Why do we never experience joy in suffering? Are we not spiritual enough?

We aren't ready for that conclusion. We would rather question God's credibility than our own behavior. If this is God's illusion of joy, then we prefer to create our own version, our own illusion. If it were up to us, we would make a world where pain and suffering don't exist, where everyone lives happily, where no one is ever disappointed. We trust ourselves to make the world a better place, trust ourselves to be more compassionate than God.

Let's be honest. We might be too shocked to say such a thing out loud, but we feel free to judge God, don't we?

Suffering provides the perfect stage for an illusion, for a game of smoke and mirrors, but the Illusionist is not our Heavenly Father. The flesh creates a house of mirrors, drawing us to focus on an illusion of suffering rather than on the real suffering. This illusion distorts our view of hardship and puts God in our blind spot. This illusion makes us feel that we are alone, that God is neither kind nor compassionate.

When we see the flesh as the true illusionist, we are freed to accept suffering in the Spirit. To accept God's use of suffering in our lives, we must know and trust Him.

Chapter

8

Suffering and Justice

One evening, while my husband and I were walking along the Mississippi River, he spied some office chairs in a dumpster. "I'm gonna get one of those chairs," he declared, and I looked at him as if he had lost his mind. This is the man who has never bought an office chair, because not a single chair in all the stores has been able to satisfy him. I had begun to think that there was no chair that would meet his criteria, yet, here he was excited about a chair in a dumpster! Surely there was a reason this chair had been rejected, so how could he know, with just one glance, that this chair would meet his standard? Baffled by this uncharacteristic display of excitement totally inconsistent with his previous behavior, I questioned if I really knew this man I had been married to for 25 years. That day I learned something about him that I had never before understood.

My husband was being consistent to a value he had held all his life, that is, if he spends money on an object, any amount of money (even just 50 cents), that object must be subjected to a rigorous evaluation of worth. If an object costs no money, however, it is free of his strict scrutiny and worthy of whatever it takes to recover it. Here is a simple truth: trying to understand your spouse (or anyone else) through your own values inevitably leads to frustration.

Many people assume they understand the values of God in the Old Testament. They assume that He is driven to seek revenge on the wicked, and conclude, therefore, that He is different from the God of the New Testament, who seems more inclined to forgive wrong-doing. Are there two Gods, with two sets of values? Does God act inconsistently from one age to another? Or might we be attempting to understand Him through our own value system? Could it be that we don't know Him as well as we think we do?

God is holy, and in His holiness He judges sin, but God is also love, and in His great love, He restores sinners. This is not inconsistent behavior, nor has God acted inconsistently in the past. He acts in holiness and love in both the Old and the New Testaments. Has God judged the wicked? Absolutely! Will He make a final judgment for the wicked? You can be sure of it. But as He always has, God also delights to forgive the sinner who turns to Him, even if he repents at the last possible moment.

> *"As I live!" declares the Lord* GOD, *"I take no pleasure in the death of the wicked."*
>
> –Ezekiel 33:11

If the righteous man turns to evil, all his righteousness will not save him. If a wicked man turns from his sin, he will live and his sins will not be counted against him. Now, Israel, you say to this, "'The way of the Lord is not right,' when it is their own way that is not right" (Ezek. 33:17).

You say, "The way of the Lord is not right." Then I say, "I will judge each of you according to your ways" (Ezek. 33:20).

------◆------

Manasseh, son of Hezekiah and Hephzibah, became king of Judah at 12 years of age. He eventually took Judah into an era more wicked than the nation had ever known, more wicked even than the nations around them. Manasseh, in his depravity, sacrificed his own sons to idols. In his 55 year reign he filled Jerusalem from one end to the other with innocent blood and led God's people to sin. Their evil so angered the Lord that He said,

> *"I will wipe Jerusalem as one wipes a dish, wiping it and turning it upside down."*
>
> –2 Kings 21:13b

Manasseh was so stubbornly evil, that the Lord sent the king of Assyria to haul him off to Babylon by a thong in his nose. "Good," you might think, "Manasseh deserved that!"

Can the most evil king of Judah receive mercy from God? Does that much mercy exist? If you were to read Manasseh's story only in 2 Kings 21, you might conclude that such an evil man would never repent, but you would be wrong. There is another record of his life in 2 Chronicles 33, a record that tells an amazing story of restoration. While in exile, Manasseh humbled himself before the Lord, turning to Him as he should have long before. The Lord heard his prayer and was moved by his pleas to bring him back to Jerusalem.

When we ask, "how can a loving God allow so much suffering in the world?" our issue isn't so much with suffering, as it is with who suffers. Like Jonah, we think it right that wicked people suffer and get angry at God when he gives them a second chance. What we find incomprehensible is that God allows suffering to come to good people who don't deserve it, but lets the wicked off the hook! Our real problem with God is that we think He is meaner than us, and we don't trust Him to be just in choosing who will receive His wrath and who His grace.

Not In My Vocabulary

As long as I can remember, I have been an advocate of fairness and equality. My first memory of encountering unfairness is when my older siblings were allowed to see "The Jungle Book" in a movie theater, but my twin brother and I were not allowed to. In those days, movie-going was a rare thing for my family, videos didn't exist, and our television was a little black and white job. I didn't need to know what a movie was to realize that I was missing out on something exciting. The explanation that I was too young made no sense to me. It was unfair! No matter how much begging and whining I did, the answer was the same. How could my parents do this to me? Why was I being deprived of this wonderful experience? Why was I being picked on? What excuse could be good enough to console me, when I was being cruelly denied pleasure? A pleasure, by the way, that was being freely bestowed on others who were no more deserving than I was. It just wasn't fair!

That began my theme song.

I have to sleep on hard boards with my brother's feet in my face, while my older siblings sleep in the camper on beds!

"That's not fair!"

She can eat anything she wants and not get fat!

"That's not fair!"

They got pregnant the first month they tried!

"That's not fair!"

God gave those missionaries a nice car that even has video monitors and didn't give us one just as nice! Are you saying we aren't as deserving as they are, God?

"That's not fair!"

Fair (according to my definition) is that which comes out the way I want it to.

Did you ever think the older brother of the prodigal son, in Luke 15, makes a fair point? I did.

"Look! All these years I've served you faithfully, never ignoring any of your commands, and you have NEVER EVER thrown a party for me. But as soon as this other son of yours, who has spent all his money on prostitutes, comes back, you show him all this honor" (Luke 15:29, paraphrase).

That's not fair!

◆

The vineyard workers, in the parable told in Matthew 20, complained to their boss about unfair treatment. "You have made them equal to us" (v. 12), they said. How had he done this? When those who had been working all day saw their co-workers who had hired on at the last hour receive a full day's wage, they started hoping for a big pay raise. Excitement built as they calculated their pay according to the new hourly wage. It would only be fair to be paid more, they concluded, since they had worked all day in the scorching heat! They deserved it!

Were they in for a big surprise when they got paid equal wages!

I imagine them thinking, "What! Are you kidding me? This is the same amount you gave the others!"

"Didn't you agree to a day's wage when I hired you?" the vineyard owner asked. "Do I not have the right to pay these men what I want with my own money? Does my generosity make you envious?" (Matt. 20:13-15, paraphrase). Jesus ends the parable with this,

> *"In this way, the first shall be last and the last shall be first."*
>
> –Matthew 20:16

You are probably familiar with this phrase, have probably even used it, though no doubt with a different spin, a spin that gives you the advantage. In this parable, Jesus means that His grace is bestowed equally, regardless of rank, order of appearance, or works. When we think that God should give us what we deserve, we begrudge Him the generosity of His grace.

When my siblings were allowed to see the "Jungle Book," I objected because they were no more deserving of this special treatment than I was. Why did I think that? Apparently, receiving equal rewards was necessary for us to retain equal value. Seeing someone rewarded more than I am tells me that I'm worth less than the other person.

"

Does it seem unfair when you suffer more than others?

"

Should reward be imbalanced? Doesn't that seem just a tad bit unfair to you? What about suffering? Should that be balanced too? Does it seem unfair when you suffer more than others?

While walking on the beach after His resurrection, Jesus reveals to Peter that his death will involve some suffering. Peter does what I would: he looks back at that other disciple John, and asks, "what about him" (John 21:21b)?

You could say that Peter and John shared an elevated position in the group of disciples. Being of the same rank, I suppose Peter might be asking this question on behalf of John because he doesn't want his friend to miss out on equal blessings. Me—I would be thinking, "I hope John will have to suffer as much as me; it wouldn't be fair if he didn't."

Jesus answers, "what I do with him is none of your concern. You, Peter, follow Me" (John 21:22)!

The idea of fairness is flesh-based, and undermines our belief in God's justice. To determine fairness, you've got to compare. "Fair" was never in Jesus's vocabulary, and it shouldn't be in ours. To live by the "fair" rule is to invite misery to walk with us. Seeking fair treatment leaves us discontent and blind to God's goodness. We compare and complain, speaking words that are unacceptable to God.

What I am most ashamed of regarding my paradigm of fairness is that I assumed God to be less than good, less than loving, less than perfect, less than God. That is sin!

Of Jesus, Peter wrote,

> *"While being reviled, He did not revile in return, while suffering, He uttered no threats, but kept entrusting Himself to Him who judges righteously."*

–1 Peter 2:23

To suffer in the Spirit, you have to know that God is just and trust Him to act justly.

> **"**
>
> *To suffer in the Spirit, you have to know that God is just and trust Him to act justly.*
>
> **"**

Cosmic Justice

Raj, in his post *Can You Escape Karma?* writes "one's acts become his/her destiny. What you give is what you get in return. Do good, and nature definitely returns you the favor. Do something wrong/evil/unethical and it sure will come back to you some day in some form."[1]

Although Karma technically relates to reincarnation, the belief that what you do in this life determines who you will be in the next, today karma is broadly defined as "what goes around comes around." This latter definition appeals to our human nature. Even if you don't believe that karma exists as some unseen force, you probably hold to this principle of karma. Isn't this the way it should be? Aren't ethical standards built on cause and effect? Do something good and good will come back to you; spend your life being nasty to others, and you will eventually get what's coming to you. That's common sense. The chickens always come home to roost.

"Nothing comes from nothing,
nothing ever could,
so somewhere in my youth or childhood,
I must have done something good."[2]

What do you think? Was Maria loved by Captain Von Trapp because of some unknown act of goodness in her past? If she had never done anything good, would she never have been loved?

Is there a direct correlation between the good things that happen to you and the good you've done?

In 2007, businesswoman and philanthropist Shari Arison established a Good Deeds Day believing that if we do enough good deeds, they will ripple out like rings in a pond, as agents of change to all mankind, bringing peace and harmony to this world.[3]

According to this way of thinking, not only do our good deeds lead to future rewards, but our actions also determine the balance of good and evil in the world. And who ensures that this happens? Why, the universe and karma. It's the law. Good creates good, bad begets bad. It is only fair, a sort of cosmic justice if you will.

Luke touches on this kind of justice in the story he tells of when he and Paul were shipwrecked on the island of Malta. While gathering wood for a fire, Paul was bitten by a snake.

When the native people saw the creature hanging from his hand, they said to one another,

> "No doubt this man is a murderer. Though he has escaped from the sea, Justice has not allowed him to live."
>
> –Acts 28:4, ESV

Justice? What are the Maltese talking about? Are they referring to a force in the universe that ensures that evil is repaid with evil? Do we humans tend to assume the existence of an unseen, cosmic force of justice that knows what we do and rewards or punishes accordingly?

Do you believe in cosmic justice, in karma?

Should we believe that doing good will bring us good, and doing evil will bring us evil? Is this the justice God seeks when He tells us to do good?

Is God Just?

It seems that in rejecting a just God, man replaces Him with the idea of a just universe. We trust "mother nature" to do right, but question whether God will. God, not mankind, becomes the target of our accusations of injustice. We may even resent God's mercy.

When Jonah settled himself on a hillside with a good view of Nineveh, what was he expecting? Did he think that cosmic justice would be served? And why shouldn't he? The Ninevites were brutal conquerors, proud of their dominance, ruthless in their attacks, ripping open the bellies of pregnant women. They deserved to be wiped off the face of the earth. Is there not an evil that goes beyond the reach of compassion?

But Jonah knew that God wouldn't see it that way.

Those wicked people had repented, and God, as Jonah had predicted, relented from destroying them. Jonah became angry with God for His compassion, bitter with Him for showing grace and mercy to such evil people. This was why Jonah had avoided Nineveh in the first place. "For I knew that you are gracious God and merciful, slow to anger and abounding in steadfast love, and relenting from disaster" (Jonah 4:2, ESV).

The prophet Joel uses those words as a promise of restoration (Joel 2:13); Jonah uses them as an excuse for disobedience. "I knew that about You" came off of his lips like drops of acid. Jonah concludes his tirade, "Lord, just kill me now, I would rather die than suffer like this" (Jonah 4:3, paraphrase).

My goodness! Jonah is suffering because God is compassionate. This doesn't make any sense! What kind of heart despises someone for his goodness? How could Jonah despise God's grace?

We will not arrive at the right perspective on suffering if we start with the erroneous premise that we or the universe can be more just than the Creator, our heavenly Father.

We can only suffer according to the will of God if we are completely surrendered to His justice, a justice that procured forgiveness of sin for us, even though every molecule of our flesh is wretchedly undeserving.

To associate suffering or reward with past or present behavior is to invite God's judgment without His mercy, without His grace.

God's words in Malachi shock us:

"Jacob I loved, Esau I hated."

–Romans 9:13

Such a statement would lead us to ask, "is God unjust?"

In Romans 9, Paul argues for the justice of God's choosing one over another. He writes that the Lord said to Moses, "I will have mercy on whom I have mercy and compassion on whom I have compassion" (v. 15).

God's choice doesn't depend on the will or actions of man, but on God who has mercy. Does the thing molded say to the molder "Why have you made me this way?" The potter has the right to make something common or make something rare out of the same piece of clay. Although willing and right to show His power by destroying vessels of wrath, God acts justly when, through great patience, He holds back His wrath and shows the great riches of His glory on vessels of mercy. Our Lord is righteous in all He does. He is also richly merciful to the unrighteous (Rom. 9:20-23).

A day is coming when each Christian's works will be tested with fire. Even if his works don't survive the fire, the man will be saved, because, in Jesus Christ, he is justified apart from his works. (1 Cor. 3:13-15)

God does not declare us right by weighing our acts of good and bad on some scale of justice. He desires to show compassion, to give His mercy to whomever He chooses. His mercy comes in buckets the size of oceans, but if you wish to have Him use thimbles and be stingy with His grace, if you want Him to give only what you deserve, if you prefer to have Him live by your standard of measurement . . . well, I pity you.

The Divine Paradox

O Man,

What do you think?

Do you think you can pass judgment on others and still escape God's judgment? Do you think so little of God's patience and kindness that brings you to repentance? Your stubborn and unrepentant heart is storing up God's wrath and righteous judgment, who will render to every man according to his deeds: to those who do good, eternal life; to those who are selfish and disobedient, wrath and indignation. There will be tribulation and distress for every soul who does evil, Jew first and then the Greek; and glory and peace for every soul who does good, same order. God is not partial (Rom. 2:1-11, paraphrase)

In his commentary on Romans, H.C.G. Moule says that, at this point in his letter, Paul is about to embark on "the divine paradox of the Justification of the Ungodly. First, so that justification "come in order and now out of it, he bids us to consider right, wrong, judgment, and retribution as if there were nothing else in the moral universe."[4]

Only Judgment.

Does the universe act as our moral judge, Paul asks. Can we be the judges of what is right or wrong? Do the Jews have a right to judge Gentiles because they don't keep the law, or by judging others, do they actually condemn themselves? Even the Gentiles instinctively know what is right and good, but that does not make them good. They condemn themselves by failing to live up to what they know. There will be a day when God will judge the secrets of men through Jesus Christ (Rom. 2:12-16).

Paul makes a powerful and clever argument.

He continues: If our unrighteousness demonstrates the righteousness of God, then isn't He unjust to inflict wrath? If my lie brings God glory, why am I being judged? And why not go ahead and say (as we have slanderously reported to be saying), "let's do evil, so good will come out of it" (Rom. 3:8). Twisted. No one is better than another, for all have sinned, all have been separated from God; no one does good to begin with.

The whole world will one day stand before God to be held accountable to Him, finally realizing how holy and perfect He is and how despicable we are. Like Job, we will put our hands over our mouths: no more arguments, excuses, defenses and self-justifications. Guilty as charged, we would all stand condemned as children of wrath. That is a universe where there is only right and wrong, judgment and retribution.

◆

Enter the Justifier.

But God, because of His great love, publicly displayed Christ on the cross. Christ, condemned to suffer the most excruciating death, satisfied God's wrath toward our sin. At the same time He demonstrated God's righteousness and patience in passing over our sins, in order that God might be just and the justifier of the one who has faith in Jesus.

Man is justified by faith in Jesus, not works. A worker gets paid what he is due according to his deeds, whereas, the one who believes in Him who justifies the wicked is declared innocent before God, not according to his deeds, but according to Christ's work on the cross (Rom. 3:21-26).

Can you believe it! No one deserves to be declared innocent before a holy God, and yet God declares guilty ones innocent, and He is just in doing so.

◆

Grace Appears.

Grace freely gives what is undeserved to the undeserving.

> **Grace freely gives what is undeserved to the undeserving.**

Have you ever been tossed aside, pushed out to make room for someone better, rejected, or made to feel useless? That's what grace does to the flesh. Grace dismisses every effort of our flesh as useless, worthless, and obsolete.

In the flesh, I like to think that I am good enough, or at least, better—better than something, anything, even just one thing. I believe in my ability to be good and want to prove it to the world.

Are you clinging to bits of your own goodness, still hoping that you can pull through and make a "good" show of it for everyone?

If so, you are despising grace.

Grace and your goodness have nothing in common. Grace cancels out your goodness, making all good efforts of the flesh worthless.

> "
> *Grace cancels out your goodness, making all good efforts of the flesh worthless.*
> "

In the flesh, I insist that I don't need help. I think of myself as self-sufficient. I don't like being dependent on others or having to ask for help. Do you too find it difficult to accept help? Are you proud of being self-sufficient? You'll find it hard to accept grace.

Grace declares us inadequate, defective, and imperfect. Grace is beautiful to us only when we are broken, empty, and spiritually destitute.

In the flesh, I am not only independent, I am also confident in my efforts, so confident that when I screw things up, I am shocked. "How could I have messed up so badly?" I cry!

Do you take pride in your achievements; relish the satisfaction of receiving what you have earned? If so, grace will leave a bitter taste in your mouth. Grace rejects all your self-effort, wipes it out, and obliterates it. Grace gives unwarranted good to us when we have made a royal mess of things. We could never earn anything that grace gives us.

Grace says bluntly, "You are undeserving." The flesh reacts to that with fierce self-defense. Flesh tells us we deserve better. When we get less than we think we deserve, flesh cries out in our defense "that's not fair!" When another person gets more than they deserve, flesh shouts "how unjust!"

We are not paid according to our deeds. God offers forgiveness to the wicked, forgiveness that is totally undeserved. It is not a justice that we consider right and fair, but it is justice according to God.

Hallelujah! That justice, crazily mixed with mercy and grace, is my blessed hope. Oh, how I need to be reminded of that every day! I have received good, and not because I have done something good in my past.

In the most beautiful paradox, my sinful soul has been justified. Through Jesus Christ, I have been ushered onto this platform of grace on which I stand, and now I have peace with God.

Suffering in the Spirit is impossible without a love of God's grace. If we insist on judging others for their works, on expecting God to judge others according to their works, then we invite Him to deal with us the same way.

> **"**
>
> *Suffering in the Spirit is impossible without a love of God's grace.*
>
> **"**

The Reward for Doing Good

In my research on karma, I was surprised to find comments that likened karma to the saying 'do unto others as you would have them do unto you'. Curious isn't it, using what Jesus taught in His Sermon on the Mount to explain karma?

> *"Treat others the same way you want them to treat you."*
> –Luke 6:3

Is Jesus teaching that you do good deeds so that good will come back to you? If we keep reading in Luke 6, we find that Jesus isn't introducing the principle that our current actions determine how we will be treated. Quite the opposite—He is introducing a new way of treating those who treat us unfairly. There is no gain, He says, in doing good to those who do good to you; even evil people can do that. He then commands us to love our enemies, do good to those who hate us, bless those who curse us. Why? Because our Father does this: He is merciful to wicked and ungrateful people.

Jesus's main point is mercy, not retribution. When He said that we should treat others the way we want to be treated, He was not teaching reciprocity, but love and mercy to the undeserving.

Jesus did not teach karma in the Sermon on the Mount.

What about another popular saying attributed to karma, "You reap what you sow." Is that in the Bible?

Paul wrote to the Galatians,

> *"Do not be deceived, God is not mocked; for whatever a man sows this he will also reap."*
>
> —Galatians 6:7

Sounds like karma, doesn't it? Sounds as though if you sow good, good will come back to you. Is that what Paul is teaching here?

"If you sow to flesh," he continues, "you reap corruption, if you sow to the Spirit, you reap eternal life." Paul is actually still on the flesh vs. Spirit theme that he began earlier in this letter. The emphasis of reaping what you sow is not on individual deeds, but on the pattern of serving the flesh or serving the Spirit. To paraphrase Galatians 6:7, "Don't kid yourself, flesh cannot do anything good, and God is not fooled by your attempts."

Paul doesn't teach that an unknown force will bring justice to this world according to our deeds. Instead, he teaches that there is a clearly defined struggle between the flesh and the Spirit, and that it is impossible for the flesh to produce the Spirit. This does not, however, excuse us from doing good. In Galatians 6:9, Paul exhorts the believers not to grow weary of doing good, not to quit doing good.

But we must not be deceived by the flesh's attempts at doing good. The flesh tries its best to make itself acceptable, to protect itself from hardship, to indulge itself in comfortable pleasures.

> *"Those who desire to make a good showing in the flesh try to compel you to be circumcised, simply so that they may not be persecuted for the cross of Christ."*
>
> —Galatians 6:12

> **Doing good for the purpose of receiving good is fleshly.**

Being circumcised was, by Jewish standards, good, but Paul says that in this situation it was an effort of the flesh to avoid suffering. Doing good for the purpose of receiving good is fleshly. Crucify the flesh and you won't fulfill its desires. We need to be strangling the flesh, not sowing to it and watering it.

On the other hand, Paul makes it clear that the life and peace we have in the Spirit is not free of suffering. We who are in the Spirit share an inheritance with Christ, if we suffer with Him. We must endure suffering in this world, endure it even when exhausted, never giving up in doing good. We must be aware of the flesh's desire to take the easy way, and realize that easy way won't include doing right.

We cheer when the wicked suffer, perhaps even tolerate our own suffering when we know that we brought it on ourselves, but we can't understand suffering that accompanies doing good. Is it possible for us to accept that suffering results when we do good? Is it possible to view suffering as a blessing? Not only is it possible, it is probable. In Peter's first letter he wrote,

> *"When you do what is right and suffer for it, you patiently endure it, this finds favor with God. For you have been called for this purpose, since Christ also suffered for you, leaving you an example for you to follow in His steps."*
>
> —1 Peter 2:20b-21

> *"But even if you should suffer for the sake of righteousness, you are blessed."*
>
> —1 Peter 3:14

(this isn't a big "if"; it's a certainty)

> *"For it is better, if God should will it so, that you suffer for doing what is right rather than for doing what is wrong."*
>
> —1 Peter 3:17

(you mean this could be God's will!)

> *"Beloved, do not be surprised at the fiery ordeal among you, which comes upon you for your testing, as though some strange thing were happening to you; but to the degree that you share the sufferings of Christ, keep on rejoicing; so that also at the revelation of His glory, you may rejoice with exultation."*
>
> —1 Peter 4:12-13).

(or as we say today, "jump for joy").

"If you are reviled for the name of Christ, you are blessed, because the Spirit of glory and of God rests upon you. Make sure that none of you suffer as a murderer, or thief, or evildoer, or a troublesome meddler; but if anyone suffers as a Christian, he is not to be ashamed, but is to glorify God in that name."

–1 Peter 4:14-16

"Therefore, those also who suffer according to the will of God shall entrust their souls to a faithful Creator in doing what is right."

–1 Peter 4:19

Don't stop doing good, even when you suffer for it. Remember that you are entrusting yourself to your faithful Lord, not to anyone else. The truth of God's Word is not that we are to do good to avoid suffering, but that we are to do good in the midst of suffering.

> ❝
> *The truth of God's Word is not that you are to do good to avoid suffering, but that you are to do good in the midst of suffering.*
> ❞

Chapter

9

Perspectives on Suffering

Eternal Weight Lifting

To live by the Spirit is to expect suffering, but if you live by the paradigm 'you get what you deserve,' suffering will seem unfair. You must drop this attitude of deserving something and welcome the suffering designed by God intended to help you die to self.

Maybe you have begun to entertain the possibility of accepting the suffering that comes from God.

A definite possibility, right?

How do you feel about accepting suffering that comes from the disobedience of others?

A definite problem.

Surely, the Lord would not intend for us to suffer the consequences of our husband's sin, our child's rebellion, our father's drinking habit, our mother's selfishness.

What if you had to endure suffering because of someone else's disobedience? How long should you be expected to endure it?

◆

Consider Caleb's story.

This was it, this was what they had been hoping for, and he had seen it himself! Beauty, richness and abundance would be theirs, ripe for the picking. His mouth watered as he remembered those grapes.

When, in his miserable life, had he tasted such sweetness! Imagine those plump, juicy little delights being made into wine! The Lord wasn't exaggerating when He called this the promised land. After slavery in Egypt, that hot, dry year at Mt. Sinai, and the trek across the desert, Caleb could hardly wait to get in there and conquer the land. Hadn't he seen the plot of land he wanted when they had gone in to scout? He was already picturing himself there enjoying the rest he had waited so long to find.

He did not doubt that God would be with them. After what God did in Egypt, He would have no trouble taking this land. Even those giants couldn't present an obstacle too big for his God. Besides, God is faithful to His promises; Caleb never stopped believing that.

Standing before Moses, Aaron, and the people, Caleb listened while his fellow spies gave their report. *Yes*, he thought, *show 'em those grapes, get them excited about the fruit of the land. Wait! No! What are you saying? You'll discourage them; it's not nearly as bad as you make it sound.* He had to speak, "Listen, we have to take the land, we can do this! Right?" Nodding his head, he turned to the others who had been with him for the last forty days. Only Joshua nodded his in agreement. The rest continued to paint horrible pictures of the people in the land and talk about the fortresses surrounding the cities. Tearing their clothes, Caleb and Joshua begged the people not to rebel against the Lord. "Don't listen to this report! The Canaanites are vulnerable, because we have the Lord with us," they cried.

They spoke, but no one listened. They begged the people to have faith, but the people preferred to take the easy route, to give in to fear. They stood alone against a nation of more than 1 million people.

Though Caleb's faith ensured that he would eventually enter the land, he still had to suffer forty long years of desert wandering and waiting. He had had faith to do what was right; he had spoken up for what was right; he had been ready to act on what was right; but in the end, he had to suffer with everyone else for their sin, not his.[1]

How did he get up each of those 14,000 days and not feel great bitterness? How did he get through those forty years of waiting for his reward, forty years of suffering? I don't like this aspect of suffering. People who make bad choices should keep their suffering to themselves, thank you. Those who do right shouldn't have to suffer just because people around them are stubborn and stupid.

Repeating Peter . . .

> *"For it is better, if God should will it so, that you suffer for doing what is right rather than for doing what is wrong. For Christ also died for sins once for all, the just for the unjust, in order that He might bring us to God, having been put to death in the flesh, but made alive in the spirit."*
>
> —1 Peter 3:17-18

(Hmmm . . . Where would I be if Jesus had shared my attitude?)

Whether our suffering lasts 8 hours, 10 days, 12 months, 40 years, or a lifetime, what is that compared with eternity with the Lord? Add together the lifetimes of every person ever born, and it only amounts to a flash in the pan. Lifetimes share something that eternity does not: an end.

> **"**
>
> *What is suffering that lasts a short time compared to eternity with the Lord?*
>
> **"**

> *"Therefore we do not lose heart, but though our outer man is decaying, yet our inner man is being renewed day by day. For momentary, light affliction is producing for us an eternal weight of glory far beyond all comparison, while we look not at the things which are seen, but at the things which are not seen; for the things which are seen are temporal, but the things which are not seen are eternal."*
>
> —2 Corinthians 4:16-18

I don't know of anything that makes suffering the consequences of others' actions seem justifiable, right, or pleasant. Honestly, though, we are not strangers to enduring pain for a reward. If you want to build muscle, you must endure pain. To weight lifters, that pain feels good. I got to thinking, what is the difference between pain in my muscles and pain in suffering? Why do I welcome one and not the other?

My first thought was the reward: you have to want what comes with the pain. But although I want and am grateful for eternity in the Lord's presence, I still don't want the pain of suffering. Looking forward to eternity doesn't help me find joy in suffering now, especially in unfair suffering. I can agree with the psalmist who wrote, "Whom have I in heaven but You and besides You, I desire nothing on earth" (Ps. 73:25), but still find it impossible to feel joy in suffering. Why can't I welcome the burn that eternal weight lifting brings?

There is one HUGE difference between painful muscles and suffering: my muscles don't have pride. It hurts my pride that I have to suffer for the sins of others, that I have to suffer for doing what is right, that I have to suffer for people who aren't acting sorry enough for what they have done to me. Pride, the beating heart of my flesh, will not have a good attitude about suffering—and that's putting it mildly.

When Evil Is Done to You

What did Joseph do to earn such hatred from his brothers? It wasn't his fault that his father loved him more, or that God had given him the ability to interpret dreams. He did nothing to deserve being dropped into a deep well and sold as a slave to traveling merchants (the kinder option; the original plan was to kill him). I wonder if, in all his sufferings, Joseph ever wished that his brothers had killed him.

People can be hateful, and that includes family.

Joseph was treated cruelly by family members. His brothers robbed him of his freedom, of the loving care of parents, of the comfort of home, of being there to see his little brother grow up. In exchange, they gave him slavery, culture shock, language barriers, strange food, and pagan practices. He endured slavery, and, as if that weren't enough, he was imprisoned for crimes he didn't commit.

What would you have done in those circumstances?

Even a fellow prisoner forgot him, left him to rot in jail after promising to help. That one disappointment alone would be enough to keep any of us in bitterness for life. I don't think many of us, myself least of all, could have borne so much suffering.

Joseph must have blamed his brothers. None of this would have happened if they hadn't plotted against him. Betrayal by family members is the worst, the most difficult to accept. You expect them to love you, to care about you. If you can't trust your family, who can you trust?

In an amazing reversal of circumstances, God raises Joseph from being a prisoner to being the most powerful man in Egypt, second only to Pharaoh. That gift of interpreting dreams, the one that had brought Joseph such misery, was finally used for his good, used to save nations, and more significantly, used to save the lives of Joseph's relatives, God's people.

Through the interpretation of Pharaoh's dream, God used Joseph to stock-pile food for the coming years of famine. The whole world sought Joseph to buy food, including his brothers. They bowed before this powerful Egyptian without a clue to his true identity. So when Joseph revealed himself to them, what do you think he said? He'd had years to plan his revenge. Now he had the power to do it.

What would you have said?

Joseph tells them "do not be grieved or angry with yourselves, because you sold me here" (Gen. 45:5).

Oh c'mon! Joseph, I think you've gone too far. If I can't be bitter with those who have hurt me, at least let me have the pleasure of knowing they hate themselves for it. They're supposed to feel bad, really bad, never forgiving themselves, living with their guilt till their dying breath. How can you wish that they not? How can you forgive them that much?

> *"It was not you who sent me here, but God."*
>
> –Genesis 45:8

Apparently, Joseph didn't hold his brothers responsible for his suffering. Instead, he looked beyond their actions and saw God's hand. In doing so, he was able to release them from their debt, and amazingly still not be angry at God. His rationale being, how could he accept only the good from God and not the bad.

Years later, when their father died, the brothers feared that Joseph would seek vengeance. In this they demonstrated not only that they had not trusted the sincerity of Joseph's forgiveness, but also that they knew their sin deserved retribution, knew that if they were in his shoes, they would seek revenge.

Once again, Joseph releases them from their debt. His reasoning this time: "you meant evil against me, but God meant it for good" (Gen. 50:20a).

Wait. Let me see if I got this right.

Joseph admits that his brothers acted against him out of pure evil. I am amazed that he doesn't have to justify, minimize, or excuse their evil as misguided or unintentional in order to forgive. Forgiveness is impossible to achieve in the flesh. Blatant evil cannot be forgiven. That would be letting someone off the hook. Therefore, we often try to make forgiveness easier by creating a false reality in which the harm is minimized. As a result, too few of us truly forgive.

Joseph's admission tells me that forgiveness doesn't diminish, deny, or change the fact that the one who harmed you has done evil against you. Joseph believes God uses man's evil for good purposes, an almost incomprehensible thought. Even if people treat us with purely evil intentions, God can use that for good. He doesn't just turn that evil around and somehow, by His goodness, make it better. He can and does, from the beginning, intend that act of evil to be for our good, and, what's more important, for the good of others. God used the evil of Joseph's suffering "to bring about that many people should be kept alive" (Gen. 50:20b, ESV) including the ones who had hurt Joseph.

If you are suffering from evil done against you, let me ask: have you forgiven as Joseph forgave? Or are you trying to make forgiveness happen in the flesh by minimizing the offense to make it seem more forgivable? That is not how Joseph forgave, and it is not true forgiveness.

> *It is impossible to walk in the Spirit while refusing to forgive.*

If you choose to hold onto the debt of those who have hurt you, choose not to forgive, your journey of walking in the Spirit ends right here. It is impossible to walk in the Spirit while refusing to forgive. I know your flesh is telling you "I would rather die than forgive." Well, here is your chance to accommodate it. Forgiveness may be the first deadly blow your flesh will have experienced, so go ahead and let 'em have it.

You have no idea how good it will feel!

The Saddest Life Award

And now, the winner of The Saddest Life Award is . . . *drum roll please* and the winner is . . . *just let me open this envelope,* and, the award goes to . . .

Jeremiah, son of Hilkiah, of the priests of Anathoth in Benjamin, for living the most disappointing life ever.

You, Jeremiah, win this award for totaling more depressing message hours than any other prophet, for not being allowed to marry and have children, for wishing your mother's womb had been your grave, for having the worst imprisonment experience—muddy seat at the bottom of a cistern—for being the most ridiculed man of your town, for receiving death threats every time you spoke, for thinking you were lucky not to have been hauled off to captivity, only to find out from the Lord that the captives in Babylon were the "good figs," and you were left behind to rot with the "bad ones."

Jeremiah, we looked high and low to find the people who showed you kindness in your sad, pitiful life. We understand that the king of Babylon treated you kindly, but unfortunately, he was unavailable to be here today (some peculiar explanation about having been turned into a mad cow—very strange).

We were able to find the one other person in your life that was kind to you. This man, upon hearing that you had been dropped into the cistern, stood up for you before the king, and then, with much ingenuity, took worn out clothes and rags from the king's palace to make a rope long enough to get you out. Jeremiah, here he is, the man who rescued you from the pit, Ebed-melech of Ethiopia.

Why Jeremiah?

The saddest life award goes to Jeremiah because, unlike the lives of Joseph or even Job, Jeremiah's life has no happy ending. It unfolds like a tragic movie that leaves you hanging at the end. Jeremiah had messages of hope for the captives in Babylon, but little hope for those in Jerusalem. The few remaining in Jerusalem had only one chance for good—to stay in Jerusalem. They chose instead to run to Egypt, hoping to escape famine and war, despite the Lord's message that both hunger and the sword would find them there. Jeremiah had to go with them in their disobedience and die in Egypt.

His tragic life makes him a character to whom we can relate. Jeremiah didn't hold back when describing his pain and sorrow. He was honest about it, asked the hard questions. I think of him as spokesman for the sufferer.

A prime example:

> *"Why is my pain unceasing, my wound incurable, refusing to be healed? Will you be to me like a deceitful brook, like waters that fail?"*
> –Jeremiah 15:18, ESV

Does Jeremiah speak for you? Do you have pain, whether physical or emotional, that refuses to heal?

> *"The thought of my suffering and homelessness is bitter beyond words. I will never forget this awful time, as I grieve over my loss."*
> –Lamentations 3:19-20, NLT

"Remember my affliction," Jeremiah says, "remember my wandering, remember the wormwood (the poison), and bitterness. Surely my soul remembers and is bowed down within me" (v. 19).

Remember, remember, remember!

I remember my misery, even when I don't want to. At times, it is all I can think about. I would love to not remember, but I can't forget pain. And the memory is not alone in consuming my thoughts. The anticipation that the pain will be endless clings as tightly as the actual suffering. Jeremiah forgets nothing, unless it is happiness (v. 17). Is that misery what we have to look forward to?

> *"But this I call to my mind, and therefore I have hope. The steadfast love of the Lord never ceases, his mercies never come to an end. They are new every morning; great is your faithfulness. 'The Lord is my portion,' says my soul, therefore I will hope in Him. The Lord is good to those who wait for Him, to the soul who seeks Him. It is good that one should wait quietly for the*

*salvation of the Lord. Let him sit alone in silence when
it is laid on him. Let him put his mouth in the dust, there
may yet be hope."*

Lamentations 3:21-29, ESV

Here's my paraphrase:

This I actively bring back to my mind, the truth of the Lord's
unfailing love, compassion and mercy. These are what will go on
without end. These are what must be remembered, must be anticipated.
My soul may remember my suffering, but it also says, "The Lord is
my inheritance," and for that hope I will wait with great expectation.
It is good for me to sit holding my words in my mouth, when I feel the
weight I think I can't bear, when it gets too heavy, when I find myself
face down in the dirt, eating humble pie.

◆

One day, our daughter unwittingly confessed to her dad that she
could cry fake tears. "Really, how do you do that?" he asked.

"I just remember things that make me sad," she said, "like my
grandfather dying, or having to give away my dog."

I think sometimes we use the same technique for the opposite effect;
we try to make ourselves happy by recalling memories that make us feel
good. Does our joy come from looking back on earthly experiences?

> **Your joy doesn't come from looking back on earthly experiences.**

Jeremiah knew very little of earthly
joy. When he speaks of the Lord's
compassion and unfailing love, he
does not have the luxury of recalling
joyful memories. In fact, the few times
he speaks of joy are like a bleep on the screen of mourning that
characterizes his life. The only joy Jeremiah knows comes from the
words of the Lord; apart from that, his life is sad and lonely.

*"I did not sit in the company of revelers," he says, "nor
did I rejoice; I sat alone, because your hand was upon
me, for you had filled me with indignation."*

–Jeremiah 15:17, ESV

He is hypersensitive in every fiber of his being, to every memory of pain, to every affliction suffered. If his rare spurts of rejoicing last only seconds between his painful memories, does that count as joy?

What does our "joy" word count have to be to say that we have rejoiced? How many times must we be joyful in our sufferings for it to count? Does it only count if joy occupies more space in our minds than misery? If we say anything that describes our pain, are we disqualified from being joyful? Or can we say what we really feel, really think, "my life is wretched" and still rejoice?

If your soul can say, "It's good that my hope isn't in this life, my hope is in the Lord," then, yeah, go ahead and say it. "My life is miserable!" You need not apologize if suffering feels more like mourning than like joy, so long as you know and can say that the Lord is your eternal inheritance. That is what counts. Your joy is in knowing what your future holds, knowing that this pain will end, but the mercies of the Lord never will.

David says of the Lord,

> "For his anger lasts only a moment, but his favor lasts a lifetime! Weeping may last through the night, but joy comes with the morning."
>
> —Psalm 30:5, NLT

> "You have turned my mourning into joyful dancing. You have taken away my clothes of mourning and clothed me with joy, that I might sing praises to you and not be silent. O Lord my God, I will give You thanks forever."
>
> —Psalm 30:11-12, NLT

Joy expressed, even if only for a second, is joy without limits, an eternal and abundant joy, an every morning fresh supply joy. Remember: momentary affliction, eternal glory.

> "
> *Joy expressed is joy without limits.*
> "

Symbiotic Relationship

"It is good for me that I was afflicted, that I may learn your statutes."

–Psalm 119:71

Those words made me choke!

Although suffering, trials, and discipline have made me dependent on God's word like a kidney failure patient is dependent on dialysis, I never thought of saying, "how good it is to suffer!" The benefits didn't excite me enough.

To be truly spiritual you must read your Bible every day, right? As a young person attending church and Christian camp, I heard this frequently. I wanted to comply, wanted to look spiritual, wanted to follow the godly example of others so that I too could be an example. I wished that I would have a desire for the Word of God, even prayed for it. Why did it never materialize?

I have at least one theory.

Let me illustrate with the two ways we desire food: craving and hunger. Cravings are lusts, seeking something sensational and tantalizing. Hunger, on the other hand, is a desperate need for food. It drives us to eat something substantial in order to survive. Hunger is the difference between life and death.

When I prayed for a desire to read the Bible, I thought I wanted to hunger for God's word, but I never let my flesh get hungry. All that was left was a chance that I might hanker for God's word. As long as I kept satisfying the flesh with sensational cravings, I wouldn't crave God's word, much less hunger for it.

> **"**
> *God's word is the satisfaction of a desperately hungry soul, and you won't be hungry unless you starve the flesh.*
> **"**

The truth was that the Bible didn't excite me. I loved reading fiction, loved the feeling of being drawn into other worlds and lost in the feelings the stories ignited. Because the Bible didn't appeal to me on that level, I chose other delights. My mistake was expecting the Bible to appeal to the cravings of my flesh. The flesh will never desire to be satisfied with God's word and God's word will never satisfy the cravings of the flesh. God's word is the satisfaction of a desperately hungry soul, and we won't be hungry unless we starve the flesh.

Psalm 119 is dedicated to a love of God's word, law, precepts, and statutes. Have you noticed that it also says a great deal about suffering? While reading this psalm, I came to understand that suffering and the word of God are in a symbiotic relationship; they cannot live without each other. Compare these two verses

"It is good for me that I was afflicted that I might learn your statutes" (v. 71), and, "If your law had not been my delight, then I would have perished in my affliction" (v. 92).

Do you see it? Suffering drives me to the Word. The Word strengthens me in suffering. They are mutually dependent.

Psalm 119 is full of encouragement, telling us what God's word does for us in the midst of suffering.

> *"My soul weeps because of grief; strengthen me according to your word" (v. 28).*

> *"This is my comfort in my affliction, that your word has revived me" (v. 50).*

> *"The cords of the wicked have encircled me, but I have not forgotten your law" (v. 61).*

> *"It is good for me that I was afflicted, that I may learn your statutes" (v. 71).*

> *"I know, O LORD, that your judgments are righteous, and that in faithfulness you have afflicted me" (v. 75).*

> *"If your law had not been my delight, then I would have perished in my affliction" (v. 92).*

> *"I will never forget your precepts, for by them You have revived me" (v. 93).*

> *"I am exceedingly afflicted, revive me, O LORD, according to your word" (v. 107).*

Every attempt I made at reading through the Bible sputtered and died before I reached the end. When that happened, I would tell myself that the Bible could be consumed in little bits here and there, that little parts were just as good as the whole. I was making excuses for my failure. I could have used Bible reading checklists, but I refused to because they seemed too mechanical. I was wrong in that. God has created me with a task finishing personality; mechanical is the best approach for me. Know how God has designed you; that knowledge can overcome obstacles. I'm now on my eighth reading. What a difference reading the entire Bible has made in my life!

When I was emerging from depression, I realized that I was dependent on God's Word as never before, that it gave me life and breathe, and that to become disconnected from it would be to lose the very oxygen I breathe to stay alive. Then I remembered my prayer. After all these years, I finally desired the Word of God. I cried tears of joy, marveling that my Lord gave me such a gift, admitting that I never would have chosen the suffering that He used to bring me to this point, thanking Him that He did.

> **God's Word sustains you and restores joy in suffering.**

"I know, O Lord, that your regulations are fair, you disciplined me because I needed it. Now let your unfailing love comfort me, just as you promised me, your servant. Surround me with your tender mercies so I may live, for your instructions are my delight."
—Psalm 119:75-76, NLT

"Your eternal word, O Lord, stands firm in heaven. Your faithfulness extends to every generation, as enduring as the earth You created. Your regulations remain true to this day, for everything serves your plans. If your instructions hadn't sustained me with joy, I would have died in my misery. I will never forget your commandments, for by them you give me life."
—Psalm 119:89-93, NLT

God's Word, eternal and faithful, sustains us and restores our joy in suffering.

Philosopher or Follower

Because we often live according to the flesh, most of what we know as suffering never produces joy.

Suffering in the flesh causes us to question the meaning of life, makes us ask questions such as "What makes life meaningful? What is the meaning of meaningful? Does meaningful mean happy, moral, significant, successful, or purposeful? Does meaning in life come from those we love, from those who love us?"

Thaddeus Metz, a Humanities Research Professor at the University of Johannesburg explores these questions in his article "The Meaning of Life."[2] Below is a summary of his thought-provoking questions.

What characteristic of God makes Him uniquely qualified to give meaning to my life? Do I need God to make my life meaningful? If my life derives meaning from fulfilling God's purposes, does that devalue me, make me less significant? Does saying that I have no purpose apart from God make me less human? If God gives meaning to my life, he would give equal meaning to all, irrespective of action, making the meaning of one life no different from another. Intuitively, this appears to be wrong, argues Metz. Is God my only source of meaning? Can I not give meaning to myself? According to Metz, for me to obtain meaning from God requires that He not be like me, for if God and I were alike, that would preclude that I could, just as easily, derive meaning from myself. But if God is utterly not like me, is utterly perfect, (which he would have to be for there to be any reason that necessitates meaning coming from him) then he is totally beyond relating to, and therefore, unable to give me meaning.

Metz goes on to ask if one can love a perfect being. Can a perfect being be a person? Why must my meaning come from a perfect being? Can't a very good being give me meaning just as well?

Asking questions can be helpful, but these leave my mind and thoughts tangled like the yarn balls in my basket.

Solomon: a Philosopher

Solomon may have got more than he bargained for when he asked for great wisdom and knowledge. At the end of his life, he wrote,

> *"Because in much wisdom there is much grief, and increasing knowledge results in increasing pain."*
>
> –Ecclesiastes 1:18

His lifetime of understanding and brilliance had burdened him, for, at the end, he said,

> *"I hated life, for the work which had been done under the sun was grievous to me; because everything is futility and striving after wind."*
>
> –Ecclesiastes 2:17

Man is never satisfied with his work. If he loves money, he will never have enough. All men, whether good or evil, face the same end; they come into the world naked and that's how they leave it.

> *"What is crooked cannot be straightened, and what is lacking cannot be counted."*
>
> –Ecclesiastes 1:15

Solomon, after achieving the highest wisdom and glory, knew that nature could not take the place of God, and that without God, life had no purpose.

> *"Consider the work of God, for who is able to straighten what He has bent? In the day of prosperity be happy, but in the day of adversity consider God has made the one as well as the other."*
>
> –Ecclesiastes 7:13-14

His conclusion was that man should fear God and keep His commandments for,

> *"God will bring every act to judgment, everything which is hidden, whether good or evil."*
>
> –Ecclesiastes 12:14

Does God have a purpose for your life? Are you interested in finding it? What if that purpose was to suffer? That's a rather odd and seemingly perverse one, wouldn't you say? I admit it sounds masochistic, but accepting suffering is only perverse if you are getting fleshly pleasure out of it. That's not the purpose Peter had in mind when he said,

> *"You have been called for this purpose, since Christ also suffered for you, leaving you an example for you to follow in His steps."*
>
> –1 Peter 2:21

What purpose could suffering have in your life?

First, it is your best weapon against sin.

> *"Therefore since Christ has suffered in the flesh, arm yourselves also with the same purpose, because he who has suffered in the flesh has ceased from sin."*
>
> –1 Peter 4:1

Second, it makes you better. You are promised that

> *"After you have suffered for a little while, the God of all grace, who called you to His eternal glory in Christ, will Himself, perfect, confirm, strengthen and establish you."*
>
> –1 Peter 5:10

Last, consider Jesus's words:

If a grain of wheat never goes into the ground to die, it just sits there, by itself, never fulfilling its purpose; but if it dies, it bears much fruit. He who loves his life loses it; and he who hates his life in this world will keep eternally.

> *"If anyone serves Me, he must follow Me; and where I am, there My servant will be also; if anyone serves Me, the Father will honor him. Now My soul has become troubled; and what shall I say, 'Father, save Me from this hour'? But for this purpose I came to this hour. 'Father, glorify Your name.'"*
>
> –John 12:24-28a

Suffering helps me to my death. That doesn't give me purpose; it is my purpose. What should I say, then, to this pain and suffering, "Father, deliver me?" No. Instead, I should say, "Father be glorified!"

At the end of your life, when you look back, what will you see? Will you see your footprints following those of Christ?

> **Suffering helps you to your death. That doesn't give you purpose; that is your purpose.**

Reservations at the Spa

"And I will bring the third part through the fire, refine them as silver is refined and test them as gold is tested."
–Zechariah 13:9a

"I have tested you in the furnace of affliction."
–Isaiah 48:10b

You know how the story goes. You've entered a trial and the heat feels unbearable. What do you want most right now? Sure, you know that God has a purpose in this, that he is making you into something better (yada yada yada), but what you want most is relief. You might want to say to God, "Hello, how long do I have to be in here? I think I'm ready now. I think I've learned enough."

When it's over you breathe a sigh of relief, thinking to yourself, "I need some serious recovery time!" *Did you make my reservation at the spa, Lord? I'm ready to receive my blessings. Sure hope they make that trial seem worth it.*

Fire destroys. Fire purifies. Fire makes hard, stiff metals bendable and malleable.

The Lord says,

> *"Because I know that you are obstinate, and your neck is an iron sinew, and your forehead bronze."*
> –Isaiah 48:4

I can see myself banging my bronze forehead against a brick wall. Hardheaded and stubborn is what I am.

How does the blacksmith get iron to take on a different shape? First he forces the iron into a burning-hot fire, and when he thinks the metal is hot enough, he pulls it out. The heat has not changed the shape; it has only prepared the metal for what comes next: the hammer. The blacksmith pounds and pounds the iron until it cools, at which point he returns it to the fire to start the process over again.

> *"Beloved, do not be surprised at the fiery ordeal among you, which comes upon you for your testing, as though some strange thing were happening to you."*
>
> —1 Peter 4:12

Does the heat catch you by surprise? It shouldn't.

Does being in the furnace feel wrong? It shouldn't.

Maybe you aren't surprised by the flame, but you are shocked by the hammer. Don't be. The furnace has prepared you for the hammer. Now is precisely when the pounding must take place, before you cool off. And don't be surprised if the Blacksmith puts you in the furnace again.

Forget about the spa, and when you throw your arms wide to receive blessings, don't be surprised if they come with a few whacks of the hammer.

> "When through fiery trials your pathway shall lie,
> My grace, all-sufficient, shall be your supply;
> The flame shall not hurt you; I only design
> Your dross to consume, and your gold to refine."[3]

Chapter

10

Getting Down

"I could easily forgive his pride, if he had not mortified mine"
–Jane Austen, *Pride and Prejudice[1]*

Pink Polyester Pants

I'm about to reveal my deepest, darkest humiliations.

In the fifth grade, a cute boy in my class noticed the black hair that grew on my arms like grass and loudly announced, "You look like an ape." I was horrified. What was I supposed to do? The hair on my arm was outside my control. I scolded God for His role in this seemingly random and unfair choice. He could have made me a blond!

Then, in the sixth grade, I had a favorite pair of pants, bright pink polyester pants that my mom had sewn for me. Polyester knit might be the worst material ever invented, but I loved those pants, until another cute boy in my class started calling me "Pink Elephant." It dawned on me that these pants I had worn practically every day, under the delusion that I looked good in them, had brought this humiliation upon me. Betrayed by my own perception, I shoved my horror deep within, but I never forgot, and I never wore those pink pants again!

For three long years after that my weight mocked me. When I finally shed those pounds, I gained a new confidence in myself. My time had come to rise to the top. No longer held back by my weight, no longer living in fear of the mockery that might jump out at any moment and mortify me, I knew freedom and power for the first time. I loved how high they made me feel.

When I realized what the Bible said about humility, I considered myself "off the hook" for two reasons. First, the commands to humble yourself could only apply to people who had never been humiliated and needed to learn the lesson. Second, I already served my "humility" sentence; I didn't need to do any more time. God wouldn't be so cruel as to humble me further!

Humility feels like going backwards, going in the wrong direction. I can't say that humility has ever achieved anything for me. I find it difficult to believe that humility is necessary in my life. I don't see where it fits into my daily activities.

Then again, why would I think I needed humility? I was daft enough to think I didn't have a problem with pride either.

To follow Christ is to take up your cross daily, to crucify the flesh, to die to self. To follow Christ is to be a dead man walking, to wake up every day with a death sentence.

Of the four tools God uses to help us die to self, we have talked about two: weakness and suffering. Flesh cleverly creates counterparts for weakness and suffering that keep us stuck in muck, but God uses authentic weakness and suffering to free us from the sludge and allow us to walk in the Spirit. Weakness and suffering require complete surrender to God's truth. The next two tools, humility and repentance, require radical changes of heart. These two go straight for the jugular of our flesh, that is, our pride and sin.

At the end of J.R.R. Tolkien's *Lord of the Rings* trilogy, a weakened and broken Frodo Baggins stares up at Mount Doom, a volcano in the black land of Mordor. Here is where his mission would end, where he would destroy the Ring, destroying the source of all the evil in Middle Earth.[2] Like Frodo, we have now arrived at our Mordor. Broken by weakness and suffering, we now face the hardest part, humility and repentance.

Humility is essential. The roots of my pride will not be pulled up with one tug, nor will the fires of my pride be quenched with a single splash. Mine is a pervasive pride that can never be humbled too much. How about yours?

◆

You know your pride needs humility when . . .

➤ you insist on being right.
➤ you want to prove that you are better than someone else.
➤ you compare yourself with others.
➤ you try to put another down.
➤ you only want to be seen with the "in" crowd.
➤ you need to show off.
➤ you refuse to give up your rights.
➤ you think of yourself as better than those you serve.
➤ you want revenge.
➤ you resent those who do better than you.

————————◆————————

You need to assume humility when . . . .

➤ you are falsely accused.
➤ someone less qualified than you is promoted.
➤ you are overlooked, not appreciated, not recognized.

————————◆————————

You need humility to . . . .

➤ wait in silence.
➤ worship God.
➤ pray.

> "Pride must die in you, or nothing of heaven can live in you."
> –William Law[3]

Parable of the Guests

A Pharisee invited Jesus to dinner on the Sabbath. The Pharisee then paraded a sick man in front of Jesus to see if He would break the Law and heal him. All were watching Jesus closely. They didn't realize that He was also watching them and had noticed that the dinner guests were picking places of honor. So after He healed the man, Jesus told them this parable.

If you are invited to a wedding feast, don't always head for the best seat. What if someone more distinguished than you has also been invited? What then? The host will have to come to you and say, 'This important person needs to have your seat, please move.' Imagine how embarrassed you will be. And by then you will have to take whatever seat you can get, probably at the foot of the table! Instead, when you come, sit at the foot of the table. That way, when the host sees you, he will say, 'My dear friend, we have a much better place for you than this!' Think of how honored you will be in front of the other guests.

"For everyone who exalts himself will be humbled, and he who humbles himself will be exalted."

–Luke 14:11

Then Jesus turned to the host who had invited a room full of self-important people.

When you throw a party, He said, don't invite friends, relatives, rich neighbors and dignitaries. Don't invite people who can repay you; instead, invite the poor, crippled, blind and lame. In other words, invite the lowest of society, the ones who can't repay you, that way you will be repaid in the resurrection.

The guests were too high in their estimation of themselves. The host sought too much exaltation from the guests he chose to invite.[4]

Remarkably, we've come full circle. The foundation of our self-worth is rich soil for the roots of pride. Anything that gives you value outside Christ provides another place for pride to put its roots. The more things you rely on for your self-worth, the more invasive is your pride.

> **Even the slightest movement away from your center in Christ is a fluctuation away from your value in Christ.**

Remember the pendulum principle in chapter one? You are on a swing and your chains are made up of those things that make you feel good about yourself. As with a pendulum, any movement starts the swing, whether the push comes from feeling good or feeling bad. Your true value in Christ is best indicated by the complete absence of swing. Even the slightest movement away from your center in Christ, in any direction, is a fluctuation away from your value in Christ. The most accurate instrument for measuring the value you have outside of Christ is the motion sensor.

Pride motivates you to impress others, to imitate what seems good. Don't be fooled. Eventually, the good crumbles and out of your flesh come the ugly manifestations that we examined in chapter three. It is not okay to ignore pride. These roots affect your life daily.

Sink Like a Rock

I like to argue. My dad used to say that I would make a good lawyer. I'm not, however, as attached to my principles as you might think. I argue because I like to be right.

Oh yes, I like to be right. My Being Right identity elevates me, gives me a lift. When you disagree with me you knock me down and I need to get back up on my high seat. I'm not interested in your being right, because I don't want you up there on my mountain, on my elevated place.

As a young person I always wanted the jobs that seemed fun or cool or had potential for recognition. If someone stood up in church to praise Sunday school teachers, then I wanted to teach Sunday school. If others were recognized for their servant-like behavior, I wanted to wash dishes for the Lord.

My life in Christ should be like a rock. A rock will not float. A rock is impervious to hot air.

Humility has one setting: "rock bottom." I've studied the movements of my pride and discovered that I'm a floater, not a sinker. I am like a balloon full of hot air, trying to rise. I keep pumping helium into my value, inflating my ego with importance, boosting my self-esteem.

Recently, a friend described himself as a helium balloon that no longer pulls upward but hovers just a few inches above the floor. He may have thought himself knocked down, but hovering, however low, is still not humility, not rock bottom.

My motion sensor needs a new calibration, one that will detect vertical movement, because any movement upward, no matter how insignificant, is a move away from humility, away from Christ. Any movement upward is a result of pumping my pride. Any movement upward will automatically bump someone else down.

In whose eyes do you want to be seen as elevated? Does God take note of your elevation? Is it possible to be elevated in God's eyes?

It is, but not by going in the direction you might imagine. Jesus showed us a different way. He showed us that in God's eyes, you move up by going down.

Down Is the New Up

Jesus told this story to some who trusted in their own goodness and looked down on others who weren't as good as they were.[5] Imagine that you are one of those self-righteous men listening.

There were two men who went to the Temple to pray. One was a Pharisee (the audience cheers), and the other a dishonest tax collector (boo). The Pharisee stood and prayed to himself.

'O God, thank you that I am not like other people, especially like that tax collector I saw come in with me! I could never be like him. I never cheat, or sleep around. I fast twice a week, and I am faithful to give you the exact amount of money you ask for.'

But the tax collector stood off to the side and wouldn't even lift his head towards heaven as he prayed. Instead, he beat his chest in sorrow, saying 'O God, be merciful to me, for I am a sinner.'

A slight pause causes you to lean in and think, "Yes . . . the point is?"

Having captured the attention of everyone there, Jesus gives the shocking revelation. In a low voice He says, "the tax collector went home justified, not the Pharisee." (gasp)!

> *"For everyone who exalts himself will be humbled, but he who humbles himself will be exalted."*
>
> –Luke 18:14

(By the way, did you notice to whom the Pharisee was praying?)

———————◆———————

The proud man thinks himself in right standing with man and God. He sees himself higher than some and scorns those who are lower.

The humble man sees himself a sinner, unworthy of standing before God. He bows low to the ground, where he cannot compare his position with that of others. His humility comes from within, not from his status among men.

Humility is not an attitude of self-degradation. Saying, "I'm just not good enough for that place of honor" doesn't mean that the flesh agrees. The person who demeans himself may, in fact, lament his inadequacies only because they have been thrust on him by others. Inwardly, he may believe himself capable of doing much more than is credited him. Or perhaps he believes that appearing humble will elevate him in the eyes of others.

Humility has a simple meaning: humility means low; haughty means high. Low and high are not difficult concepts.

Instinctively, we know that it is better to be at the top than at the bottom. Rising in status is honoring, but going down is humbling. We honor what elevates and despise what humiliates. We are most content when we're up, when we're valued, and when we're not, our pride seeks to console us with the reminder that we're better than we seem.

"But I don't have to be at the top," you say, "as long as I'm not at the bottom. Doesn't that count as humility? Surely that must mean I'm not proud."

Think about what takes you up, elevates your status, makes you better, keeps you from being at the bottom, keeps you from being the worst. Maybe it is education, friends, ministries, salary, spiritual gifts, appearance, your social network, number of retweets, approval of those you admire, or what others say about you. Maybe it's being in a relationship, being admired, being liked, being perfect, being chosen, being talented, being the leader, the confidant, the favorite, the wise one, or the top of your class. Do any of these pull you up when you've been knocked down? Does the lack of any of these test your humility?

When God humbles us, our first reaction is to inflate ourselves so that we will rise up, if only a few inches. This need to boost ourselves is an automatic reaction to the downward pull of humility. God uses a multitude of circumstances to teach us to be humble. Humility pulls us down when we are treated unfairly or misjudged, when someone yells at us, when we are not the best, the smartest, or the prettiest, when we are passed over for a position, when we have to take the second best, when another person is praised, when we aren't the center of attention, when our contribution goes unrecognized, when our kids misbehave. Humility tugs at us when we feel unwanted, excluded, when we aren't asked for or needed, when we aren't consulted or chosen, when we feel useless, when we feel like a burden.

Are you familiar with these tugs of humility? How often do you feel the pull? Maybe your tugs look different from these. Whatever the case, humility gets you down.

The problem is that what humbles us does not always make us humble. We are not content to stay down. We will squirm and whine, get angry, expend lots of effort to improve ourselves, and make it a priority to get back up to where we think we were, just so we can be okay with who we are. We will repeatedly ask

> **"**
> *The problem is that what humbles you does not always make you humble.*
> **"**

ourselves "why": "Why am I not the favorite? Why was she chosen over me, what does she have that I don't? Why did they laugh at her story and not mine? Why did they take her suggestion and not mine? Why am I not good enough?" We will not rest until we are up there again.

Failure to be as good as we thought we could be may bring us down in guilt and shame, and even though this feels low, it's not humility. Fear that others don't think of us as highly as we would like them to may cause us to sink into self-pity and self-loathing, but our slime pit does not make us humble.

Pride hates that which humbles us, hates the failures, hates the features, hates what keeps us from rising. Loathing what humbles us does not make us humble; it is a fleshly reaction to being humbled. Pride motivates us to hate ourselves, and self-hatred does not produce humility. Self-hatred is simply a twisted form of self-love.

---◆---

We also elevate ourselves by elevating others. Do you perceive some people as better? What traits elevate them in your eyes? What makes you wish you could be like them? Are they creative, funny, cool, or witty? Are they confident, logical, and smart? Do they hold a respected position such as president, doctor, executive, manager, or department head? Are they opinionated, cutting edge, trendsetter, outspoken, powerful? Do you look up to famous singers, conference speakers, preachers, authors? Do riches, possessions, name brand clothes, accessories, car, or house draw your attention to a person? Do popularity, friends, rugged good looks, beauty, appearance increase another's value? Do you honor someone in a relationship more than someone who is single?

Some people you elevate will give you a sense of increased value. When you are accepted by them or included in their inner circle, you feel elevated too. Others will have the opposite effect, eroding your sense of worth and value. You may find yourself hating them, wanting to bring them down a few notches. Valuing or devaluing others in order to change your own status is a practice of the flesh motivated by pride.

The value of an item is determined either by the one who made it or by how much someone is willing to pay for it. Jesus Christ is both our Creator and Redeemer. Redemption means to buy back. Imagine the value Christ gives with the price He paid for you and me when He died on the cross for our sins. On second thought, don't bother. You can't dream up a worth that comes within light years of reaching the edge of the immense value that Christ set.

Yet we practice the folly of elevating!

When we exalt one person over another, we are exchanging their value, determined by God, with a value we determine for ourselves. Let that sink in. This is so second nature to us that we play this ludicrous game in our sleep.

That we would even consider exchanging the price Christ paid for any person with our own estimate of value is horrific! Any value we could assign is so obscenely inferior to the value assigned by God, that to deposit a penny of His worth would make us millionaires by comparison. Even then, a penny fails to demonstrate the true disproportion between the value we have in Christ and the value we gain from those things we think make us better.

> *"Do not hold your faith in our glorious Lord Jesus*
> *Christ with an attitude of personal favoritism. For if*
> *a man comes into your assembly with a gold ring and*

dressed in fine clothes, and there also comes in a poor man in dirty clothes, and you pay special attention to the one who is wearing the fine clothes, and say, 'you sit here in a good place', and you say to the poor man, 'you stand over there, or sit down by my footstool', have you not made distinctions among yourselves, and become judges with evil motives?"

–James 2:1-4

> *If you are looking down on anyone, you have put yourself higher than the Lord would have you be.*

Seeking to elevate either myself or others is a dangerous game of arrogance, requiring an attitude of superiority, and, according to James, it is pure evil. Any attempt to elevate myself or others forces someone else to a lower position. To make some into celebrities inevitably makes others into peasants. This does not glorify God! It assigns a value, a glory to another. That is idolatry.

If you are looking down on anyone, you have put yourself higher than the Lord would have you be. The Lord says that, if you want to be great, you have to lower yourself to serve; if you want to be exalted, go from low to the lowest.

——————◆——————

Recently I read Ephesians 3:8 in which Paul says he is less than the least of all the Lord's people. What an odd and illogical thing to say, I thought. How can something be less than the least? The phrase caught my attention, but I was later frustrated to read other versions which said, "the very least of all saints" or "the least deserving of all God's people." That didn't sound as catchy, didn't fit with my initial thought on humility. Which is it, I wondered.

I know very little Greek, but I must look at the Greek text if I am to avoid one of my pet peeves: extracting a special point from a specific phrase only to find that the translation was inaccurate, thereby discounting the wonderful lesson I had imagined to be there.

In Ephesians 3:8, Paul added a comparative to a superlative, and made a new word, "elachistoteros," the equivalent of combining the words lower and lowest. So "less than the least" is what Paul was saying, and he coined this word for this one instance. This makes me think that he couldn't find a regular word to say how low he was willing to go, so he had to make one up. He is most emphatically emphatic that he is lower than the lowest, and that, therefore, no one can get below him. Paul creates a single word, "elachistoteros" that perfectly describes the humility we should be striving for.

If we were to think of this striving as a competition, we would each be striving to go lower than the other person. Imagine fighting each other for the lowest position rather than for the highest one. What attitude would we have if we were always trying to outdo each other for the lowest position instead of always trying to "one-up" someone else?

We would need to invent a new word, "to one-under."

Back in the Butter

Missionaries are often elevated to celebrity status. They are in a position to which people give respect, earned or not. When my husband and I were missionaries, we noticed that everyone listened to us, sought our advice, and chose our side in an argument. Then we moved back home and suddenly we were just like everyone else, with no power, no authority, no opinion. We had to start at the bottom and pretty soon, we found ourselves longing for the good old days when we were important, when our opinion mattered.

Remember when you were important? Hold that thought because you'll need it to relate to this story about Job.

Job's story is told in a series of painful speeches between him and some friends who have come to offer comfort, though I doubt that "comfort" was their true purpose. They argued that Job must have done something bad, that his current suffering revealed wickedness beneath his apparent righteous behavior. Their arguments provoked defensiveness in Job. He could produce plenty of examples of men much more wicked than himself, living blissful lives, thereby proving the friends wrong. Where was the justice of God in this?

Job won't curse God, but you get the feeling that he had a few choice things to say, if he could just get an audience with God. In his final impassioned defense, Job described the position he used to have in the community, when his steps were "bathed in butter", when he went out to the gate of the city where the dignitaries gathered. Here the young men would step back, the old men would stand up, and princes would stop talking, putting their hands on their mouths. A hush would descend on the group when Job arrived, as if their tongues were stuck to the roofs of their mouths. "To me they listened and waited and kept silent for my counsel," Job said.

But now, Job was humiliated, now young men mocked him, the sons of men that Job would not have considered worthy to mingle with his sheep dogs. They taunted him and made fun of him. He had become one who was despised, one whose condition was so disgusting that no one came near him except to spit on him. Job was humbled and afflicted.[6] Looking up at the height of his former glory made his fall harder, and the distance of his fall more painful.

Elihu, the youngest, who had kept quiet because of his youth, got fed up with the useless arguing. His anger burned at Job for defending himself rather than defending God, and at the others for condemning Job without answering him. Elihu says, "Job, you speak senseless words without knowledge. You are a fool, who defiantly claps your hands in front of us and multiplies your words against God. You have only succeeded in adding rebellion to your sin" (34:35-37, paraphrase).

Then the Lord spoke out of a whirlwind, and Job finally stopped multiplying words, saying only,

> *"I am unworthy, how can I reply to you? I put my hand over my mouth."*
>
> –Job 40:4, NIV

Isn't that how Job had been shown respect by others, how he longed to be respected again? How ironic!

———————◆———————

How is it Job was left out of the discussion on suffering, and yet here, in this chapter on humility, his story surfaces?

I have often struggled to understand where Job went wrong. He was right to say he wasn't suffering because of sin, right to declare his own righteousness. Hadn't God Himself said Job was righteous? Didn't He tell Satan that Job was the most upright man on earth? All Job wanted was a chance to defend himself, a chance to question God. What was wrong with his demand to know why he was suffering? When the Lord speaks, He is annoyed with Job, but why? I could never put my finger on it, and that bothered me. I needed to know so that I wouldn't make the same mistake. Where did Job go wrong, what did he fail to understand, what has he grasped at the end that marks a turning point in his story?

Job's problem was his pride that surfaced in his suffering. Through all his suffering, he wouldn't stop defending his exalted self, wouldn't stop seeing himself as a man worthy of commanding silence from those around him. Despite the extreme physical humiliation he suffered, Job had been caught in the current of his pride, swirling in the pool of his own significance, because he had not lowered his spirit to match his circumstances, had not yet been humbled.

Pride is idolatry. Pride seeks worship. It hates being brought down from its lofty place. As long as we seek to elevate our own worth, we cannot worship God.

My Prickled Pride

My Pride is sensitive, full of nerve endings and prickle points. It hurts when I don't get my way, when I'm overlooked, and when I feel insignificant. At one time or another, every one of my pride's feelings has been hurt, and many times I have had to rise up in defense of my delicate sensitivities.

In the countless times I have been offended, it never occurred to me that I had a choice. I took offense because I thought I had to, thought the other person was solely responsible for my being offended, thought I was within my rights to be offended.

However, when my pride is prickled I can choose to not be offended.

Paul pricks my pride when he scolds the Corinthians for taking each other to court and bringing up lawsuits. He suggests,

"Why not rather be wronged? Why not rather be defrauded?"

–1 Corinthians 6:7

Have you been wronged, cheated, robbed, or deprived of what you are due? First thing you wanted to do was lay down and let the other person win.

Oh, it wasn't?

Really Paul, this is a hard pill to swallow. How in the world can I let others think I'm wrong when I know I'm right!

Jesus said,

"You have heard that it was said 'an eye for an eye, and a tooth for a tooth.' But I say to you, do not resist an evil person; but whoever slaps you on your right cheek, turn the other to him also. If anyone wants to sue you and take your shirt, let him have your coat also. Whoever forces you to go one mile, go with him two."

–Matthew 5:38-41

Furthermore, Jesus teaches us by example that if you are falsely accused, beaten, tortured, mocked, forced to carry your own cross to your execution, then use your last breaths to plead for their forgiveness.

You have a choice.

Next time the feelings of pride are hurt, see it as an opportunity to take up your cross, as a chance to die.

Pulverized in His Presence

Suffering and weakness hit us from outside our control. God aims them specifically at the areas that need His work to accomplish His purposes. They hurt for sure, but our involvement with them is only in exposing flesh and building endurance. Now, in seeking humility, we are at that point of digging and scraping, of tweezers and magnifying glass, of being more refined, more purposeful, and more brutal. Now is the time for a steady hand and strong resolve.

Pain causes hesitation. It is much harder to agree to something once you know the pain involved. Only on his first dentist visit can you make a child think that the procedure will be fun. I'm not trying to deter you from proceeding, but I do want you to count the cost. Living is dying, and dying hurts. You can't be a bystander anymore. You are the living sacrifice bound to the altar. You are the one carrying the cross.

> **Living is dying, and dying hurts.**

"Do you say, "I am not willing to be poured out right now, and I don't want God to tell me how to serve Him. I want to choose the place of my own sacrifice. And I want to have certain people watching me and saying 'Well done.'" It is one thing to follow God's way of service if you are regarded as a hero; it is quite another thing if the road marked out for you by God requires becoming a "doormat" under other people's feet. God's purpose may be to teach you to say, "I know how to be abased . . ." (Phil. 4:12). Are you ready to be sacrificed in that way? Are you ready to be less than a drop in the bucket, to be so insignificant that no one remembers you even when they think of those you served? "Bind the sacrifice with cords to the horns of the altar" (Ps. 118:27). You must be willing to be placed on the altar and go through the fire, willing to experience what the altar represents—burning, purification, and separation for one purpose—the elimination of every desire and affection not grounded in or directed toward God."

–Oswald Chambers *My Utmost for His Highest*[7]

John the Baptist, when confronted with the problem of his successful ministry shifting to someone else (John's disciples were comparing him with Jesus), replied, "A man can receive nothing unless it has been given him from heaven" (John 3:27). In the end, "He must increase, but I must decrease" (v. 30), he says, speaking of Jesus as the one who must increase.

It can be unbearably humiliating to know that you are dependent on the charity of another for everything that you have, to realize that, without the help of a benefactor, you are impoverished. We do not like shrinking so much that we become invisible, reducing so much that we become insignificant, emptying so much of ourselves that we are no longer seen. We are too proud to be empty handed.

> *"Do nothing from selfishness or empty conceit, but with humility of mind regard one another as more important than yourselves."*
>
> –Philippians 2:3

> *"Have this attitude in yourselves which was also in Christ Jesus, who, although He existed in the form of God, did not regard equality with God a thing to be grasped, but emptied Himself, taking the form of a bond-servant, and being made in the likeness of men."*
>
> –Philippians 2:5-7

Man prefers his own importance, not only in the company of others, but also in religion. He values whatever he brings to the object of his faith, whether it be to God, to a god, to humanity, or to himself.

God says to each of us what could you bring to me that I didn't make? You cannot approach me as if you have anything that might make you more valuable in my sight. Your attitude is wrong. This is how you should come to me: humble, contrite and trembling (Isa. 66:1-2, paraphrase).

The Hebrew word for *contrite* (Ps. 51:17, Isa. 57:15) means to be crushed to powder, pulverized.

> **You cannot be humble without being emptied and crushed.**

We cannot gain humility through our efforts; rather, we gain humility by emptying ourselves. We cannot be humble without being emptied and crushed. If we think we have something to offer to God, even if that thing is our humility, we are not yet humble.

◆

"For though the Lord is exalted, yet He regards the lowly; but the haughty He knows from afar.
—Psalm 138:6

"Crawl into caves in the rocks. Hide in the dust from the terror of the Lord and the glory of His majesty. Human pride will be brought down, And human arrogance will be humbled. Only the Lord will be exalted on that day of judgment."
—Isaiah 2:10-11, NLT

"For thus says the high and exalted one who lives forever, whose name is Holy, I dwell on a high and holy place, and also with the contrite and lowly of spirit in order to revive the spirit of the lowly and to revive the heart of the contrite."
—Isaiah 57:15

"Thus says the Lord, 'Heaven is my throne, and the earth is my footstool, where then is a house you could build for me. And where is a place that I may rest? For my hand made all these things, thus all these things came into being,' declares the Lord. 'But to this one I will look, to him who is humble and contrite of spirit, who trembles at my word.'"
—Isaiah 66:1-2

"On that day you will no longer need to be ashamed, for you will no longer be rebels against me. I will remove all proud and arrogant people from among you. There will be no more haughtiness on my holy mountain. Those who are left will be the lowly and humble, for it is they who trust in the name of the LORD."
—Zephaniah 3:11-12, NLT

"God is opposed to the proud but gives grace to the humble . . . humble yourselves in the presence of the Lord and He will exalt you."
—James 4:6, 10

> *"You younger men likewise, be subject to your elders;*
> *and all of you, clothe yourselves with humility toward*
> *one another, for God is opposed to the proud, but gives*
> *grace to the humble. Therefore humble yourselves under*
> *the mighty hand of God, that He may exalt you at the*
> *proper time, casting all your anxiety upon Him, because*
> *He cares for you."*
>
> —1 Peter 5:5-7

According to these verses, what does our pride get us? It gets us God on the opposing team, it gets us far from Him, and it gets us banished from His Holy Mountain.

I wonder that I'm not more sobered by the exclusion of the proud and exclusive entry of the humble, wonder that I don't tremble more at the severity of God's judgment on the proud. I do think, *uh-oh, I better put on more humility, just to be on the safe side, you know.*

I have a sneaking suspicion that my flesh might just make a costume of humility and slip it on over my pride. Unless I choose to decrease, to be pulverized, I'm in danger of reverting to my natural inclination to improve myself. But the High and Exalted One who lives forever will see right through that disguise.

Only the lowly will be with Him in that high place, only the contrite will dwell in His presence, only the humble will call Him Holy.

If I were to write a "contract" for humility, I would be inclined to write something like this:

> I agree to not think too highly of myself, but to think of myself only as I deserve, and if, by chance, others think more highly of me, I agree to think less of myself than they do.

Let me recommend the following prayer written by Raphael Cardinal Merry del Val for a set of terms that will achieve more dying to self than mine.

O Jesus meek and humble of heart, hear me.
From the desire of being esteemed,
from the desire of being loved,
from the desire of being extolled,
from the desire of being honored,
from the desire of being praised,
from the desire of being preferred to others,
from the desire of being consulted,
from the desire of being approved,
from the fear of being humiliated,
from the fear of being despised,
from the fear of suffering rebukes,
from the fear of being falsely accused,
from the fear of being forgotten,
from the fear of being ridiculed,
from the fear of being wronged,
from the fear of being suspected,
Deliver me, O Jesus.
That others may be loved more than I,
That others may be esteemed more than I,
that, in the opinion of the world,
others may increase and I may decrease,
That others may be chosen and I set aside,
That others may be praised and I unnoticed,
That others may be preferred before me in everything,
That others become holier than I,
provided that I may become as holy as I should.
Jesus, grant me the grace to desire it.[8]

Chapter

11

Turning Around

We are dead men walking, and I don't mean zombies. We live every day with a death sentence; every day we pick up the dying of Jesus. Every day we embrace weakness, accept suffering, and choose humility. There is one more step in this walk of dying: repentance, the final nail on the coffin, the critical step between dying and living. Without repentance there is no change of heart or mind, without repentance you continue in the wrong direction, without repentance you can't live by the Spirit.

> **"**
> *To die to self, your pride must be dealt a fatal blow.*
> **"**

Pride is the heartbeat of the flesh. Living by the unmerited favor of God's grace weakens the heartbeat of the flesh and silences the protests of our pride. To die to self, pride must be dealt a fatal blow. Weakness hurts it, suffering offends it, and humility suffocates it. Repentance finishes it off.

Too Much Talk, Not Enough Walk

Venting has been my excuse for saying some harsh words. As a teen, I said many things that hurt my mom, and though the wounds my words inflicted were apparent, I refused to apologize, preferring to retreat to my room and wait for the dust to settle. I vividly remember the first time I sought out my mom to say I was sorry. She too had retreated to her room. All the way there I rehearsed the words in my mind, but when I opened my mouth, nothing came out. Talking is as natural as breathing for me, but I realized that saying, "I'm sorry for . . ." would never be easy.

"Sorry"—a word that by itself says very little. "Oh, sorry!" we say, meaning "excuse me." We tell a child who has made another child cry, "Say you're sorry." "Sawwwy" he says, but what does he think that means? Does he think it is a magic word like "please"? Saying sorry could be the means of avoiding punishment, a loophole that gets you out of trouble. "I'm sorry," we say, but we don't mean it.

Once I thought I would see if my daughter knew why she was sorry, so rather than accept a simple "I'm sorry," I asked her to finish the sentence, "I was wrong for . . ." You would have thought her mouth was glued shut. She had the same problem as I did. No surprise there!

Try it yourself. It is much easier to say, "I'm sorry" than to admit what you did wrong.

I wonder about this sorry business. If I feel sorry, does that mean I've repented? What am I usually sorry for? Sometimes I feel sorry for getting caught or for letting myself down or for disappointing others. I often feel sorry for making a mistake, for being less than perfect, for opening myself up for blame, criticism, and judgment. I feel sorry for myself when I make someone angry at me. I feel sorry for the consequences of my mistakes. Do any of these feelings mean I have repented?

The dictionary says that repentance is sincere regret or remorse. I'm familiar with regret, familiar with reliving, over and over again, each of my regrets.

➢ Why didn't I learn faster?
➢ Why didn't I shut my mouth before I said those things?
➢ Why couldn't I do it right?
➢ Why did I get jealous?
➢ Why wasn't I strong enough to avoid depression?
➢ Why did I lose my temper?
➢ Why was I destructive to others and to my relationships?
➢ Why did I eat that donut?
➢ Why didn't I say "no"!

Regrets. First they torment, then they anger.

I regret my failures because I want to think of myself as better than that, because I fear that others will think less of me.

My regret is always sincere. Does that mean I have repented?

The Biblical definition of repentance is very different from the dictionary definition. Biblical repentance is to change your mind and turn to the Lord. This definition was lost in the Latin translation, so that today, all we have is this idea of feeling sorry and regret. The problem is that regret and remorse have nothing to do with true repentance.

Charles Spurgeon describes this conflict surrounding repentance in his book *All of Grace.*

> "I desired to repent, but I thought that I could not do it, and yet all the while I was repenting. Odd as it may sound, I felt that I could not feel. I used to get into a corner and weep, because I could not weep; and I fell into bitter sorrow because I could not sorrow for sin. What a jumble it all is when in our unbelieving state we begin to judge our own condition! It is as a blind man looking at his own eyes. Remember that the man who truly repents is never satisfied with his own repentance. We can no more repent perfectly than we can live perfectly. However pure our tears, there will always be some dirt in them: there will be something to be repented of even in our best repentance. But listen! To repent is to change your mind about sin, and Christ, and all the great things of God. There is sorrow implied in this; but the main point is the turning of the heart from sin to Christ. If there be this turning, you have the essence of true repentance, even though no alarm and no despair should ever have cast their shadow upon your mind."[1]

The essence of repentance is the turning of the heart from sin to Christ. Spurgeon has observed our tendency to linger and stumble and get stuck in despair over our sin, saying that we want to be forgiven, yet insisting we don't feel repented.

Why don't we know true victory over sin? Why do our efforts at repentance distance us from God?

The first principle of repentance is to turn. The problem is that we can sit in remorse and regret indefinitely, never turning around. What's worse, regret and remorse can be born of the flesh, born of self-love, self-hate, and self-centeredness. In fleshly regret we label our sin as "mistakes," and, given enough time, we work out our own justification for having "made a mistake." Fleshly regret and remorse dump us in a cesspool of guilt and shame where we wallow until the pain subsides and we feel strong enough to keep going. In this, we have not repented nor have we turned to God!

> **"**
>
> *Repentance is to turn. The problem is that you can sit in remorse and regret indefinitely, never turning around.*
>
> **"**

Dead Men Don't Wear Fig Leaves

Reading fiction books was my addiction. I would read for hours, losing myself in the imaginary world of my books. It was horribly annoying to be jerked back to reality to do some boring chore. And that is what my mom would do, without fail, if she discovered me reading. I hated it! I would read where she couldn't see me. If I heard her moving about, I would think to myself, "please, don't let her come in here and find me, please." Even those moments of holding my breath were rain on my party. I wanted to be left alone to do what I wanted, free of even the fear of being discovered.

When the Spirit pricks my conscience, I am annoyed at His persistent interference with my pursuits. My flesh wants to be left alone, and my pride pouts at being judged, at being told to stop doing what I enjoy. I try to brush away the Spirit as if He were a bothersome mosquito. I want to silence the conviction because guilt is annoying; it makes me feel bad about myself. I want to return to thinking positive things about myself, return to freedom from guilt and shame, return to feeling good about myself again.

Our natural selves like to be left to do as we please with no consequences, with no interference, and with no one to make us feel guilty. We are offended by our judges and punishers. Their judgment and punishment disrupt our pursuit of happiness. In fact, just knowing that someone might judge us is enough to take the fun out of our self-centered pursuits and make us angry. We prefer to be left alone to feel confident and strong in ourselves.

So we're tempted to hide from the Spirit. We look for a private place to lick our wounds and indulge in our pleasures. After a while, when we feel a little better and our wounds of regret don't sting quite as badly, we sheepishly open the door a crack to see if the coast is clear. Full of thoughts that this time we'll do better, this time we'll succeed, we tip-toe back out and hope that all has blown over, that no one noticed our absence, that we can move on as if nothing had happened. We feel ready now, feel strong enough to do this. Our confidence is back and we think "this is who I really am."

Maybe God won't notice the fig leaves I'm wearing.

Melville's Father Mapple

Herman Melville was not, to my knowledge, a religious man, yet he wrote a chapter titled "The Sermon" in his whaling tale *Moby Dick*. In this sermon, the preacher, Father Mapple, tells an imaginative version of Jonah's experience in the Bible, an appropriate topic for a whaling ship. He concludes his sermon with this: "Then Jonah prayed unto the Lord out of the fish's belly. But observe his prayer, and learn a weighty lesson. For sinful as he is, Jonah does not weep and wail for direct deliverance. He feels that his dreadful punishment is just. He leaves all his deliverance to God, contenting himself with this, that spite of all his pains and pangs, he will still look towards His holy temple. And here, shipmates, is true and faithful repentance; not clamorous for pardon, but grateful for punishment."[2]

Remember that look from mom or dad when you had gone too far? Suddenly, you've been grabbed by the arm and you start pleading "I'm sorry, I'm sorry, I'm sorry," hoping that your parent will have pity on you. You are too busy clamoring for pardon to even think about repenting. Imagine coming to your mom or dad, prepared for punishment, and saying, "thank you."

Imagine that!

Drop the Slop and Turn Around

What if you just blew it—lost your temper, yelled at your kids, lied to your boss, looked at porn, got jealous? Whatever it was, you blew it. What now? You might feel sorry because you've embarrassed yourself, exposed yourself to the possibility that others will think less of you. You might go to your mental room where you alternate between convincing yourself that you aren't that bad, fretting about what others think, excusing your lapse of perfection, and beating yourself up for having failed to keep it together. Wasn't it just two days ago that you said you would never do that again?

Often we retreat until the bad feeling passes, but we should turn to God and admit defeat. Like the prodigal son who comes to his senses, we should drop the slop and return, broken and humble, to the Father. Retreating is easier than accepting defeat, but it doesn't produce a change of heart, doesn't change direction to face God. Our habit of retreating causes us to repeat the same sins over and over again.

> **"**
> *To pick up your cross you'll have to put something else down.*
> **"**

To pick up your cross you'll have to put something else down.

➢ You'll have to put down your rebellion.

➢ You'll have to put down your sin.

➢ You'll have to put down your pride.

➢ You'll have to put down that thing you refuse to give up.

➢ You'll have to put down those other loves.

➢ You'll have to put down your will.

To walk by the Spirit you'll have to put it down and turn around.

What Is True Repentance?

True repentance is turning around and standing before the One greater than you, who has the right to judge you, and saying, "Here I stand Lord, wretchedly out of reach, with no hope of crossing over to You. Here I stand in the stench of my filthy rags of sin. What an offensive mess I bring into Your presence! No Lord! I am undone. I have sinned against You, and You are right to call me out on it and have the right to punish me."

True repentance is . . .

➢ seeing your sin as God sees it, without trying to justify it.

➢ acknowledging God's perfect justice and rightness in punishing your sin, abandoning all hope of being able to make things right, and throwing yourself on God's grace and mercy.

➢ recognizing that you cannot, in any way, recover from your sin.

➢ making your appeal based on who God is, not on anything that you have done.

➢ action.

➢ bending down in submission to accept the cross that identifies you with Christ.

➢ dying to self.

➢ freedom from sin.

➢ the step that finally breaks the cycle of defeat —completing it instead of repeating it.

Do you need to change your mind about . . .

➢ the reward for doing good.

➢ the idea that you have rights.

➢ the view that weakness is bad.

➢ the pursuit of feeling good about yourself.

➢ the justice of God.

➢ the practice of elevating.

➢ the fluctuation of self-worth.

> *The flesh will not offer itself up to die.*

The flesh will not offer itself up to die, will not surrender, will not release us to the Spirit's control. Living by the Spirit means a walk of dying to self. How do we do that? God has built the method into our Christian lives by making us weak, bringing us suffering, and humbling us. We need to embrace weakness, accept suffering, and choose humility. But those, on their own, will not be enough. We must also take this most fatal step for the flesh, the step of repentance. Don't say, "Oh I need to repent" and then walk away staying stuck in discouragement over your failings and forget to put it down and turn around.

Acknowledging your mistake, or poor choice, or even failure to yourself won't empower you to be different, won't empower you to stop repeating your defeat. And while confession to others may make you feel better, you haven't humbled yourself before the One who is worthy.

It's easy to rely on self-correction and think you've repented, but nothing can replace the physical act of getting on your knees before God and confessing your sin. In His presence you see your sin through His eyes and that is where you are when true repentance occurs.

This chapter on repentance is short because action, not explanation, is needed. Nothing can be said that will make you feel more ready to begin this walk of dying. Take the first step: drop the slop and turn around.

Repent!

Part 3

◆

Walking Empowered by the Spirit

Chapter

12

Walking in Truth

"I have no greater joy than this, to hear of my children walking in the truth."

–3 John 4

As we walk by the Spirit we should expect to find that a divine presence does things in and through us that we can't do. We should not expect to better our walk by diligent human effort. The Bible teaches us about four significant areas in this life of following Christ in which the Spirit's role is so indispensable that any fleshly input is detrimental. These areas are walking in truth, walking in love, serving with gifts, and praying.

The Spirit of Truth

It was the day of the feast when the Passover lamb was to be sacrificed. Jesus spent that evening alone with his disciples, feasting in a large, furnished upper room. Knowing the agony that was coming, He was eager to celebrate with them His last Passover on this earth. John begins his account of that night by saying of Jesus,

> *"Having loved His own who were in the world, He loved them to the end."*

–John 13:1

Already loving these men that his Father had given him, He is about to love them to the complete end, all the way to the outer limits.

How did He love them so fully that night? Was it by taking up a basin and towel and washing the disciples' feet? Was it by taking up the cross and dying in their place? Was it both of those things and everything He promised in between? Was it the promise of beautiful dwelling places in Heaven, and the promise that He would receive them there? Was it His promise to do whatever they asked in His name, or the promise that the Father loves those who love the Son, those who keep his commandments?

Did He show the extent of His love to them and to us by calling us friends, by praying for us, by giving us peace, joy and eternal life? Did He show us the extent of His love by promising not to leave us as orphans, but to give us the Helper, the Spirit of truth, who would guide us into all truth?

John, reclining next to Jesus, must have been captivated by the love talk he witnessed that night, must have listened intently to Jesus's every word, for he recorded the conversation in great detail. He remembered how Jesus spoke of the Helper. The subject was so important that Jesus emphasized it at least four times throughout the night.

> *"And I will ask the Father, and He will give you another Helper, that He may be with you forever; that is the Spirit of truth, whom the world cannot receive, because it does not behold Him or know Him, but you know Him because He abides with you, and will be in you."*
>
> —John 14:16-17

> *"But the Helper, the Holy Spirit, whom the Father will send in my name, He will teach you all things, and bring to your remembrance all that I said to you."*
>
> —John 14:26

> *"When the Helper comes, whom I will send to you from the Father, that is the Spirit of truth, who proceeds from the Father, He will testify about Me."*
>
> —John 15:26

> *"But when He, the Spirit of truth, comes, He will guide you into all the truth."*
>
> —John 16:13a

Have you ever considered how important the promise of the Spirit was to that small group of weak men? Was it love that prompted Jesus to give them what they would desperately need, before they even knew they would need it?

In a letter John wrote to the churches he said,

> *"By this we know that we abide in Him and He in us, because He has given us of His Spirit. And we have seen and testify that the Father has sent the Son to be the Savior of the world. Whoever confesses that Jesus is the Son of God, God abides in him, and he in God."*
>
> —1 John 4:13-15

> *"The one who believes in the Son of God has the testimony in himself; the one who does not believe God has made Him a liar, because he has not believed in the testimony that God has given concerning His Son. And the testimony is this, that God has given us eternal life, and this life is in His Son."*
>
> —1 John 5:10-11

It is a simple equation,

> *"He who has the Son has the life; he who does not have the Son of God does not have the life. These things I have written to you who believe in the name of the Son of God, so that you may know that you have eternal life."*
>
> —1 John 5:12-13

Have you agreed that Jesus Christ is God? Have you believed that He came to this world to be your Savior, to die for your sins? There is no witness without the Spirit; there is no Spirit without new life in Christ. If you believe in the Son, you have life and the Spirit is the witness within you to that life.

> *"It is the Spirit who testifies, because the Spirit is the truth."*
>
> —1 John 5:6b

"In Him, you also, after listening to the message of the truth, the gospel of salvation—having also believed, you were sealed in Him (Christ) with the Holy Spirit of promise, who is given as a pledge of our inheritance."
—Ephesians 1:13-14a

The Spirit, always there, always sure, bears witness within me, reminding me of my position in God's family, of the love of the Father, of the truth, of the words of Christ, of the mind of God. He is a gift with infinite proportions.

The Truth Is Out There

"I have not written to you because you do not know the truth, but because you do know it, and because no lie is of the truth."
—1 John 2:21

What is truth? How do you arrive at the truth, and how do you know what truth you should believe? Is truth based on facts, is it measured by the mounds of evidence, is it found in consistency, is it discovered through the most convincing argument?

We seek truth, but can we find it?

Is That a Fact?

"Facts are the world's data," says Stephen J. Gould, evolutionary biologist. "Theories are structures of ideas that explain and interpret facts. Moreover, 'fact' doesn't mean absolute certainty, there ain't no such animal in an exciting and complex world."[1]

In the scientific world, a fact is a truth based on highest probability arrived at by testing. A scientific fact is never final; it can be changed or discarded. It was once considered a fact that the world was flat, that the atom could not be split, that man has evolved from something else.[2] (The last one is still considered a fact.)

It is widely accepted that sugar causes children to be hyper, yet the results of a double blind study published by the Journal of the American Medical Association disproved it.[3] In fact, according to a study published in the Journal of Abnormal Child Psychology, parents who thought their children had been fed sugar, when the children had actually been given a placebo, were more likely to report hyperactivity than parents who thought their children had not received sugar, when, in fact, their children had been fed sugar.[4]

Expectations affect our perception of the truth.

We are all prone to consider true whatever we already believe to be true, and to filter any further evidence as reliable if it supports our truth, or as unreliable, irrational, or conspired if it doesn't. I like hearing my truth being proclaimed. It makes me downright euphoric.

> *Expectations affect your perception of the truth.*

We are also prone to believe to be true that which we want to believe is true. "Do you think he likes me?" the young woman asks her friends, as if a consensus would confirm truth. A boy says, "I love you," and a girl loses her virginity because she wants to believe that he does. She's not interested in her friends' warnings, doesn't believe the rumors of infidelity, ignores the red flags. Is that rational?

Juan Diego saw an apparition in 1531, and Mexico converted to the worship of the Virgin of Guadalupe. The vision and interpretations of Joseph Smith in the 1820's led to a religion that has swept the world. Since 610, when the prophet Muhammad began receiving visions from the angel Gabriel while alone in a cave, Islam has grown to include more than 23% of the world's population. Why do so many accept a truth built on the unwitnessed vision of one person?

"Truth has power," Dan Brown, author of *The Da Vinci Code* says, "and if we all gravitate toward similar ideas, maybe we do so because those ideas are true . . . written deep within us. And when we hear the truth, even if we don't understand it, we feel that truth resonate within us . . . vibrating with our unconscious wisdom."[5]

Remember how we thought society would collapse on January 1, 2000? Did you feel the gravitational pull of that "truth"? Oh, it vibrated with all our wisdoms when we heard it, yet that didn't make it true.

184 ◆ UnStuck: Moving Beyond Defeat

The reality of human nature, the flesh, is that we are not good at knowing or finding truth, not as consistent with truth as we like to think we are. We may say that we arrive at the truth through inquiry, proof, and logic, but we have consistently proven that we are irrational, that we are predisposed to believe certain things, and that we are easily intimidated into believing something, even without supporting evidence.

We are naturally skeptics and doubters. That does not mean we are naturally truth seekers.

Do not be deceived in thinking that the flesh will guide you into truth—only the Spirit can do that. The flesh is a master deceiver.

> **"**
> *Do not be deceived in thinking that the flesh will guide you into truth—only the Spirit can do that.*
> **"**

Are We Delusional?

Delusional disorder, according to the Encyclopedia of Mental Disorders, appears in the person who is convinced of an irrational belief to such an extent that he or she refuses to change his mind even when presented with proof that contradicts that belief.[6]

That could describe me a little, but the definition actually applies to people with serious delusions, people who are convinced they are under surveillance or who believe that Brad Pitt secretly loves them. Delusional people might be irrationally convinced that their spouse is cheating on them, or that they have been given a special revelation from a spiritual power, or that aliens have planted a creature inside them that is eating their brain.

Okay, I don't have the disorder; but that earlier definition still hits close to home.

Cambridge Neuroscience published an article titled "The Deluded Brain" that includes recent findings on why our brains are subject to delusional thoughts. "We learn by our mistakes," a group of Cambridge neuroscientists explain. Dopamine neurons in our brain cells receive information and from that information we learn to predict what will probably happen next time. If future information presents a contradiction to the first prediction, our brains should find a way to choose the more likely prediction and adjust our beliefs. But our brains don't always do that; they can't be relied upon to choose what is most probable.[7]

In answer to his question, "Is healthy belief formation optimal, or are we all deluded?" Rob Hoskin, PhD student in the Neuroscience Department of Sheffield University, writes this: "most people display a 'belief bias,' the tendency to evaluate the validity of evidence based on their prior beliefs, rather than on the inherent validity of the evidence as could be assessed through logical reasoning." He continues, "We have a bias towards evaluating beliefs more in terms of their inherent probability (as we see it) without fully taking into account new evidence." He concludes that, since the coded transmission of neural signals is influenced by a significant amount of noise, "differences in beliefs between people are presumably therefore inevitable, as is the likelihood that we all, at some time, adopt irrational convictions. Of course these are just things that I believe, and I may be deluded in believing them!"[8]

So why do we sometimes choose the least probable option? Why do we give more credence to some evidence than to other evidence? Are we biased in our beliefs? Are we predisposed to accept one system of truth over another, even in the absence of evidence or in the presence of a more logical explanation? Others may tell us we are wrong, but we stubbornly stick to what we have experienced, disregarding any evidence presented because it cannot outweigh the bias toward what we are already convinced is true. Sure, we don't all suffer from delusional disorder, but doesn't it seem that we are all genetic cousins to it?

I too am prone to think that I am able to accurately conclude what is the most probable truth, but that is not always the case. The other day my daughter told me, "Mom, sometimes you couldn't see truth even when it was staring you in the face." "Really?" I challenged her, "Give me an example." (I know, what was I thinking?) She proceeded to dramatize an evening at the dinner table where she, my husband, and I were eating. I had asked how the food tasted. She reminded me how the conversation went, "We said, 'It's good, but a little salty,' and suddenly you, Mom, threw up your hands (this was where she got dramatic) and said 'Fine! I'm never going to cook again.' We said,

'Mom, it's good,' but it didn't matter. You kept arguing, 'No, no, it's too salty, I'm a terrible cook. You won't have to eat my food anymore,' continuing to mutter, 'that's the last time I'll ever cook.'"

As I said before, we like to think that we are rational beings, capable of thinking our way to truth. But then, our version of the truth makes total sense to us, seems rational from our perspective. We have all the proof we need to be convinced of our truth, and can't understand why others don't see it.

> **You can't arrive at truth in the flesh. Revealing truth is the role of the Spirit.**

Don't be duped, you can't arrive at truth in the flesh. Revealing truth is the indispensable role of the Spirit.

Whoa, Nellie, Whoa

As a child, I had a romantic view of horses and always dreamed of owning one. When I was 12 years old, we moved to a 20 acre lot in Louisiana and my dream came true. My dad bought two old horses. But when I got close to "old Nellie," as we called her, my illusions evaporated and in their place I saw a muscle-bound, powerful creature who, every now and then, released intimidating power through her nose by loud snorting. I was terrified, but I got on her anyway. And then my brother warned me not to let Nellie step into the fence-post holes that he and my dad had just finished digging, but had not yet filled. The moment I hear a warning, I'm certain that I am somehow destined to screw up. I got extremely nervous, and some helpful spectator shouted, "Don't get nervous; they can sense your fear." "Great!" I thought, "too late now." And, as if she could sense my fear, Nellie took off galloping down our gravel driveway, knocking me flat on my back, but not out of the saddle.

Thus began the most terrifying ride of my life.

I knew that in a half mile we would come out on the highway, so as my head bounced on the horse's rump, I started thinking about my options. How was I going to get out of this muddle? I could roll off the horse onto the ground, but I abandoned that brilliant idea as soon as I glanced over the side and saw the speed with which the gravel was streaking by. For a moment I resigned myself to my fate. "Oh well, there's nothing I can do about it," I thought. "I'm at the mercy of this horse. I'm going to die." I didn't think I could sit up on the horse, let alone stop her. Then, out of nowhere, "do something" swooped in like a super-hero and I did. Miraculously still holding onto the reins, I managed to pull myself up and bring Nellie to a standstill just short of the highway, and just in time to see my big brother coming after me on the other horse.

Sometimes our thoughts run away with us. We find ourselves flattened by the things we think. They carry us away, bouncing us along against our will. Do you ever feel as if you are at the mercy of your mind, that it chooses to run off with your thoughts and you can do nothing to stop it?

Do you ever find that your thoughts have built walls around you, blocking out reality?

> *"For though we walk in the flesh* (as in, we are in these bodies until we die or are taken up with Christ)*, we do not war according to the flesh, for the weapons of our warfare are not of the flesh, but divinely powerful for the destruction of fortresses. We are destroying speculations and every lofty thing raised up against the knowledge of God, and we are taking every thought captive to the obedience of Christ."*
>
> –2 Corinthians 10:3-5

Fortresses, according to Strong's concordance, is not a common word in koine Greek, but is used here, figuratively, of false arguments which often serve as a refuge from reality.[9]

Where are those fortresses that divine weapons can tear down?

> ❝
> *If you go to battle with weapons of the flesh, you are guaranteed defeat, guaranteed to give up.*
> ❞

This war is being waged in our mind every waking moment and sometimes even in our sleep. We feel completely unprepared for it, most often cowering behind the rubble trying not to get hit. Sometimes we fight back, rising up and launching a counterattack, shooting arrows of arguments, only to drop and hide from the bombardment that comes in response. We're feeble. We're tired. We want to give up. We long for it to stop. We want to lie down and sleep.

Oh, no you don't! If you go to battle with weapons of the flesh, you are guaranteed defeat, guaranteed to give up and give Satan a foothold. But you have divine weapons, you have been given spiritual power. Don't bother with whether you feel like fighting; that's a waste of time. You are in this, whether you want to be or not. Are you ready?

Be strong in the Lord. Put down your flesh and put on the full armor of God. Stand firm—with truth, righteousness, and salvation strapped on. Don't launch arguments anymore. You will never win. Instead, take up the shield of faith, blocking and deflecting those fiery darts. With the helmet of salvation on your head and the Word of God in your hand, lies will no longer have a foothold in your mind. Speak truth to yourself in the Spirit, and never stop praying (Eph. 6:10-18, paraphrase).

If you can't remember all of that, but you know you need something quick to help when you do catch your mind running away, picture yourself grabbing the reins and saying to those thoughts, "whoaaa Nellie, whoaaa!"

Unpacking the Mind

As I meditate on the Spirit's role in this area of truth and my thoughts, I find the Spirit bringing to mind other teachings in God's Word about the mind. For instance, "loving God with all your mind" (Deut. 6:5), and "the mind set on the flesh is death" (Rom. 8:6), and "set your mind on things above" (Col. 3:2). We are exhorted to "gird up our minds" (1 Peter 1:13), and to "renew our minds" (Rom. 12:2).

The other day, my husband was observing how the variety of words used to describe the same thing in a language reflects the importance of that particular thing in the culture. Do you know how many Greek words are used in the Bible for the mind? There are six. I plan to explore each one here, so that we will grow in understanding how walking by the Spirit should affect our minds.

nous: [10]

This Greek word means mind, reason, or intellect.

Not every occurrence of this word in the Bible is included here. I have specifically chosen ones that relate to our walk. You will find the form of the word in bold type.

> *"But I see a different law in the members of my body, waging war against the law of my **mind**, and making me a prisoner of the law of sin which is in my members. Wretched man that I am! Who will set me free from the body of this death? Thanks be to God through Jesus Christ our Lord! So then, on the one hand I myself with my **mind** am serving the law of God, but on the other, with my flesh the law of sin."*
> —Romans 7:23-25

> *"For who has known the **mind** of the Lord or who became His counselor."*
> —Romans 11:34

> *"And do not be conformed to this world but be transformed by the renewing of your **mind**."*
> —Romans 12:2

> *"Now I exhort you, brethren, by the name of our Lord Jesus Christ, that you all agree and that there be no divisions among you, but that you be made complete in the same **mind** and in the same judgment."*
> —1 Corinthians 1:10

> *"For who has known the **mind** of the Lord, that he will instruct him? But we have the **mind** of Christ."*
> —1 Corinthians 2:16

> *"For if I pray in a tongue, my spirit prays, but my **mind** is unfruitful. What is the outcome then? I will pray with the Spirit and I will pray with the **mind** also; I will sing with the Spirit and I will sing with the **mind** also. In the church, I desire to speak five words with my **mind**, so that I may instruct others also, rather than ten thousand words in a tongue."*
> —1 Corinthians 14:14-15, 19

*"So this I say, and affirm together with the Lord, that
you walk no longer just as the Gentiles also walk,
in the futility of their **mind**, being darkened in their
understanding."*

–Ephesians 4:17-18a

*"In reference to your former manner of life, you
lay aside the old self, which is being corrupted in
accordance with the lusts of deceit, and that you be
renewed in the spirit of your **mind**, and put on the new
self, which in the likeness of God has been created in
righteousness and holiness of the truth."*

–Ephesians 22-24

*"And the peace of God, which surpasses all
comprehension, will guard your hearts and your mind
in Christ Jesus."*

–Philippians 4:7

*"Let no one keep defrauding you of your prize by
delighting in self-abasement and the worship of the
angels, taking his stand on visions he has seen, inflated
without cause by his fleshly **mind**, and not holding fast
to the head, from whom the entire body, being supplied
and held together by the joints and ligaments, grows
with a growth which is from God."*

–Colossians 2:18-19

> **When you serve the
> law of God with
> your mind, you find
> freedom from sin.**

In summary, what do we learn from the Word about the mind, reason, and intellect? We are told that, though the Lord's mind is beyond our grasp, we have the mind of Christ! We serve the law of God with our minds and, in doing so, find freedom from sin. The fleshly mind does not hold fast to the mind of Christ, but leads us astray to fleshly things like visions, the worship of created beings, and pleasure in self-harm. Before Christ, our minds took us in useless directions, but our minds are transformed when we abandon the old lusts of the flesh and put on the new self, created in righteousness and truth.

In the church, we pray and sing with both the Spirit and the mind, and we seek for agreement of mind and judgment with our brothers and sisters in Christ.

Finally, that is not a typo in Philippians 4:7. "Nous" is indeed translated comprehension, while another word is used for "mind," which leads us to . . .

noema:

This Greek word means the mind, thought, purpose, or scheme.

With the exception of Philippians 4:7, it is used exclusively in 2 Corinthians.

> "If I have forgiven anything, I did it for your sakes in the presence of Christ, so that no advantage be taken of us by Satan, for we are not ignorant of his **schemes**."
> —2 Corinthians 2:10b-11

> "But their **minds** were hardened; for until this very day at the reading of the old covenant the same veil remains unlifted, because it is removed in Christ."
> —2 Corinthians 3:14

> "And even if our gospel is veiled, it is veiled to those who are perishing, in whose case the god of this world has blinded the **minds** of the unbelieving so that they might not see the light of the gospel of the glory of Christ, who is the image of God."
> —2 Cor. 4:3-4

> "We are taking every **thought** captive to the obedience of Christ."
> —2 Corinthians 10:5b

> "I am afraid that as the serpent deceived Eve by his craftiness, your **minds** will be led astray from the simplicity and purity of devotion to Christ."
> —2 Corinthians 11:3

> *"And the peace of God, which surpasses all comprehension,*
> *will guard your hearts and your **minds** in Christ Jesus."*
> —Philippians 4:7

This word unpacks quite differently, doesn't it? Here we see Satan's scheming mind, see him blinding the minds of unbelievers, and leading our minds astray. It also seems to reveal weak minds, hardened minds, vulnerable minds, and desperately needy minds.

I feel intimately connected to this kind of mind, but Truth tells me I have the mind of Christ. Which will I live by?

Let's recap Paul's exhortation to the Philippians. Don't worry about anything, but pray about everything. Make your requests known to God. And God's peace, which is vastly beyond all your reasoning and intellect, will act as a guard, surrounding and protecting your heart and mind from attack.

phroneo:

This Greek word means to think, to have understanding, to observe, to have in mind. The list below includes most occurrences of *phroneo.*

> *"He (Jesus) rebuked Peter, and said, 'Get behind me*
> *Satan; for you are not **setting your mind** on God's*
> *interests, but man's."*
> —Mark 8:33

> *"For those who are according to the flesh **set their***
> ***minds** on the things of the flesh, but those who are*
> *according to the Spirit, the things of the Spirit."*
> —Romans 8:5

> *"**Set your mind** on the things above not on the things*
> *that are on earth."*
> —Colossians 3:2

> *"For through the grace given to me I say to everyone*
> *among you not to **think more highly** of himself than*
> *he ought to **think**; but to **think** so as to have sound*
> *judgment, as God has allotted to each a measure of*
> *faith."*
> —Romans 12:3

*"Be of the same **mind** toward one another; do not be
haughty in **mind**, but associate with the lowly. Do not be
wise in your own estimation."*

–Romans 12:16

*"Now may the God who gives perseverance and
encouragement grant you to be of the same **mind** with
one another according to Christ Jesus."*

–Romans 15:5

*"Make my joy complete by being of the same **mind**,
maintaining the same love, united in spirit, **intent** on one
purpose."*

–Philippians 2:2

*"Have this **attitude** in yourselves which was also in
Christ Jesus."*

–Philippians 2:5

*"I urge Euodia and I urge Syntyche to **live in harmony**
in the Lord."*

–Philippians 4:2

*"I press on toward the goal for the prize of the upward
call of God in Christ Jesus. Let us therefore, as many
as are perfect, have this **attitude**; and if in anything you
have a different **attitude**, God will reveal that also to
you; however, let us keep **living by** that same standard to
which we have attained. Brethren, join in following my
example, and observe those who walk according to the
pattern you have in us. For many walk, of whom I often
told you, and now tell you even weeping, that they are
enemies of the cross of Christ, whose end is destruction,
whose god is their appetite, and whose glory is in their
shame, who **set their minds** on earthly things."*

–Philippians 3:14-19

Oswald Chambers wrote, ". . . thoughts about myself hinder my
usefulness to God."[11] And to that I say AMEN! But how do I stop
thinking about myself?

My favorite ride at the waterpark is the lazy river. I love the sensation of being carried along by the current. Put me in the middle of the Niagara River, however, and I would swim as hard as I could to change direction, futile though that would be.

When I approach the current of my mind as if it were a lazy river, I'm easily lulled into letting my fleshly mind direct me whichever way it wants to, and invariably that way is self-centered. The mind is a powerful current of thinking that reflects attitude and dictates the standard by which we live. If I'm not fighting it, I'm drifting with it, right into danger.

Walking with my mind set on the Spirit takes intention and effort. Look at these two verses in Philippians again: "make my joy complete by being of the same **mind**, maintaining the same love, united in spirit, **intent** on one purpose." and "I urge Euodia and I urge Syntyche to **live in harmony** in the Lord." Unity

> **"**
> *Walking with your mind set on the Spirit takes intention and effort.*
> **"**

in the body of Christ is achieved in the mind. Harmony is a way of thinking, and the biggest obstacle to unity is our self-consumed thoughts. The mind set on the Spirit is a team player. It doesn't seek its own glory, but looks out for the interests of others. If you are living in discord and division with your brothers and sisters in Christ, seeing them as enemies or yourself in opposition; if you typically function independently from your church or tend to pull away rather than bond, you are not looking out for God's interests.

> *"Therefore I, (Paul), prisoner of the Lord, implore* (plead with) *you to walk in a manner worthy of the calling with which you have been called, with all humility and gentleness, with patience, showing tolerance for one another in love, being diligent to preserve the unity of the Spirit in the bond of peace."*
> –Ephesians 4:1-3

phronema:

The Greek word for thought, purpose, aspirations, thought that results in behavior.

It appears only four times, each of those in Romans 8.

> *"For the mind set on the flesh is death, but the mind set on the Spirit is life and peace, because the mind set on the flesh is hostile toward God."*
> –Romans 8:6-7a

> *"And He who searches the hearts knows what the mind of the Spirit is, because He intercedes for the saints according to the will of God."*
> –Romans 8:27

dianoia:

This word represents the mind, understanding, intellect, and disposition. It is the word for mind that we find in the most important commandment the Lord gave us, to

> *"Love the Lord your God with all your heart, and with all your soul, and with all your mind."*
> –Mark 12:30, NIV

> *"Among them we too all formerly lived in the lusts of our flesh, indulging the desires of the flesh and of the mind, and were by nature children of wrath, even as the rest."*
> –Ephesians 2:3

> *"Being darkened in their understanding, excluded from the life of God because of the ignorance that is in them, because of the hardness of their heart."*
> –Ephesians 4:18

> *"And although you were formerly alienated and hostile in mind, engaged in evil deeds, yet He has now reconciled you in His fleshly body through death, in order to present you before Him holy and blameless and beyond reproach."*
> –Colossians 1:21

> *"I will put My laws into their **minds**, and I will write them upon their hearts."*
>
> –Hebrews 8:10

and

> *"I will put My laws upon their heart, and on their **mind** I will write them."*
>
> –Hebrews 10:16b

> *"Therefore, prepare your **minds** for action, keep sober in spirit, fix your hope completely on the grace to be brought to you at the revelation of Jesus Christ."*
>
> –1 Peter 1:13

The word "prepare" draws from the custom of preparing for active exertion by tucking a flowing tunic into the belt to keep it from getting in the way.

> *"And we know that the Son of God has come, and has given us **understanding**, so that we may know Him who is true; and we are in Him who is true, in His Son Jesus Christ."*
>
> –1 John 5:20

I'm humbled by the reality that, if God had not written on our wicked minds that which is true, we would be unable to love Him. We can't let our minds go to chaos; we must discipline them to always be on the alert, ready for battle.

> **❝**
>
> *You must not let your mind go to chaos!*
>
> **❞**

logizomai:

This Greek word can be interpreted a number of ways: reckon, consider, think, compute, or reason. *Logizomai* occurs about 20 times in the book of Romans; more than half the occurrences are in chapter 4 and translated "reckon." It shows up here in my list because of its use in Philippians 4:8.

> *"Finally, brethren, whatever is true, whatever is honorable, whatever is right, whatever is pure, whatever*

*is lovely, whatever is of good repute, if there is any excellence and if anything worthy of praise, **dwell** on these things."*

–Philippians 4:8

*(Love) "does not **take into account** a wrong suffered."*
–1 Corinthians 13:5c

*"Blessed is the man whose sin the Lord will not **take into account**."*

–Romans 4:8

*"Even so, **consider** yourselves to be dead to sin, but alive to God in Christ Jesus."*

–Romans 6:11

*"For I **consider** that the sufferings of this present time are not worthy to be compared with the glory that is to be revealed to us."*

–Romans 8:18

These verses focus on the determination and duration of the thoughts of our minds. We cannot always control what enters our minds, but we can determine what our minds dwell on. The thoughts we dwell on are those that we engage our mind to think on for an extended time in order to draw a conclusion.

> *You cannot always control what enters your mind, but you can determine what your mind dwells on.*

We must not let our minds dwell on those things we are warned to avoid. Just as the Lord chooses not to dwell on our sin, so we should not let our minds dwell on the wrongs that others have committed against us. Just as He chooses not to keep a list of our offenses against Him to bring them up over and over, so we should not keep an account of the offenses made against us. Don't let your mind keep that list of wrongs tucked away for those times you can pull it out to review and relive the hurt. Don't let your mind linger on lies, on lusts, on evil plots, on the ugly, or on another's bad reputation. Don't let your mind dwell on others' sin or on your own sin, but instead forgive and be forgiven.

Similarly, on the other end of the spectrum, those things we should dwell on are not to be wisps of thoughts that last no longer than a puff of smoke, nor to be conclusions we arrive at in a matter of seconds. We should think on thoughts that, like numbers in a mathematical problem, have been calculated and written as the perfect solution, the infinite answer.

Do let your mind dwell on the truth. Do let your mind linger on the honorable, the right, the pure, the lovely, the good reputation, the excellent, and the praiseworthy. Do let your mind think about sufferings, but only if in doing so, your sum totals up to be far inferior to the glory awaiting you in heaven; otherwise, don't let your mind go there.

And stand ready to do this for the rest of your life.

Loving Aletheia

"You shall know the truth and the truth shall set you free."

When I studied Spanish at the University of Guanajuato, I passed this slogan everyday on my way to class. It is a popular saying that has been adopted by many institutions. In fact, this verse, complete with the reference John 8:32, is etched on the wall of the Old Headquarters Building of the CIA.

Why is it so popular? What truth, I wonder, do they think sets them free? From what do they imagine it will free them: from tyranny, from poverty, from servitude?

"If you continue in my word," Jesus said, "you will know the truth, and the truth will make you free" (John 8:31-32). The Jews answered, "We are Abraham's children, slaves to no one; from what, then, could we be set free?" (v. 33, paraphrase).

Aha! Exactly! What did Jesus mean by this?

"The one who sins is a slave to sin; therefore, if the Son will make you free, you are free for sure" (v. 34 & 36, paraphrase).

Jesus sets us free from sin.

He said to the Pharisees, who claimed to be Abraham's children, "If you were Abraham's children, you would follow his deeds, but instead you are seeking to kill Me, the man who has spoken truth to you. You follow the desires of your true father, the devil. He doesn't stand in the truth, because there is no truth him. He lies because it is in his nature to lie, because he is a liar and the father of lies. But because I speak the truth, you do not believe Me" (vv. 39-47, paraphrase).

In *Philosophy Now*, a magazine of ideas, Andrew Warren wrote about truth, "The lack of objective truth leaves us free to carve our own truths. As in Sartre's existentialism, we aren't trapped by objectivity; rather the lack of eternal, immutable truths allows us to create truth for ourselves. Truth is mine. My truth and your truth have no necessary relevance to each other. Because truth is subjective, it can play a much more unique and decisive role in giving life meaning; I am utterly free to choose my truths, and in doing so, I shape my own life. Without subjective truth, there can be no self-determination."[12]

It appears to Warren that subjective truth will set you free.

Our society has come to equate absolute truth with dogmatism and self-righteous arrogance, which has contributed to the call to dismantle absolute truth altogether. According to this reasoning, when we eliminate or redefine truth, we no longer have grounds to be right, and we become a more tolerant and loving people.

Does believing in absolute truth make us mean-spirited and narrow-minded? Did God intend to make His children into mean people by teaching us what is true? Does He support this idea that truth and love cannot coexist? Not at all! He designed truth and love to exist together.

> *"Do not let kindness and truth leave you; bind them around your neck, write them on the tablet of your heart."*
>
> –Proverbs 3:3

◆

I used to believe my emotions, convinced that whatever I felt was true. I never questioned whether my flesh was telling me the truth, but I always questioned everyone else's concept of truth. Now I realize that flesh does not buy and sell truth. Skepticism and doubt are not fruits of the Spirit.

To walk by the Spirit is to walk in truth, to choose truth over all other thoughts, to commit to think only on those things that are true. Dwelling on the uncertain events of the future is appealing. It distracts us from the present reality with which we can and should be engaged. We are commanded not to worry about tomorrow, since today has enough troubles of its own. Yet we keep choosing to dwell on what might happen, on what others might think of us, or on what we can't change. Worrying is not loving the truth.

> **"**
> *Worrying is not loving the truth.*
> **"**

"She hates me," you may say, either to yourself or out loud. Why are you convinced? Because you feel that she does, and your feelings have become your source of truth. To dwell on such thoughts or, worse still, to say them out loud is to entertain lies, and entertaining lies is not loving the truth.

When you blur truth, "lies" don't exist, only misconceptions. That is not loving the truth.

God justly preserves the existence of absolute Truth and yet is full of grace and mercy. In turn, He commands that we be as merciful as He is. It is not Truth that must die but our flesh.

> "Truth is so obscure in these times, and falsehood so established, that, unless we love the truth, we cannot know it."
> –Blaise Pascal[13]

Living by the Spirit will mean an unwavering commitment to thinking and loving truth, and only in the Spirit can you do this!

> *"Buy truth and do not sell it, get wisdom and instruction and understanding."*
> –Proverbs 23:23, ESV

Chapter

13

Walking in Love

"If we live by the Spirit, let us also walk by the Spirit. Let us not become boastful, challenging one another, envying one another."

–Galatians 5:25-26

It hit me—right between the eyes: walking in the Spirit isn't for my own benefit!

Called to Freedom

Before tackling the list of fleshly dominance in this letter to the Galatians, Paul wrote,

> *"For you were called to freedom, brethren; only do not turn your freedom into an opportunity for the flesh, but through love serve one another. For the whole Law is fulfilled in one word, in the statement, 'you shall love your neighbor as yourself.' But if you bite and devour one another, take care that you are not consumed by one another. But I say, walk by the Spirit, and you will not carry out the desire of the flesh."*

–Galatians 13-16

In the past, my desire to walk in the Spirit was mainly motivated by my desires to promote myself, to avoid blundering into sins involving public humiliation, and to impress others with good "spiritual" qualities. The ugly side of my flesh is embarrassing, so naturally I wanted to fix it before anyone noticed. That was my problem. I wanted to fix myself naturally, selfishly.

"Discouragement is disillusioned self-love."

–Oswald Chambers[1]

When I became disillusioned with myself, I would slip into despair over having failed to make any real change in my life. Then I would indulge the flesh in order to feel better, because, of course, what I wanted more than anything was to feel good about myself. My sole purpose in spiritual growth was to hold back the waves of discouragement brought on by failing to be good enough. Missing the most opportune moment to crucify the flesh, I would instead look to the flesh to be victor and fixer, reformer and comforter. I would go to battle under flesh's flag, making whatever "good" I accomplished, whatever "spirituality" I conjured up, done in flesh's strength. Because I would choose to redeem the flesh in the flesh, I wouldn't find the Spirit trailing along, just off to the side, so that, when I thought I had it together, I could switch over to the Spirit.

> **If you're not crucifying the flesh, your're carrying out its desires, and its desires are selfish.**

The Spirit and the flesh do not share the same road. If I'm not crucifying the flesh, I'm not walking in the Spirit. If I'm not crucifying the flesh, I am carrying out its desires, and its desires are selfish.

> *"If you are living according to the flesh, you must die; but if by the Spirit you are putting to death the deeds of the body, you will live. For all who are being led by the Spirit of God, these are sons of God. For you have not received a spirit of slavery leading to fear again, but you have received a spirit of adoption as sons by which we cry out, 'Abba! Father!' The Spirit Himself testifies with our spirit that we are children of God, and if children, heirs also, heirs of God and fellow heirs with Christ, if indeed we suffer with Him in order that we may also be glorified with Him."*
>
> –Romans 8:13-17

*"Because you are sons, God has sent forth the Spirit of
His Son into our hearts, crying, 'Abba! Father.'"*

–Galatians 4:6

The child is free; the slave is not.

———————◆———————

When we came before the judge to adopt our daughter, he
charged us to give to her, and likewise, for her to give to us, all the
responsibilities that come with being a part of the family. When I
received the Spirit, I could say, "abba," that is "daddy," to my Heavenly
Father. I am an adopted child of God, and with that adoption come
certain responsibilities.

*"Whoever believes that Jesus is the Christ is born of
God; and whoever loves the Father loves the child born
of Him."*

–1 John 5:1

> **"**
>
> *The evidence of a
> walk of dying is in
> your relationships.*
>
> **"**

The evidence of a walk of dying is
in our relationships. Scripture shows us
that God is intensely interested in how
we relate to others in His family. As a
member of this family, we are charged to
love the other children. The freedom to
call God Abba brings with it the freedom not to walk in the flesh, the
freedom to suffer, the freedom to serve one another in love.

All You Need is Love[2]

Love is one need we all have in common. Every human being wants
to be loved, but how much do we want to give love? This disparity in
wanting and giving is a problem; somebody will be left out. We long
to be loved, but equal to that desire is our capacity to hate.

Do you have a hard time accepting love from others because you
don't feel you deserve it? Do you find it easier to accept love when you
feel you have done something to earn it?

Likewise, do you believe that some people don't deserve to be
loved? Have you ever felt that you wasted your love on someone? Do

people have limited opportunities to gain your love? It is natural to think of love as a reward.

All you need is love, but it's not that simple, is it?

Our idea of love comes with guidelines.

➢ Love should never be difficult.
➢ Love should bring out the best version of you.
➢ Love should make you feel good.
➢ Love should never hurt or make you cry your eyes out.
➢ Love should let you be yourself.
➢ Love should make everything better.
➢ Love should come naturally and easily; you shouldn't have to work at it.

There are two inherent dangers with this concept of love. First, if real love is easy, then we will think that it wasn't difficult for God to love us. Second, if we expect love to be easy, we won't succeed in walking in the Spirit. We will turn back to flesh the moment love gets hard, and it will get hard.

Let's be honest, we know that love is painful. Love hurts. Love is risky. Love is not free.

"To love at all is to be vulnerable," says C.S. Lewis. "Love anything and your heart will be wrung and possibly broken. If you want to make sure of keeping it intact you must give it to no one, not even an animal. Wrap it carefully round with hobbies and little luxuries,

> **"To love at all is to be vulnerable."**
> —C.S. Lewis

avoid all entanglements. Lock it up safe in the casket or coffin of your selfishness. But in that casket, safe, dark, motionless, airless, it will change. It will not be broken; it will become unbreakable, impenetrable, irredeemable. To love is to be vulnerable."[3]

One day my husband told his class that he loved me out of obligation. You should have heard the girls howl. They were outraged. How could he say that! Love should be wrapped up in warm feelings before it is given, but this . . . this obligatory love, this committed love—it sounded naked and cold. They would never accept that kind of love! I understood what my husband meant. He loves me the way Christ loved the church, and I gladly accept that kind of love, because I trust my husband's faithful integrity to his promises more than I trust my ability to earn his love.

"A new commandment I give to you," Jesus told his disciples on that fateful night he was taken by soldiers to be tortured and crucified. That new commandment is "that you love one another, even as I have loved you, that you also love one another. By this all men will know that you are my disciples, if you have love for one another" (John 13:34-35).

Imagine yourself in that upper room when Jesus said this. Imagine looking around at each person there. What are you thinking about them?

"Really Lord? Love Peter! Have you seen the way he behaves? He is loud, always talking without thinking. He's pushy and a show-off. And I don't think I should have to love John either. He already gets enough love and attention from you. Why should I give him more? And what about that big move for power he and his brother made? They used their mother to try to influence you. Sick! I have never trusted them since, and you can't love someone you don't trust. Thomas has to question everything, and that can get old. I'd rather avoid him and his negativity altogether. He's a hard one to love. Poor Philip, it always takes him twice as long to catch on. He's rather dense, which tries my patience. He's a loser, Lord. Loving him would be a waste of my time."

We can easily dismiss people we find hard to love, but Jesus doesn't. Look at the men in this room through His eyes. Did any of them deserve to be loved? One friend has sold his trust and is ready to betray him; another will deny ever knowing him. His closest friends won't be able to stay awake to pray for him and support him in his pain. And right now all they can do is argue about who will be the greatest.

Do you think it was easy for him to love them?

Despite this, knowing they will abandon him, he says to them, "You are those who have stood by Me in My trials" (Luke 22:28). "But I have prayed for you, Simon, that your faith may not fail. And when you have turned back, strengthen your brothers" (Luke 22:32, NIV).

To love in the Spirit is to love even the most difficult people you will ever meet, without merit and without limit. "I can't love them that way!" you say. Jesus would answer, of course you can't: "Apart from Me you can do nothing" (John 15:5c).

> **"**
> *To love in the Spirit is to love even the most difficult people.*
> **"**

"To love means to open ourselves to suffering."
—Elizabeth Elliot, *The Path of Loneliness*[4]

This is hard. When we think about walking by the Spirit, are we prepared for this kind of dying, for walking in this kind of love?

Did you realize that walking in the Spirit is a team sport?

Loving in the Spirit

Are you trying to love someone in the flesh? It won't work, because the flesh only knows selfish love. The flesh corrupts and destroys love. Think about your relationships in your home, in your church, in your life, and compare them with this list. What corrupting influence has the flesh had in your relationships?

Of others, are you ever . . .

➢ suspicious
➢ jealous
➢ critical
➢ harsh

➢ resentful
➢ dismissive
➢ intolerant
➢ indifferent

To others, do you ever respond with . . .

➢ impatience
➢ insecurity
➢ negativity
➢ competition
➢ self-pity
➢ bragging

➢ gossip
➢ revenge
➢ partiality
➢ ultra-sensitivity
➢ blame

Also consider these questions to determine if you are loving in the Spirit:

➢ Whom can you not stand to be around?

➢ Whom do you make fun of with your friends?

➢ Who gives you pleasure when you see them fail?

➢ Who has a weakness that you recall to mind in order to feel superior?

➢ Whom are you cutting off because they don't recognize your abilities or value you enough?

➢ Who are you trying to impress?

➢ Who has something you wish you had?

➢ Whom do you avoid because they aren't popular?

➢ Who has hurt you deeply, and seems impossible to forgive?

➢ Who owes you?

➢ Who tries your patience?

➢ Whom do you frequently get angry with and yell at?

➢ Whom do you criticize?

➢ Whom do you complain about?

➢ Who has let you down?

➢ Whom do you never pray for?

➢ Whom have you cut-off from your concern?

➢ Whom do you want to be better than?

➢ Whom do you tell yourself you could love if only they were more loving to you first?

> **Jesus commanded us to love others, not to be loved.**

Do you wish that people in your church were more loving? Do you complain about their lack of love? Maybe it hasn't occurred to you that you are one of those people who aren't loving? The Lord has placed you with these people to teach you to walk in the Spirit.

Jesus commanded us to love others, not to be loved.

208 ◆ UnStuck: Moving Beyond Defeat

Do You Know Calvary Love?

> *"Whoever covers an offense seeks love, but he who repeats a matter separates close friends."*
> —Proverbs 17:9, ESV

Once I tried to love someone. I wanted to love this person, but my attempts were met with cold responses. After a while, I gave up. "Oh well," I said to myself, "you can't win them all." I had done what I could; she just didn't want to be loved. Apparently.

And then someone else loved her, and she accepted that love. Apparently she did want to be loved, just not by me. I felt rejected, wondered what was wrong with me, wondered why I wasn't good enough. I have a hard time loving someone who has rejected me, but I had to try again. I wish I could say that I tried again because I wanted to love in the Spirit, and that may have been a small part of why I tried. Mostly my flesh wanted to prove that I was good enough to be loved. Little wonder that my efforts kept failing.

Then the day came when I discovered that, based on hearsay, I had been tried and found guilty of an offense that broke all trust with this person and severed any chance of recovery. At first I was distraught that she thought this of me, contemplating how horrible I must appear to her and how she must hate me. Then I began to feel offended that she had believed this report so easily. I thought that my friendship had been worth more than that, that she would have been slower to judge me guilty, slower to make me the enemy. I burned at the thought that, after all the sacrifices I had made for her, this was how she treated me!

Outraged and hurt, I told myself that I was done. This time when the Spirit convicted, I argued. I wasn't willing to push myself where I wasn't wanted. Sunday after Sunday I sat in church and shared communion, while justifying my attitude. I was right to be careful, right to hold back, right to protect myself from being hurt again.

Was I loving her? No, but I wasn't hating her, so I told myself it was okay. I was excused from trying hard to love. I thought I could get away with it, that I could go on forever this way. I couldn't think of another option. But the Lord wasn't content to leave it.

One Sunday, as I sat across from her at the Lord's Supper, reviewing, once again, all the reasons that she didn't deserve my love, the Lord said to me, "Look at what you are doing. You dare to sit here remembering My death for you, enjoying all the benefits of My sacrifice and at the same time denying one of My own the love I have commanded you to give. Do you think that My love for you is worth so little, that it didn't cost Me much? I never said it would be easy. No, you are not excused from loving her with all your heart. I will not accept your weak and feeble attempts at half love." I broke down ashamed and immediately repented.

When Jesus told us who to love, he said to love each other. He also said to love our enemies. Loving someone doesn't require that he or she be your best friend.

Sometimes I feel that I will never graduate from this commandment. If I had my choice, I would much rather clean up after fellowship, teach Sunday School, decorate, sing, watch babies, do anything other than love the unlovable, other than love someone who doesn't love me back.

> **If you withhold even a spoonful of love, then you're not loving as Christ has loved you.**

If we withhold even a spoonful of love, or if we love based on whether we believe the person deserves it, then we are not loving as Christ has loved us, and, as Amy Carmichael said in her book *IF*, we "know nothing of Calvary love."

In the introduction to her book, Amy says that one evening a fellow worker came to her with a problem involving a younger sister in Christ who had lost the way of Love. Amy stayed awake all night, wondering if she had failed this sister somehow, wondering what she truly knew of Calvary love. And then, one by one, the "ifs" came to her as if, she says, "spoken aloud in the inward ear."

As I read Amy's book, I wept over my own lack of Christ-like love; her book radically changed my perspective on how I love others. Here are a few lines that still speak powerfully to me today.

"I know nothing of Calvary love . . .

➤ if I hold on to choices of any kind, just because they are my choice;

➤ if I give any room to my private likes and dislikes;

➤ if my thoughts revolve around myself;

➤ if I cannot in honest happiness take the second place (or the twentieth);

➤ if I cannot take the first without making a fuss about my unworthiness;

➤ if I do not give a friend "the benefit of the doubt," but put the worst construction instead of the best on what is said or done;

➤ if I take offense easily;

➤ if I am content to continue in a cool unfriendliness, though friendship be possible;

➤ if a sudden jar can cause me to speak an impatient, unloving word;

➤ if I feel bitterly towards those who condemn me, as it seems to me unjustly, forgetting that if they knew me as I know myself, they would condemn me much more;

➤ if monotony tries me and I cannot stand drudgery;

➤ if stupid people fret me and little ruffles set me on edge;

➤ if something I'm asked to do for another feels burdensome; and yielding to an inward unwillingness, I avoid doing it;

➤ if the praise of men elates me and his blame depresses me;

➤ if I cannot rest under misunderstanding without defending myself;

➤ if I love to be loved more than to love;

Then I know nothing of Calvary Love."[5]

The Critical Element of Love

As I meditate on the four areas in which the Spirit is indispensable in our lives, on truth, love, gifts, and prayer, I am surprised to find that they are deeply interconnected. Before we move to spiritual gifts in the next chapter, let's explore their connection to love.

In the four Bible passages on spiritual gifts, Ephesians 4, 1 Peter 4, Romans 12, and 1 Corinthians 12, we learn this about love.

> *"But **speaking the truth in love**, we are to grow up in all aspects into Him, who is the head, even Christ, from whom the whole body, being fitted and held together by that which every joint supplies, according to the proper working of each individual part, causes the growth of the body **for the building up of itself in love**."*
> —Ephesians 4:15-16

> *"Above all, **keep fervent in your love for one another**, because **love covers a multitude of sins**. Be hospitable to one another without complaint."*
> —1 Peter 4:8-9

> *"**Let love be without hypocrisy**. Abhor what is evil; cling to what is good. **Be devoted to one another in brotherly love**; give preference to one another in honor."*
> —Romans 12:9-10

> *"If I speak with the tongues of men and of angels, **but do not have love**, I have become a noisy gong or a clanging cymbal. If I have the gift of prophecy, and know all mysteries and all knowledge; and if I have all faith, so as to remove mountains, **but do not have love, I am nothing**. And if I give all my possessions to feed the poor, and if I surrender my body to be burned, **but do not have love**, it profits me nothing."*
> —1 Corinthians 13:1-3

The body of Christ is where we do our internship for Loving Others 101.

Chapter

14

Walking with Gifts

"**S**piritual gifts are just one more area in my Christian life where I can fail."

That's how I used to feel about spiritual gifts. "Discover your spiritual gift," I would hear, but it seemed an impossible task. What was my problem? Why did I have such a negative attitude toward spiritual gifts?

The Christian life, in my mind, was a demand to perform perfectly. I wanted to be popular and compared myself to others. I wanted to be affirmed by public acknowledgement and praise, even pursuing ministries for that purpose. Frustrated and discouraged, I finally concluded that it wasn't necessary to know your spiritual gift. I only needed to keep serving, doing what needed to be done, and God would "exercise" my gift through me. Knowing what the gift or gifts were wouldn't change that. Besides, where in the Bible does it say that we have to know what our gift is?

So there, on the shelf, sat my closed book of spiritual gifts, untouched for years because I no longer considered the subject useful for my spiritual growth. Then, out of the blue, I was invited to a women's conference in Dallas. God had been behind the scenes of this surprise, orchestrating it like a well-planned con game and I was the mark; only the benefit was mine. Having seen His hand at work, I flew to Dallas wondering what special message God had for me, confident that He had something for me to learn that would revolutionize my life and help me overcome the depression I was battling. When I arrived and heard the topic, my heart sank into disappointment and confusion. The topic was, you guessed it, spiritual gifts. I wondered if God had "messed up" somehow, had not understood what I needed. I was certain He wanted me there, so why had He arranged this topic? Did He get the scheduling mixed up? "How could this be helpful?" I thought, convinced that it wouldn't be.

From the first session, I knew that, along with a good dose of humility, I was getting what God wanted me to learn. He had brought me there so I would know my spiritual gift—of this I am certain—and in doing so, He changed my life completely.

Flesh and the Five P's

Should you know your spiritual gift(s)? I believe you should for three reasons:

Stewardship:

Peter says,

> *"As each has received a gift, use it to serve one another, as good stewards of God's varied grace."*
>
> −1 Peter 4:10, ESV

When you don't know what your gift is, you can't be a good steward of it.

Purpose:

When you know your spiritual gift, you are better able to live according to the purpose for which God created you, able to discern right priorities and even the will of God.

> "
>
> When you know your spiritual gift, you are better able to live according to the purpose for which God created you.
>
> "

Contentment:

When you know your gift, you'll stop comparing yourself to others, stop feeling inadequate, stop wishing you were like someone else. And you will be free to function better with the strength that God supplies.

There are many spiritual gift surveys online designed to help you discover your gift(s); you've probably taken at least one. I never found them helpful, probably because I tried to work them to fit who I wanted to be instead of who I am. Linda McGregor-Clark, the speaker at the conference mentioned earlier, introduced me to the idea that our spiritual gifts manifest themselves differently if we are walking in the flesh. When I got a good picture of that ugly side of things, my spiritual gifts became clear to me. It made sense. I had not been able to identify or appreciate my spiritual gifts because the flesh and the five P's—performance, perfectionism, popularity, praise and pride—were dominating my Christian life. Now that I recognize the ways the flesh distorts the spiritual gifts, I have a better vision of where I need to crucify the flesh and of where I need to surrender to the Spirit's control.

> **Understanding your unique combination of spiritual gifts frees you to serve God by His design.**

So, in an attempt to debunk the five P's, I searched for a spiritual gift survey that included statements about the flesh. In the end, I created my own. Over the past few years, after conversations with many people about the results of this survey, I have noticed a few patterns. I have noticed that, although each person has a variety of gifts, differing from one to another, the combination is divinely grouped to uniquely equip each person. I've seen how God has combined gifts so that the combination itself takes on its own personality. I've been amazed at our Lord's sovereign creativity. Understanding your unique combination of spiritual gifts frees you to serve God by His design, which He created to cause the mature growth of the church into the stature of Christ. It is truly beautiful!

I have also noticed that some gifts are more prevalent than others. Based on my surveys taken in the American Midwest, the gift of exhortation/encouragement appears in almost 3 out of 4 people, while the gift of evangelism appears in as few as one out of ten. That tells me that those with the gift of evangelism are not meant to be doing all the evangelizing. We need those with the gift of evangelism to motivate others in the church rather than bear the burden themselves. Similarly, those with the gift of giving, which also has a low ratio, serve by motivating others to give.

I don't have the gift of mercy, but I know women in my church who do. These women have young children and often can't act on the need they see, so they sometimes call me. I would never think of it, but I'm happy to visit someone in the hospital if someone with the gift of mercy tells me to. The parts of the body need to work together as a whole, and we do that by using our gifts together. If you have the gift of leadership, but lack administration, then don't just build your team with your friends or with the people you get along with; build your team with persons who have the gifts needed.

> **The parts of the body need to work together as a whole, and we do that by using our unique gifts together.**

Four Points on Spiritual Gifts

Here are four main points from the four passages on spiritual gifts that, if put into practice, will help us to deny the participation of the flesh.

1. Stay humble. There is no pride to be gained from your spiritual gift.
2. Let the Spirit drive. You should always be in the passenger seat.
3. No amputee parts. Your gift is given for use in the body to "cause the growth of the body for the building up of itself in love" (Eph. 4:16).
4. Not self-centered. Your spiritual gift is not meant for your personal edification. You can't be selfish and exercise your spiritual gift in the Spirit at the same time.

> **Walking in the Spirit doesn't mean doing nothing; it means that your motivations are radically changed.**

Often when we hear that all fleshly effort must be abandoned in order to walk in the Spirit, we conclude that abandoning fleshly effort means sitting back and doing nothing. Nothing could be farther from the truth. Walking in the Spirit doesn't mean doing nothing; it simply means that our motivations are radically changed. It means, for example, that you will stop exercising your spiritual gifts . . .

➤ in your own strength.

➤ for selfish reasons.

➤ for personal gain.

➤ for your own edification.

➤ for the boosting of your pride.

➤ for being seen by others.

➤ for acknowledgement.

➤ for praise.

➤ for position.

➤ for your own good, your own satisfaction, your own righteousness.

Instead, you'll be exercising your gifts in God's strength . . .

➤ to serve others.

➤ to cause others to grow.

➤ for another's honor.

➤ by God's grace.

➤ with diligence.

➤ cheerfully.

➤ for the common good.

➤ in love.

➤ to equip another for service.

➤ to see maturity in another.

➤ as a good steward.

➤ that God may be glorified.

Spiritual Gifts Survey

Spiritual gift surveys are not inspired by God; they are only tools to help you see how God may be gifting you. You do not have to identify with 100% of the statements in a category to have that spiritual gift. If you see that God has equipped you to fulfill a majority of the statements regarding a particular gift, then it is possible that those you don't fulfill are areas where you need to grow as you walk in the Spirit. Unless, of course, they are fleshly characteristics: those need to be surrendered to the Spirit.

You may identify with a few characteristics of several gifts, but look specifically at the gifts where the majority of the statements are true of you. These are traits that you find to be true more than 75% of the time. Avoid selecting the traits you wish you had. Recognize that any traits from spiritual gift surveys that you find in yourself reflect the Spirit's power, not your worth. You may find that genetics come into play through your God-given personality, and you may even find traces of your parents' gifts. Remember, however, these are not fleshly abilities, but divine gifts empowered by the Spirit. Approach the results of any survey with prayer and seek truth from the Spirit. Ask others to confirm what they see in your life.

Spiritual Gifts Defined

What follows is a description of each gift I included in the survey along with some suggestions for improving your walk in the Spirit. You will find the survey in the appendix of this book.

A. Administration

God has given you the ability to organize, make plans, and manage details. You like events to go smoothly and feel frustrated with disorder and inefficiency. The church needs administrators to help the visionaries bring their ideas to fruition. God has placed many administrators in the church. He is a God of order.

Develop skills in delegating rather than doing everything yourself.

B. Discernment

God has given you the ability to distinguish between good and evil, truth and lies. He has equipped you with an instinctive sense for motives and intentions, and for deception or inconsistency with Biblical truth, so much that you may feel like a negative person. Beware, you can easily judge others if you are walking in the flesh.

Make prayer as natural as breathing; it is the first thing you should do when God gives you discernment. Also, develop mercy and humor to counter the feelings of judgmental negativity that often overwhelm people with this gift.

C. Evangelism

God has given you the ability to share the Gospel in a way that people respond to in faith. He has given you a special burden to see people saved, a unique awareness of when an unbeliever needs to hear the Good News, a gift for sharing the Gospel clearly, and an ability for answering arguments against Christianity. You tend to develop friendships outside the Christian community and may find it frustrating to be around Christians all the time.

Since the majority of Christians score 0 in this gift, if you answered yes to at least four of the related statements, I encourage you to develop this gift of evangelism. Learn how to be clear in sharing the Gospel. Study the arguments against Christianity and learn creative ways to respond. Be patient with the rest of the church body. We know that we should evangelize, so rather than criticize or guilt trip us, organize and motivate us.

D. Exhortation (Encouragement)

God has given you the ability to come alongside those who are discouraged and encourage them to stand firm in their faith. You are sensitive to others' emotions, prefer to work with people one on one, and find yourself getting frustrated and eager to move on if someone is slow to change.

Since you are drawn to individuals, focus on not being exclusive with your love and loyalty. Work on building unity in the church. Avoid thinking that you are the only one who can help the person in need, and making your ministry to the individual more important than your ministry to the church as a whole.

E. Faith

God has given you the ability to know with confidence that He will do what He says. You see God's powerful activity in the lives of

220 ◆ UnStuck: Moving Beyond Defeat

others and believe that God answers prayer. You don't question God's faithfulness to his promises, even when others lose faith or doubt. Obstacles do not intimidate you. You easily lose patience with people who doubt God.

You know that prayer is powerful; pray more! Don't become frustrated or critical with doubters, but rather be a positive witness to God's power. Patiently remind others of God's promises. Set a goal of reading through the Bible every year so that you build your faith on knowing who God is and not in your own confidence.

F. Giving

God has given you the desire and the ability to give of what He has given you. He may also have given you the ability to earn money, or He may use other means to provide for you abundantly. You are God's money launderer. You frequently see needs before others do, and would rather give what you have than keep it. This gift requires lots of prayer to discern to which needs God would have you give.

Learn how to manage money well. Begin developing this gift through consistent and regular giving to your church. Develop a habit of praying about giving, becoming more and more sensitive to the Spirit's leading, and seeking the Lord's mind about giving first. Since the gift of giving is as rare as the gift of evangelism, think about ways to encourage others in the body to give. Communicate needs to the body and seek the help of those with the gifts of administration and leadership to organize giving projects.

G. Helps

God has given you a drive and an ability to serve. All Christians are called to serve one another, but you are especially gifted to see needs. You enjoy working behind the scenes, feel satisfaction in doing difficult jobs, and often see things to do without being asked. You are content knowing that your labor improves the ministry of others.

Keep yourself physically healthy so that you can serve. Be cheerful in labor. Do not complain when others aren't helping you. Since you can't meet every need, learn to ask for help.

H. Leadership

God has given you the ability to motivate and lead people. You see the vision for the group before others do and take the responsibility of inspiring action. You usually step in when direction is lacking, leading by example. You enjoy building a team of people who can carry out your vision.

Develop a servant-leader's heart, following Christ's example. Avoid seeing people as tools for your vision. Learn humility; practice submission.

I. Mercy

God has made you especially sensitive to the feelings of others. You reach out to those who are suffering and hurting with love and understanding. You are compassion in action. You easily detect when others are in pain and think of ways to ease that pain. Because you are warm and caring, people tend to respond to you in the same way, except for those who have the gift of discernment. Your gift seems to contradict and challenge theirs, since they tend to see negative motives where you see only good ones.

Learn to bring your emotions under the Spirit's control. Rather than avoiding those who have the gifts of discernment or prophecy because of their harshness, learn to work well with them. Your compassion and their discernment balance each other.

J. Pastor (Shepherding)

God has equipped you to care for and protect His people. Much like someone with the gift of encouragement, you have a burden for others' spiritual growth, but you interact with people in a group more than one on one. You desire to build relationships with those in the group, nurturing them and helping them grow spiritually. You are not discouraged by the thought of investing in these people over a long time. You are concerned for the spiritual welfare of each, and believe that the group provides safety.

Seek to serve in group settings, and develop skills in spiritual warfare so that you will be better able to defend yourself and the group. Strengthen your knowledge of the Bible and your habit of prayer.

Become adept at putting out the fires of sins that can destroy the unity of the group. Know how to share the Gospel.

K. Prophecy

God has given you the ability to proclaim His word, to speak His truth, and to warn against unbelief. You believe that God's word tells others how to change the way they are living, and have a burden to speak the word to others, holding yourself to the same standard. You cannot overlook sin in the lives of others, and you speak truth in order to bring them to repentance. You are often as harsh and blunt with yourself as others accuse you of being with them.

Read and meditate on God's word every day, to ensure that you are speaking God's truth and not your own. Learn to weave love into the truth you speak.

L. Teaching

God has given you a love for the Bible and an ability to study it, understand it, and make it relevant to others. You enjoy studying the Bible, getting excited about breaking down a passage and observing the details. It thrills you to communicate Biblical truth to people and see them understand it. You love sharing what you have learned.

Be diligent to set aside a time every day, not only to read the Bible, but also to study a passage, take it apart, meditate on it, digest it, and apply it. Your long term goal should be to know the whole Bible. If you aren't teaching anyone, begin by teaching children.

A Spiritual Nose Job

Remember how awkward it was during the teen years, how much you hated the traits that kept you from fitting in. Some of us made it into the cool kid group. Others of us were excluded, pushed to the fringes, taunted, and laughed at by the "in crowd." Many of us moved through puberty hating almost everything about ourselves, angry at the genetic curse that gave us those ears or that nose, a low metabolism, stringy hair, or bad acne. Our gene pool was out of our control. Our design was not our choice.

Like a teenager, my flesh was discontent with the divine genetics that didn't give me the spiritual gifts I wanted, the ones I thought would gain me acceptance, make me popular. Since I perceive love through affirming words, I longed for the gifts that others admired and praised. Just as I needed to learn contentment with God's sovereign wisdom in who I am and where I come from, I also needed to learn contentment with God's sovereign wisdom in who I am as His child and the purpose for which He has placed me in His family.

People who get extreme makeovers on television often comment that now "the real me can be seen," as if what was visible before was hiding who they believed themselves to truly be. We often approach spiritual gift surveys like a shopping list for plastic surgery, picking the way we wish to be perceived, trying to become the person we believe we are inside. "The real me is not like that," we tell ourselves when our ugly exterior of the flesh results in rejection.

By discovering my spiritual gifts, the Lord helped me have better clarity about the flesh, helped me accept how He has made me, gave me a new vision of His purpose for my life, and brought me into a refreshing total dependence

> **Spiritual gifts are practical.**

on the Spirit that I had never experienced before. Spiritual gifts are practical. They are about the body of Christ, about unity and bonding, about growing, about needing each other, and about being dependent on the Spirit to guide.

Just as your physical body is one body with many parts, so the body of Christ is not one part, but many. So . . .

> *"If the foot says, 'because I am not a hand, I do not belong to the body,' that does not make it any less a part of the body. And if the ear should say, 'because I am not an eye, I do not belong to the body' that would not make it any less a part of the body."*
>
> –1 Corinthians 12:15-16, ESV

What would happen to the body if the whole thing were an eye? Think about it. Is there any part of the body that we don't need (with the possible exception of the appendix)?

Do you ever think that because you don't have the spiritual gift someone else has, you are less important in the church? Do you ever feel that you are not needed in the body, or have nothing to contribute? Should you be thinking that way?

Well, that's how others make me feel, you say. Ultimately, who is responsible for that attitude—you or others?

Paul says,

> *"The eye cannot say to the hand* (and this is important, because you cannot say or even think this about your brother or sister in Christ!), *'I have no need of you.'"*
> —1 Corinthians 12:21, ESV

Here is the truth:

> *"The parts of the body that seem to be weaker are indispensable, and on those parts of the body that we think less honorable, we bestow the greater honor, and our unpresentable parts are treated with greater modesty, which our more presentable parts do not require. But God has so composed the body, giving greater honor to the part that lacked it, that there may be no division in the body, but that the members may have the same care for one another. If one member suffers, all suffer together; if one member is honored, all rejoice together. Now you are the body of Christ and individually members of it."*
> —1 Corinthians 12:22-27, ESV

Do you know what surprises me about this? Disparity exists among the parts; some people in the church will have more honor than I do. My assumption had been that unity in the body is achieved by all of us looking equal in presentation, and therefore equal in honor. That had always been my mindset, and yet, the truth is, God will not balance the scales. He chooses for us to learn to walk in the Spirit by turning our assumptions on their heads, by doing the opposite of what our flesh desires. Our flesh gives honor to the greater parts, yet reacts to such inequality with jealousy, division, and rivalry. Lamenting and moping about my lack of honor is not the way to unity. Showing preference to those who have the greater gifts is not the way God would have us treat the body. Unity is the responsibility of each of us, whether that responsibility means changing the way we view others, or changing the way we view ourselves.

> **Unity is the responsibility of each of us.**

Living by the Spirit in the body of Christ is not about me changing my nose to look like someone else's; it's about me being the nose that God made me to be so that the body, i.e. the church, functions at her best.

───────◆───────

Here is what I have come to see as the primary way for me to exercise the gift of discernment: I must pray. When the Spirit shows me that "red flag" about someone else, I must pray. Since this is His gift that He chooses to use as He pleases, I must pray! In fact, no spiritual gift should be practiced without praying first.

> **No spiritual gift should be practiced without praying first.**

Walking in Prayer

Spiritual Thoughts, Spiritual Words

"Some friends and I are getting together to pray and I would love for you to come," my friend Lisa said, "but, just so you know, we aren't going to share any prayer requests." She must have seen the puzzled look on my face—Lisa could always read my face—so she explained, "we're going to wait on the Holy Spirit to tell us what to pray about."

I'm a skeptical person, and her comment produced such an uneasy skepticism in my gut that you would have thought she was inviting me to a séance. Maybe this was too mystical for my upbringing, but I decided to give it a try.

We met on the floor around a coffee table. Some of us were stretched out, some leaning over the table, some leaning back on the couch. We were silent and we waited.

I don't think I had ever been to a prayer meeting where we didn't spend the majority of the time sharing requests. To be honest, I think that was the part I preferred, because I always seemed eager for the prayer time to end. As I sat there silently, I noticed that I was in the habit of waiting, but not on the Spirit. I was used to waiting for who would pray next, used to waiting for my turn to pray. (Remember how you would pass prayer around the room like a game of electricity, tapping the person next to you if you didn't want to pray.) I was especially used to waiting for the clock, waiting for the typical 10 minutes of prayer to be done.

228 ◆ UnStuck: Moving Beyond Defeat

After waiting for the things I was used to waiting for, I found myself relaxing into an easy place of waiting. What I experienced then was a prayer time like nothing I had known before. My heart and mind had never felt this quiet, never felt more free of my flesh.

Ephesians 6:18 tells us to "pray at all times in the Spirit." Can we infer from this that it is possible to pray in the flesh?

Jesus warned against praying like the Pharisees or Gentiles.

> *"And when you pray, you are not to be like the hypocrites; for they love to stand and pray in the synagogues and on the street corners so that they may be seen by men. Truly I say to you, they have their reward in full. But you, when you pray, go into your inner room, close your door and pray to your Father who is in secret, and your Father who sees what is done in secret will reward you. And when you are praying, do not use meaningless repetition as the Gentiles do, for they suppose that they will be heard for their many words. So do not be like them; for your Father knows what you need, before you ask Him."*
>
> –Matthew 6:5-8

When I pray I do a lot of thinking. I think about what I'm going to say, about what others will think of what I say. I think about how long that person is praying, about how I wish I sounded as worshipful as she does. I think about what I will do after the prayer time is over, about what I want to say to the person next to me, about my next task.

If I'm being particularly fleshly, I'll critique what others are saying, thinking about the triviality of their prayer requests, and judging them for the mess they make of their lives. I'll wait for my requests to be prayed for, comparing whether sufficient time was given for my concerns and my needs, wondering why people don't care about me or think about me as much as they do another person.

That's what I mean by being burdened by my flesh when I pray. Frustrating indeed! On this unprecedented occasion, the patient waiting succeeded in letting that fleshly thinking slip away and in its place I found myself listening.

I'm not the best of listeners. I talk to think, which results in a lot of talking. When I'm talking, I'm not listening, and when I'm not talking, I'm thinking about what I want to say next. So, whether I'm talking or thinking, I don't do much listening—ok, I don't do any listening.

You know how it is when someone is talking at you, not with you? Prayer ought to be a two way communication, but it often looks like us talking at God. How much do we listen to God? Do we expect Him to talk to us?

Usually I hesitate to welcome other people's ideas because I'm satisfied with my own. I think mine are good, maybe the best. Why consider another idea when I'm not interested in changing mine?

> **When you pray, do you come to God with a closed mind, unwilling to change yours?**

When I pray, do I come to God with a closed mind, unwilling to change my thoughts? Am I interested in what God thinks, in what's on His mind? Maybe I don't want to know; maybe I don't want to change my plans.

In his book *Experiencing God*, Henry Blackaby suggests that, "what God says in prayer is far more important than what you say," and with that he poked me just where I needed it.[1] I had always felt that what I had to say was very important, so I had never considered that God's part of the conversation might be more important than mine.

What was I doing in prayer? Was I trying to communicate to God what was on my mind or listening to learn what was on His? Which is more important—that He knows my will, or that I know His? Doesn't He already know what I am thinking, even the motives of my heart, far better than I do?

> **Which is more important—that God knows your will, or that you know His?**

Our prayers and our thoughts are intertwined. God has made it possible for us to know His will, and listening to Him to understand His will ought to be the primary focus of our prayer life.

> *"Just as it is written, 'things which eye has not seen and ear has not heard, and which have not entered the heart of man, all that God has prepared for those who love Him.' For to us God revealed them through the Spirit; for the Spirit searches all things, even the depths of God. For who among men knows the thoughts of a man except the spirit of the man, which is in him? Even so the thoughts of God no one knows except the Spirit of God. Now we have received, not the spirit of the world, but the Spirit who is from God, so that we may know the things freely given to us by God, which things we also speak, not in words taught by human wisdom, but in those taught by the Spirit, combining spiritual thoughts with spiritual words."*
>
> —1 Corinthians 2:9-13

> *"In the same way the Spirit also helps our weakness; for we do not know how to pray as we should, but the Spirit Himself intercedes for us with groanings too deep for words; and He who searches the hearts knows what the mind of the Spirit is, because He intercedes for the saints according to the will of God."*
>
> —Romans 8:26-27

I cannot know one tiny smidgen of God's will, whether through His inspired written Word or through prayer, without the Spirit. So I must ask, "Whose mind or thoughts am I expressing when I pray?" Do I start praying by admitting my incapacity to know how or what to pray?

I love the story Henry Blackaby tells illustrating this. When his son was six years old, Henry bought him a blue Schwinn bike, but his son didn't know he wanted a blue Schwinn bike. He kept asking for smaller, inferior toys, but Henry kept working to get his son to want a blue Schwinn bike. By the day of his birthday, his son had asked for a blue Schwinn bike. Blackaby says, "The bike was already in the garage, I just had to convince him to ask for it."[2]

The Holy Spirit knows the mind of God. The Holy Spirit knows what God already has planned for us "in the garage." When we learn to wait on Him in prayer, to want God's will first, the Holy Spirit will show us what to ask for. And we can be certain that the Spirit of truth will not lead in opposition to the Word of truth. The only way to pray according to the will of God is to pray in the Spirit.

> *"No prophecy was ever made by an act of human will, but men moved by the Holy Spirit spoke from God."*
>
> –2 Peter 1:21

The same should be said about prayer: that no request has its origin in my will, but has come from God through the Holy Spirit.

Maybe we need to reverse the customary order: pray first and then share requests. Who knows, we might not even have time to share requests because we'll be talking about God's will.

Praying in the Spirit

Paul wrote to the church in Ephesus,

> *"With all prayer and petition pray at all times in the Spirit, and with this in view, be on the alert,* (be watchful, not asleep, vigilant, no time off, staying awake) *with all perseverance,* (with all persistence, tenacity, steadfastness) *and petition for all the saints."*
>
> –Ephesians 6:18

> *There is only one way to gain perseverance in prayer: through the Spirit.*

To walk in the Spirit is to pray in the Spirit, and to pray in the Spirit is to pray with perseverance. So how can we gain perseverance in prayer? Stubbornness may help for a while, but stubbornness is just the flesh imitating perseverance. There is only one way to gain perseverance in prayer: through the Spirit.

◆

When I was fifteen years old I was baptized at camp, and returned home that August at the height of my spiritual enthusiasm. I was determined to get up early every morning and spend time with the Lord, but I soon found that nothing could keep me awake when I prayed.

Whose bright idea was it to pray with your eyes closed?

Frustrated with my failure, I tried praying on my knees, thinking that discomfort would keep me awake, but even then, I couldn't stay awake long enough to get through one prayer! Ugh! Finally, I tried praying while walking in circles around the island in our kitchen. That worked, for a time, but I eventually gave in to the comfort of my bed and quit getting up early altogether.

The flesh cannot produce alertness and tenacity in prayer.

In college, my husband had the most awful time waking up and getting to class on time. He rigged his bed with wires so that he had to get off it to silence the alarm. But then he realized that he could sleep on the floor. Then he fixed the alarm so that he had to go to the bathroom to turn it off, only to discover that he could also sleep on the bathroom floor. That changed at the birth of our daughter. He was so aware of her tiny presence that he wanted to remain watchful for her every need. He became a light sleeper, alert to any little sound she made.

> **The flesh cannot produce alertness and tenacity in prayer.**

I understand that my computer has some programs that lay sleeping until I "wake them up," while others, such as the one that runs the mouse, are always on, always watchful and alert for action.

According to Ephesians 6, prayer in the Spirit is always alert and watchful, ready to swing into action, ready to pray at a moment's notice, ready to keep praying.

◆

If there was ever a time that Jesus needed prayer it was that night in the garden before he was arrested. His agony was so deep that he asked his three closest disciples to watch and pray while he went off to pray by himself. Returning to where he had left them, he found them sleeping.

> *"Could you not watch one hour?" he said. "Keep watching and praying that you may not come into temptation; the spirit indeed is willing, but the flesh is weak."*
>
> –Mark 14:37b-38

Jesus went away by himself a second time and returned to find them sleeping again "for their eyes were heavy" (Matt. 26:43).

I can relate. I'm no different from Peter, James and John. When it comes to praying, I'm a wimp, not a warrior.

The One who created our physical bodies to need sleep tells us to "stay awake." How are we to accomplish this? Does He mean that we are never to sleep? That's impossible! But staying awake for an hour is not impossible. I do it all the time, unless, of course, I'm praying, or reading the Bible, or riding in a car. An all-night prayer vigil sounds excruciatingly painful, yet how easy it is for me to stay up all night reading a good fiction book. The flesh doesn't find it impossible to stay awake when what we want to do excites or appeals to us. Jesus may as well be saying to us what he said to Peter, "Could you not stay awake for an hour?"

Don't Be Caught Sleeping

The physical weakness of the flesh in prayer is falling asleep. The emotional weakness of the flesh is growing weary and giving up when our prayers are not answered immediately.

> *"And he* (Jesus) *was telling them a parable to show that at all times they ought to pray and not lose heart."*
> —Luke 18:1

There was a judge in a certain city who didn't fear God or respect people. Now in that same city was a widow who kept coming to this judge, relentlessly asking for justice. Finally, the judge gave in, not because he became a God fearer or people respecter, but because she pestered him to no end.

The Lord wants us to see how the unjust judge gave in to persistence. That parable should cause us to ask ourselves, "Won't God also come to the aid of those who cry to him night and day? Will he be slow about it?"

> *"I tell you that he will give them justice quickly."*
> —Luke 18:8a

Then he asks this question:

> *"But when the Son of Man comes will he find*
> *faithfulness on earth?"*

–Luke 18:8b

Why does Jesus close the parable with this?

The purpose of the parable is stated at the beginning: to teach us to always pray without growing weary. Why is He concerned with whether He will find us faithful when He returns? What does He want to find us faithful in doing? Is there a relationship between prayer and end times?

About those last days Jesus warns,

> *"Be on guard, so that your hearts will not be weighted*
> *down with dissipation and drunkenness and the worries*
> *of life, and that day will not come on you suddenly like*
> *a trap; for it will come upon all those who dwell on the*
> *face of all the earth. But keep on the alert at all times,*
> *praying that you may have strength to escape all these*
> *things that are about to take place, and to stand before*
> *the Son of Man."*

–Luke 21:34-36

He has just told them, as recorded earlier in this chapter, of the end of time, of how there will be terrifying signs from heaven, and they will be persecuted and betrayed even by family members. They will be hated by all because of Jesus, but if they endure they will be saved. When they see the Son of Man coming in a cloud with power and glory, they will know that the kingdom of God is near.

A parallel description of this discourse records Jesus saying,

> *"But concerning that day or that hour, no one knows,*
> *not even the angels in heaven, nor the Son, but only*
> *the Father. Be on guard, keep awake. For you do not*
> *know when the time will come. It is like a man going on*
> *a journey, when he leaves home and puts his servants*
> *in charge, each with his work, and commands the*
> *doorkeeper to stay awake. Therefore stay awake—for*
> *you do not know when the master of the house will*
> *come, in the evening, or at midnight, or when the rooster*

crows, or in the morning—lest he come suddenly and find you asleep. And what I say to you I say to all: Stay awake."

–Mark 13:32-36, ESV

What do praying and the coming of the Son of Man have in common? They both require watching, being alert, staying awake and praying with faithfulness. Watch and pray until the Lord returns. Don't be caught sleeping.

"On your walls, O Jerusalem, I have set watchmen; all the day and all the night they shall never be silent. You who put the Lord in remembrance, take no rest, and give him no rest until he establishes Jerusalem and makes it a praise in the earth."

–Isaiah 62:6-7, ESV

Our prayers are to have an annoying persistence about them. Our prayers are to put the Lord in remembrance. We take no rest from them, nor do we give Him rest from them.

Our prayers must also be watchful, anticipating the Lord's return. We pray so that we can resist temptation, we pray so that we remain ready and alert, we pray to show that we are vigilant, we pray at all times because we don't know when His return will be.

> **"**
>
> *Faithfulness is a fruit of the Spirit, so to be faithful in prayer, you must pray in the Spirit.*
>
> **"**

Faithfulness is a fruit of the Spirit, so to be faithful in prayer, we must pray in the Spirit. In the flesh, we cannot hope to know how or what to pray, cannot hope to stay awake or be tenacious enough to pray.

I offered to pray for someone once saying, "It's the least I can do." As soon as I uttered those words I realized how upside down my view of prayer was. My friend's story was heart-wrenching, and there was nothing I could do to help. So out of my own inadequacy I offered the only thing I could. Sadly, I viewed that as the least.

Prayer is the MOST we can do!

"Devote yourselves to prayer, keeping alert in it with an attitude of thanksgiving."

–Colossians 4:2

"Rejoice in hope, be patient in tribulation, be constant in prayer."

–Romans 12:12, ESV

Conclusion

◆

"You'd find it easier to be bad than good if you had red hair," said Anne reproachfully. "People who haven't red hair don't know what trouble is. Mrs. Thomas told me that God made my hair red on purpose, and I've never cared about Him since."
–L.M. Montgomery, *Anne of Green Gables[1]*

There came a day when I realized that I had inherited my dad's temper and my mom's controlling nature. I remember asking God why He gave me negative traits from both my parents. What a mean set-up!

These things were interfering with my attempts to be good, to be loved, to be honored. It would be much easier to be His servant if I weren't being criticized or rejected, if I were beautiful and sweet. How could I do great things for Him if I was always driving people away?

> *Do you fuss and squirm at the circumstances that make your life harder, wondering why God doesn't make life easier for you?*

We fuss and squirm at the circumstances that make our lives harder, wondering why God doesn't make life easier for us.

Why did He make Peter with a loud mouth and give Paul a permanent thorn in the flesh?

Why did Mary have to endure the shame of an illegitimate pregnancy and watch the brutal death of her son?

Why did God create sexual desire and then command us not to have sex outside of marriage and say that some are never to marry?

Why does He let us be born with a sin nature, and then tell us to be holy?

Put simply, we whine, "Why can't I have what I want, be what I want? God, if you won't let me have my way, you're mean."

God and I don't see eye to eye on what my goals should be. I'm working toward self-promotion, self-protection, and self-pleasure; God is working toward my self-execution.

Remember: God hasn't put you in charge of the dying process.

When we take charge, we come with our own purposes, our own stipulations, our own expectations. We feel entitled to give God suggestions on how, when, where, and by whom our execution should be done. So when the process gets difficult, we detour, make a bypass, or take any route that shortens the track. Doing so only ensures that we circle back to the beginning instead of moving forward. We will always have the flesh with us, but we don't have to live by the flesh, we don't have to be stuck in this perpetual looping.

> You will always have the flesh with you, but you don't have to live by the flesh, don't have to be stuck in this perpetual looping.

A walk of dying is the moment by moment choice to die to self, to step with the Lord into the circumstances He designs—circumstances that make us feel weak, take us through suffering, pierce our pride, and lead us to humble repentance.

A walk of dying means living a life of power in the Spirit—power to know the Truth, power to love as Christ loved, power to pray, and power to serve with the Spirit's gifts.

In God's paradigm, only the dead can live, only the dead are free to walk by the Spirit.

Appendix

◆

Guidelines for Loving Others from 1 Corinthians 13[1]

- ➢ Never give up
- ➢ Care more for others than for yourself
- ➢ Don't want what you don't have
- ➢ Don't strut
- ➢ Don't have a swelled head
- ➢ Don't put yourself first
- ➢ Don't fly off the handle
- ➢ Don't keep track of the sins of others
- ➢ Don't revel when others grovel
- ➢ Take pleasure in the flowering of truth
- ➢ Put up with anything
- ➢ Trust God always
- ➢ Never look back
- ➢ Keep going to the end
- ➢ Always look for the best
- ➢ Be kind
- ➢ Be patient
- ➢ Never be jealous

- ➢ Never boast
- ➢ Never be proud
- ➢ Never be rude
- ➢ Never be selfish
- ➢ Don't be quick tempered
- ➢ Don't keep a record of wrongs committed against you
- ➢ Rejoice in the truth, not in evil
- ➢ Always be supportive
- ➢ Always be loyal
- ➢ Always be hopeful
- ➢ Always be trusting
- ➢ Never fail the other person
- ➢ Don't demand your own way
- ➢ Don't be irritable
- ➢ Never be glad about injustice
- ➢ Rejoice whenever the truth wins
- ➢ Never lose faith
- ➢ Endure through every circumstance
- ➢ Don't be arrogant
- ➢ Don't be resentful
- ➢ Bear all things
- ➢ Believe all things
- ➢ Hope all things
- ➢ Endure all things
- ➢ Don't show-off
- ➢ Don't be conceited
- ➢ Don't be self-seeking
- ➢ Don't be easily irritated
- ➢ Don't fret
- ➢ Don't pay attention to an offense
- ➢ Bear up under anything and everything that comes

- ➢ Be ever ready to believe the best of every person
- ➢ Never let hope fade
- ➢ Endure everything without weakening
- ➢ Don't get easily angered
- ➢ Don't delight in evil
- ➢ Always protect others
- ➢ Always persevere
- ➢ Don't brag
- ➢ Don't let yourself be provoked
- ➢ Don't get upset with others
- ➢ Patiently accept all things

Spiritual Gifts Survey:
Highlight the ones that describe you.

Gift A

- ➢ I like to get things done by organizing or delegating.
- ➢ I'm good at delegating.
- ➢ I need to know the purpose of what I'm doing.
- ➢ I get frustrated when a leader is not organized.
- ➢ I think that careful planning is what makes things go smoothly.
- ➢ It really bothers me when plans are changed.
- ➢ I love to take charge of a project.
- ➢ I don't find other people's suggestions helpful.
- ➢ I forget to ask God for help, since I usually have a good idea of what I need to do.

Gift B

- ➢ I frequently question others' motives.
- ➢ I feel strongly about right and wrong.
- ➢ I am deeply troubled when I see others doing wrong.

> ➤ I want everyone around me to see the truth.
> ➤ I spot phony or manipulative people.
> ➤ I feel as though something is burning inside me when I see injustice.
> ➤ I often find myself judging others.
> ➤ I see good and evil as clearly as black and white.
> ➤ I help others identify the root of their spiritual problem.
> ➤ I am usually hesitant to restore a repentant sinner; I want to see evidence of change first.
> ➤ I feel like a negative person.
> ➤ I believe that sometimes people just need a swift "kick in the pants."
> ➤ I tend to see "red flags" when discussing plans or situations.

Gift C

> ➤ I love to talk about Jesus with unbelievers.
> ➤ I get animated when I'm sharing the Gospel.
> ➤ I can easily tell someone how to be saved.
> ➤ When I share about Jesus, people often trust in Christ.
> ➤ I'm always telling my Christian friends that people are lost and need salvation.
> ➤ I enjoy thinking about how many people I have led to Christ.
> ➤ I'm always burdened to pray for someone who is lost.
> ➤ I can sense when someone I meet needs to be saved.
> ➤ I am critical of Christians who are not talking to unbelievers about Jesus every day.
> ➤ I easily make friends with unbelievers.

Gift D

> ➤ People tell me I encourage them to follow Christ.
> ➤ I love to help others make Scripture practical in their lives.
> ➤ I often help others get God's perspective when they are in difficult trials and suffering.

- I deeply care about spiritual growth in the lives of others.
- I want to help those who want help.
- I believe people will grow through counsel and the Word of God.
- I am sensitive to suffering, troubled and discouraged people.
- I like to find the practical application of a message or Bible passage.
- I think people will respond to the truth if it is presented in an understanding and gentle way.
- I enjoy encouraging others to take practical steps.
- I want to help others find the solution to their problems quickly.
- I am frustrated when people aren't changing fast enough.

Gift E

- I truly believe that God can and will do supernatural actions.
- I seem to be more confident than those around me that God can change impossible situations.
- I'm not discouraged by enormous difficulties or obstacles.
- I act on faith when others may say I'm being irresponsible.
- I'm impatient with believers who doubt God.
- I don't listen to people who tell me it can't be done; I trust God anyway.
- I am often frustrated by others' lack of faith.

Gift F

- I will do without so that I can give.
- When I hear of a financial need, I feel great urgency to help.
- I enjoy working at being a wise consumer and a good steward.
- I usually want to give more than I am able; I don't know how much is enough.

- ➢ I want to give to everyone who has a need.
- ➢ I always have enough money, even though I never worry about it.
- ➢ I like to learn how I can support a cause or a missionary.
- ➢ I seldom forget to take an offering to church.
- ➢ I love to give away my things.
- ➢ I like it when people recognize how unselfish I am with my possessions.
- ➢ I often give people money just when they need it.
- ➢ I can sometimes pressure others to give.
- ➢ I hope that someday I can give 30% of my income.

Gift G

- ➢ It is hard for me not to respond to a request for help.
- ➢ People often ask me for favors and I enjoy doing them.
- ➢ I do not mind giving time and effort to help another.
- ➢ I enjoy physical jobs, even if they are boring or dirty.
- ➢ Sometimes I get involved in doing too much for too many people.
- ➢ The first thing I notice when I walk in a room is what needs to be done.
- ➢ Often I find myself helping without having been asked or told what to do.
- ➢ I'll find a way to meet a need, even if someone in authority discourages me from doing so.
- ➢ I am often helping others rather than fulfilling my own responsibilities.
- ➢ I sometimes resent that others are not helping me.
- ➢ I want people to notice that I am always serving at Church.
- ➢ I like to be the first to meet a need.
- ➢ I feel good about myself when I am helping others.

Gift H

- ➤ I like being in charge.
- ➤ At times I find myself thinking of how I would do something better than the current leader.
- ➤ People seem to enjoy following my directions and plans.
- ➤ Sometimes I fear being too authoritative or "bossy."
- ➤ I might like projects and programs more than people.
- ➤ I love motivating people towards a goal.
- ➤ I often have a vision of how things could go better.
- ➤ I like being put in a position of authority.
- ➤ It frustrates me to have to follow another's leadership.
- ➤ It is easy for me to run ahead of God and forget to let Him lead.
- ➤ I get enthusiastic about inspiring others in a ministry.
- ➤ I evaluate people based on how useful they are in accomplishing my goals.

Gift I

- ➤ I am sensitive to people's feelings and immediately notice if someone is upset, discouraged, or burdened.
- ➤ I find being firm and direct with people difficult; I usually feel sorry for them.
- ➤ I am often guided more by emotions than by logic in responding to others' needs.
- ➤ Sometimes my understanding heart has been misunderstood by the opposite sex as romantic intentions.
- ➤ I would never think of reprimanding someone in pain.
- ➤ I enjoy working with suffering people.
- ➤ I tend to see only good motives in people.
- ➤ I withdraw from insensitive people.
- ➤ I am patient with sick people.
- ➤ My feelings of pity get in the way of giving good advice.

Gift J

> - I feel responsible for the spiritual lives of others and give my time to help them.
> - I love being with and ministering to people.
> - I can tell when someone needs counseling and will make myself available.
> - I would much rather do a task with people than by myself.
> - My day is often filled with giving guidance to others.
> - It is difficult for me to make a decision until I have heard from everyone.
> - I enjoy having others need me or depend on me.
> - I feel a burden for wandering Christians.
> - I am protective of those in danger of being deceived.
> - I want to ensure that those close to me don't make bad decisions.

Gift K

> - When I hear error or see it in another's life, I find it difficult to keep quiet.
> - Self-righteousness, sin, worldly behavior, etc. bother me, and when I see these in a person, I want to correct them.
> - I love communicating biblical truth.
> - I'm frustrated by Christians who don't obey Scripture.
> - I think the Bible is clear on what actions we need to take in order to change.
> - I speak my mind bluntly.
> - I tend to see how something can go wrong before it is even started.
> - I am direct and persuasive in what I say.
> - I hold others to a high standard.
> - When telling people what to do, I have to be careful not to go beyond what Scripture says.
> - I believe more Christians would change if we spoke to them directly about their sin.

Gift L

- ➤ I consider accuracy of facts to be crucial when I study.
- ➤ I like to answer questions about the Bible and explain confusing passages to others.
- ➤ Sometimes people think my explanations are too long.
- ➤ Having knowledge gives me a sense of pride.
- ➤ I place importance on what people know.
- ➤ I get excited about studying.
- ➤ I thoroughly enjoy researching a passage, digging into it and taking it apart.
- ➤ Sometimes I appear to have all the answers.
- ➤ I can give out too much information too quickly for others to absorb.
- ➤ I love to explain a Bible passage.
- ➤ People usually understand my explanations.

————————◆————————

Read the definitions in Chapter 14 that correspond to the gift or gifts that you highlighted more than others. Consider whether this gift describes you and begin walking with your gift in the Spirit.

Endnotes

Chapter 1 — Our Obsession

[1] *American Heritage Science Dictionary* (Boston: Houghton Mifflin, 2005).

Chapter 2 — Deadly Desire

[1] Joni Eareckson Tada, *When God Weeps* (Grand Rapids, MI: Zondervan, 1997), 174.

Chapter 3 — The Opposition

[1] Henry Haven Windsor, "Safe Moorings for Motorboats", *Popular Mechanics* (1909) vol. 11, 474.

[2] Amy Carmichael, *IF* (1938; repr., Fort Washington: CLC Publications, 2009), 57.

[3] John Piper, *5o Reasons Why Jesus Came to Die* (Wheaton, IL: Crossway, 2006), 95.

Chapter 4 — Dead Man Walking

[1] Oswald Chambers, *My Utmost for His Highest* (Grand Rapids, MI: Discovery House, 1995), May 16.

Chapter 5 — Embracing Weakness

[1] J.R.R. Tolkien, *The Hobbit* (London: HarperCollins, 2012).

[2] Jane Austen, *Pride and Prejudice* (New York, NY: Signet Classic, 1996), 19.

[3] "It's a Good Day" FFH; words and music by Michael D. Boggs and Tony W. Wood.

[4] Conversation compiled from Matthew 26:31-35, Mark 14:27-31, and Luke 22:31-34.

[5] "Ten Thousand Angels" words and music by Ray Overholt.

Chapter 6 — Enduring Weakness

[1] The account of the raising of Lazarus is in John 11.

[2] Hebrews 12:1 challenges us to run this race with endurance. I noticed that the author, further into the chapter, seemed to list practical instructions for how to run the race, so I adapted it and gave it the name, *Manual for Runners*.

Chapter 7 — Counterfeit Suffering

[1] C.S. Lewis, *Grief Observed* (San Francisco: HarperCollins, 2001), 36.

[2] Joseph Stowell, *Simply Jesus* (Sisters, OR: Multnomah, 2002), 69.

[3] Well-known expression of Anne Shirley, L. M. Montgomery, *Anne of Green Gables* (New York: Grosset & Dunlap, 1908).

[4] Elizabeth Elliot, *Passion and Purity* (Grand Rapids, MI: Fleming H. Revell, 1993), 163.

[5] Webster's Dictionary.

[6] Nancy Leigh DeMoss, *Lies Women Believe* (Chicago: Moody, 2001), 75.

[7] Chambers, *My Utmost for His Highest*, March 8.

[8] David Roper, *The Song of a Passionate Heart* (Grand Rapids, MI: Discovery House, 1996).

[9] Chambers, *My Utmost for His Highest,* November 1.

Chapter 8 — Suffering and Justice

[1] Raj, "Can You Escape Karma?" *Random Wisdom Blog* http://randomwisdomblog.wordpress.com/2009/02/11/can-you-escape-karma/

[2] "Something Good" from the soundtrack *The Sound of Music,* words and music by Richard Rodgers, starring Julie Andrews and Christopher Plummer, 1965.

[3] Shari Arison is the founder of Good Deeds Day http://gdd.goodnet.org/about

[4] H.C.G. Moule *The Epistle to the Romans* (London: Hodder and Stoughton), 63.

Chapter 9 — Perspectives on Suffering

[1] Caleb's story is found in Numbers 13 and 14.

[2] Thaddeus Metz, "The Meaning of Life" *The Stanford Encyclopedia of Philosophy* (Summer 2013 Edition), Edward N. Zalta (ed.), URL = <http://plato.stanford.edu/archives/sum2013/entries/life-meaning/>.

[3] Third verse of "How Firm a Foundation" by John Rippon, music by Joseph Funk.

Chapter 10 — Getting Down

[1] Austen, *Pride and Prejudice*, 19.

[2] J.R.R. Tolkien, *Lord of the Rings* (London: Collins, 2001).

[3] William Law, *The Spirit of Prayer* (London: R. Hawes, 1782), 74.

[4] Parable told in Luke 14:7-14.

[5] Parable told in Luke 18:9-14.

[6] Job's last defense can be read in Job chapters 29-32.

[7] Chambers, *My Utmost for His Highest,* February 5.

[8] Raphael Cardinal Merry del Val, *A Litany of Humility* (Chicago: Loyola University Press, 1963).

Chapter 11 — Turning Around

¹ Charles Spurgeon, *All of Grace* (Springdale, PA: Whitaker House, 1981), 69.

² Herman Melville, *Moby Dick* (London England: Penguin Group, 1994), 62.

Chapter 12 — Walking in Truth

¹ *"Evolution as Fact and Theory"*, Stephen J. Gould; Discover, May 1981.

² Hermann Joseph Muller, *"One Hundred Years without Darwinism are Enough"* (School Science and Mathematics 1959), 304.

³ Based on the findings of a double blind study revealed in the November 22, 1995 issue of the *Journal of the American Medical Association.*

⁴ *Journal of Abnormal Child Psychology* (August, 94).

⁵ Dan Brown, *The Lost Symbol* (New York: Doubleday, 2009).

⁶ "Delusional Disorder", *Encyclopedia of Mental Disorders* http://www.minddisorders.com/Br-Del/Delusional-disorder.html

⁷ "The Deluded Brain", *Cambridge Neuroscience* (British Science Association Brainwaves blog, August 12, 2012).

⁸ Rob Hoskin, PhD, "Is healthy belief formation optimal, or are we all deluded?" *Science for All Brainwaves* (British Science Association, August 27, 2012). http://www.sciencebrainwaves.com/uncategorized/how-delusions-occur-and-why-they-may-be-widespread/

⁹ James Strong, *Strong's Exhaustive Concordance* (Peabody, MA: Hendrickson, 2007).

¹⁰ The definitions of the Greek words were compiled from biblehub.com

¹¹ Chambers, *My Utmost for His Highest,* December 2.

¹² Andrew Warren, "What Is Truth?" *Philosophy Now*, https://philosophynow.org/issues/86/What_Is_Truth

[13] Blaise Pascal, *Pascal's Pensees* (New York: E. P. Dutton, 1958), 259.

Chapter 13 — Walking in Love

[1] Chambers, *My Utmost for His Highest,* August 18.

[2] "All You Need is Love" The Beatles, words and music by John Lennon.

[3] C.S. Lewis, *The Four Loves* (New York: Harcourt Brace, 1960), 121.

[4] Elizabeth Elliot, *The Path of Loneliness* (Nashville, TN: Thomas Nelson, 1988), 83.

[5] Carmichael, *IF,* 10, 28, 30, 31, 33-36, 40, 43.

Chapter 15 — Walking in Prayer

[1] Henry Blackaby, *Experiencing God* (Nashville: Lifeway Press, 2008), 107.

[2] Blackaby, *Experiencing God* 109.

Conclusion

[1] L.M. Montgomery, *Anne of Green Gables* (New York: Grosset & Dunlap, 1908), 71.

Appendix

[1] Guidelines compiled from the following Bible translations:

New Century Version

The Message

New American Standard Version

New International Version

The Amplified Bible

English Standard Version

New Living Translation

Contemporary English Version

A Walk of Dying

Study Guide

There's a weed in these parts called a pokeweed. It grows 12 feet tall and produces grape-like berries that will give your digestive tract a nightmare if you try to eat them. When the weed is tiny, it slides right out of the ground with an easy tug, but leave it to grow just 8 inches tall and the plant snaps right off when I pull on it. To get rid of it, I have to get the shovel and dig hard at the roots.

We've all let the flesh grow too tall. If we really want to get unstuck, we're going to need to find those roots and do some digging.

It took writing most of this book before I realized that learning to walk by the Spirit isn't to remake me or realize me—it's about the end of me. But "me" is deeply rooted in the flesh and isn't about to lay down and die without putting up a fight.

This study guide is about asking questions that help you dig deeper. It may be too personal to share in a group. On the other hand, it may be the perfect study for a group if what you are looking for is genuine vulnerability and growth with others.

Use it anyway you like, just know that . . .

. . . every day is a good day to die.

Chapter 1

Our Obsession

1. Do you need a little "pick-me-up" now and then to feel okay or worthwhile? What would those be?

2. When you feel undervalued, or question your worth, in what ways do you typically try to increase your value or restore your worth?

3. Review the list on pages 14 and 15, and identify the contents of your value closet. Which items do you look to, or try to improve on, in order to gain value?

4. How does your need to boost your worth influence your relationships? Try to think of specific ways.

5. How do you react when your value is threatened? Do you . . .

- ☐ become defensive
- ☐ blame others
- ☐ draw attention to yourself
- ☐ try to convince others you've got it all together
- ☐ get angry
- ☐ lash out
- ☐ mope
- ☐ sink into self-loathing

6. How do you define self-worth and should you have any? Why or why not?

7. Do you ever feel that you aren't good enough? How do you react to that feeling? Do you react with . . .

- ☐ anger
- ☐ depression
- ☐ food
- ☐ sex
- ☐ sleep
- ☐ self-inflicted harm
- ☐ distractions
- ☐ chemical substances
- ☐ self-hate

8. What does it mean to say your identity is in Christ? When are you likely to want to affirm your identity in Christ? When your identity is in Christ, should you expect your value to fluctuate? Explain your answer.

Chapter 2

Deadly Desire

1. What is your flesh capable of doing for you? (Checkmark all that apply.)

- ☐ help you find truth
- ☐ deceive you

- ☐ desire what is good for you
- ☐ convict you of sin
- ☐ lead you out of an emotional storm
- ☐ satisfy your wants

2. In what ways does your flesh offer solutions for what is wrong with you? Have any of these "fixes" been achievable?

3. When we trust the flesh to want what is good for us, we will question God's goodness. In what ways do you doubt the goodness of God in your life right now? In what ways have you trusted your flesh to know what is good for you? Would the Spirit ever cause you to doubt God's goodness?

4. Is feeling good about yourself a flesh goal or a Spirit goal? Explain your answer.

Does the Bible say anything about feeling good about yourself? Give examples if you say yes.

5. Think of some instances in which you have made feeling good about yourself your goal. What has typically been the outcome of those times?

STUDY GUIDE

6. Would the flesh ever make bad things look appealing? What might those things be in your life? (ex. sin, drugs, self-harm, sex, self-condemnation, etc.) Be specific.

7. How does the flesh enslave us?

8. Feelings are voices of the flesh that give misleading directions. How have you been, or are being led, by your feelings? What are some examples?

9. When I want to look good is that the Spirit or my flesh talking? When I try to do good is it always the Spirit leading me? What else could it be?

If what I achieve as "good" is really done in the flesh, can that good have any power to overcome the flesh? Why do you think this?

10. What are the four things the flesh does? (Review the chapter subtitles.)

Chapter 3
The Opposition

1. In what spiritual muck do you find yourself continually stuck?

2. Read Galatians 5:13-26, then review the lists on pages 37-39. What characterizes your flesh? (Write your own personal list.)

3. Should you avoid feeling bad about yourself? Why or why not?

4. Satisfying desires can often help us escape that bad feeling. How does doing this make it difficult to live by the Spirit?

5. How do you pamper your flesh?

Too much flesh pampering leads to obvious warning signs. Are any of these signs indicating an overactive flesh in your life?

- ☐ defensiveness
- ☐ outburst of anger
- ☐ self-pity
- ☐ only doing what you feel like doing
- ☐ bitterness
- ☐ discouragement

STUDY GUIDE

- ☐ resentment
- ☐ keeping a list of hurts
- ☐ running away/ avoiding reality
- ☐ panic
- ☐ hopelessness
- ☐ indulging in "feel good" behavior

6. Identify the positive side of your flesh. Next, consider your answers to these questions:

When your confidence is shaken, what do you instinctively reach out for to restore your confidence?

What do you believe you have to do in order to be loved?

What are you good at?

Why do people usually compliment you?

7. How can you tell the difference between the flesh and the Spirit?

8. How is the flesh making you look good? How is the Spirit making you look good? (This might be a trick question.)

Chapter 4
Dead Man Walking

1. Read Colossians 3:1-17. What comes "naturally" to you?

2. Read 2 Corinthians 4:5-12. In what ways are you investing time and energy in your jar of clay? What have you gained by making yourself a priority?

3. Read 1 Corinthians 4. How does Paul view himself?

4. Read Romans 13:14. What do you think it means to "put on the Lord Jesus Christ"? What will putting on the Lord Jesus Christ help you do?

5. What rewards are you expecting to get here on earth in exchange for your "sacrifices"?

6. How familiar are you with the slope of self-pity? How familiar are you with self-hatred? What is the root of these?

STUDY GUIDE

7. Do you need to confess the practice of self-pity or self-hatred to the Lord? Take time to do that now. Write your prayer in a journal and date it.

8. Do you have the hope of the living Christ in you? Why do you need it?

Chapter 5

Embracing Weakness

1. Do you ever say to yourself "I should have been able to do that"? Should we expect that to be true? Why or why not?

♣ **2.** When we think we can be strong, are we looking to strengthen the flesh or strengthen the Spirit? Is "trying harder" the solution to weakness? Why or why not?

3. What is your optimistic delusion regarding the flesh?

4. What makes you feel weak? Do any of these things make you feel weak?

- ☐ crying
- ☐ losing
- ☐ stupid
- ☐ fear
- ☐ apologizing
- ☐ failure
- ☐ being vulnerable
- ☐ inferiority
- ☐ being wrong
- ☐ rejection
- ☐ loneliness
- ☐ neediness
- ☐ poverty
- ☐ handicaps
- ☐ dependence on others
- ☐ inadequacy
- ☐ not being good enough

5. How does weakness make you feel? Does it make you feel any of these?

- ☐ desperate
- ☐ a failure
- ☐ trapped
- ☐ afraid
- ☐ hopeless
- ☐ angry
- ☐ suffocating
- ☐ frustrated
- ☐ embarrassed
- ☐ discouraged

✓ **6.** Often we feel that if we can't pull ourselves up "by the bootstraps," then our best option is to give up. Why would the flesh prefer defeat over enduring weakness?

✓ **7.** Read 2 Corinthians 1:8-11. According to Paul, what was the reason for his extreme weakness?

✓ **8.** Can weakness ever be a good thing? Why or why not? (Explain your answer with God's Word.)

2 Cor 12:9-10

✓ **9.** Think of a time when God showed His strength in your weakness. Describe how He did that.

✓ **10.** Read 2 Corinthians 12:9-10. What attitude should you have toward your weaknesses?

11. Where does true strength come from? Which are you most often desiring, true strength or the appearance of strength?

✓ **12.** Describe the difference between human joy and Crazy Joy? (pages 77-80)

13. Do you have to feel happy in order to be happy, in order to rejoice? Can you have authentic joy while feeling weak? Why or why not?

14. Make a plan for how you can have Crazy Joy this week. Think of at least one specific thing you can do this week to experience Crazy Joy.

15. Read Matthew 26:31-35. Was Peter expecting to be strong? Did Jesus expect him to be strong? Was Peter set up for failure? What was God's purpose for Peter's failure? What was God's purpose in crushing Jesus?

Chapter 6

Enduring Weakness

1. How would you rate your endurance? If offered the choice of enduring weakness or giving up, which one are you likely to choose?

2. What trial are you facing that is testing your endurance?

3. Read Hebrews 10:32–12:3. What motivation can you find from this passage that inspires you to endure? How long should you expect to endure?

4. Read Hebrews 10:19-25. Describe the hope you have in Jesus Christ. How does having Jesus Christ as your Great High Priest make a difference in your life today?

5. Read Hebrews 4:14-16. What promises about Jesus can you claim that will help you endure today?

Which is more likely to be an anchor for you in the midst of trials: truth in doctrine or comfort of feelings? How can the Lord be your anchor?

6. Read Hebrews 12:7-17

Look at the "Runners Manual" on pages 95 and 96. Which items do you need to remind yourself to observe on the race?

Chapter 7
Counterfeit Suffering

1. What are the "numbing agents" your flesh turns to when suffering or in pain? Why should you not give in to the flesh's ways of avoiding pain?

2. Why does suffering seem wrong?

3. Is it okay to say that God is responsible for suffering? Why or why not?

4. What is the difference between suffering in the flesh and suffering in the Spirit?

5. Use the questions on page 104 to help you make an inventory of your "warehouse." On a separate piece of paper, try to make as complete a list as possible. Review the list, drawing a circle around those things that you aren't willing to lose. How will you react if the Lord takes any of those things away?

6. Do you have rights? What do you believe you have a right to? (See pages 106-107.)

7. Are you experiencing empty longings right now? What do you long for?

8. In the darkness of empty longings you should stay put rather than run, listen to God's voice rather than scream, trust God rather than doubt Him. Read Psalm 63:1-8. How can your soul thirst for the Lord in a way that surpasses all other longings?

9. According to God's Word, how should we view suffering?

10. How does suffering challenge your view of God?

Chapter 8

Suffering and Justice

1. With which of these statements do you agree?

- ☐ I think God should keep everyone from suffering.
- ☐ I think it is okay for bad people to suffer.
- ☐ I think God should keep innocent people from suffering.
- ☐ I think God should keep good people from suffering.
- ☐ I think it is okay for people to suffer the consequences of their choices.

2. Define fair. Who decides what is fair? What unfair circumstances have occurred in your life?

3. Should reward and suffering be equally distributed? Why or why not?

4. Is the paradigm of fairness a desire of the flesh or a goal of the Spirit? Why do you think this?

5. Read Romans 9:10-23

Do you believe that God is right and just in all that He does? Explain why you believe this.

6. Which do you prefer to live by: grace or karma? Why? Which one does God's Word support?

7. Read Romans 2:1-16. Paul is describing a world where only judgment exists. Now read Romans 3:5–4:8. What does this passage teach you about God's justice?

8. Read Romans 5. What does this passage teach you about God's grace?

9. In what ways, if any, are you despising God's grace? (Review page 126)

10. What do you usually think should be the reward for doing good?

11. Read Galatians 6:7-10. Now read 1 Peter 2:20b-21 and 4:19. What should we be doing in the midst of suffering?

Ask the Lord to show you how you can apply this to your situation today. Write specific ways you should change how you are responding to suffering.

Chapter 9

Perspectives on Suffering

1. Have you ever suffered due to the disobedience of others? Describe the situation.

2. How does your pride keep you from finding joy through suffering?

3. Read Genesis 45:1-15; 50:15-21. Describe the characteristics of Joseph's forgiveness? How does that compare to yours?

4. Is there anyone that you believe does not deserve forgiveness? Is there someone you find impossible to forgive?

5. Read Jeremiah 15:15-18. Are you suffering physical or emotional pain that refuses to heal? Describe your pain.

6. Read Lamentations 3. As Christians we often feel that we must hide our sorrow and pain, that somehow we aren't spiritual if we aren't talking about joy all the time. What do you learn about joy and sorrow from Jeremiah's life and words?

7. Does our joy come from looking back or looking forward? Following Jeremiah's example, write your own honest words of sorrow and joy.

STUDY GUIDE

8. Do you wish that you desired more of God's Word? Will your flesh ever desire God's Word? Why or why not?

9. Read Psalm 119. What role does the Word of God play in your suffering? In what practical way can you make use of God's Word? Make a plan.

10. What does following Christ look like?

Are you a philosopher or a follower?

Are you expecting your suffering to end with a trip to the spa or the hammer?

Chapter 10

Humility

1. Review your list of what gives you value in Chapter One. Identify the places where pride has put down roots.

2. In what ways does your pride motivate you personally?

3. Read Luke 14:7-14. Is it possible to be elevated in God's eyes? How do we do that?

4. What do you do when you feel inferior? Do you put others down? Do you mock others? Do your use others' weaknesses to make you feel better about yourself? Do you look for others with whom by comparison, you will feel superior?

5. Read Luke 18:9-14. What is the attitude of the proud man? What is the attitude of the humble man?

6. What elevates you in your own eyes?

7. Pride is the strongest opposition to humility. What hurts your pride? Do any of these?

- ☐ unfair treatment
- ☐ misjudged
- ☐ overlooked
- ☐ rejected
- ☐ ignored
- ☐ unwanted
- ☐ excluded

STUDY GUIDE

- ☐ needy
- ☐ public shame
- ☐ criticism
- ☐ second best
- ☐ misbehaving kids
- ☐ feeling useless
- ☐ being a burden
- ☐ expressing gratitude
- ☐ asking for help
- ☐ appearing stupid

8. What traits elevate people in your eyes? Think about those people you see as better than others. How can the practice of elevating others be a trap for your pride?

9. In what two ways has Christ set your value? (page 157)

10. What should humility look like for you?

Chapter 11

Repentance

1. When you do something wrong or get into trouble, what are you usually sorry for?

Do any of these make you feel sorry?

- ☐ getting caught
- ☐ disappointing others
- ☐ not being perfect
- ☐ consequences
- ☐ bad opinion of others

2. Define Biblical repentance.

Which of these reflect true repentance?

- ☐ feeling bad you messed up
- ☐ sorry you got caught
- ☐ turning around
- ☐ disappointing yourself and others
- ☐ failing to be perfect
- ☐ regret
- ☐ confession
- ☐ guilt
- ☐ anger at yourself
- ☐ complete change of direction
- ☐ not forgiving yourself
- ☐ disillusionment
- ☐ change of heart
- ☐ accepting grace and punishment from God

STUDY GUIDE

3. Do you need to change your mind about one or more of these?

- ☐ the reward for doing good
- ☐ you have rights
- ☐ weakness is bad
- ☐ you deserve to feel good about yourself
- ☐ God is not always just in all He does
- ☐ the practice of elevating
- ☐ your worth in Christ
- ☐ God's right to give free grace

Describe what your attitude should be.

4. Is there anything for which you need to repent? Take time to do that now. Write a prayer of repentance here or in your journal.

Chapter 12

Walking in Truth

1. Read John 13:1–16:15. What do you learn about the Spirit from this passage?

2. Have you believed in the Son of God? Do you have life? Do you have the Spirit?

3. How important is the gift of the Spirit to you? What important role does the Spirit play in your life as a child of God?

4. How do you usually go about finding truth?

- ☐ asking other people's opinions
- ☐ looking on the internet
- ☐ relying on your intuition
- ☐ taking a poll
- ☐ trusting only in yourself
- ☐ asking the Spirit to reveal it to you
- ☐ reading your Bible
- ☐ believing what you have been taught
- ☐ doubting the existence of truth
- ☐ basing it on how I feel
- ☐ researching proof
- ☐ going with the most probable or logical option

5. Do your thoughts ever seem to run away with you? Describe how this happens.

Do your thoughts sometimes build walls around your mind that block out reality? In what way?

6. Read 2 Corinthians 10:3-5. Do you ever feel that there is a battle going on in your mind? In what ways are you trying to fight this spiritual battle with the flesh? What is the spiritual battle strategy that you should use?

STUDY GUIDE

7. The mind is a powerful current of thinking that reflects attitude and dictates actions. Read the verses about the mind on pages 189-197. Pick a verse (or verses) that challenges your thought life in a new way. How will you apply that to your life this week?

8. *Aletheia* is the Greek word for truth. Do you really love *aletheia*? Rate yourself with these statements:

- ☐ I get anxious.
- ☐ I worry about future events, about things that might happen.
- ☐ I am concerned about what other people think of me.
- ☐ I have a habit of lying.
- ☐ Talking about others is okay as long as what I am saying is true.
- ☐ I'll stretch the truth if it makes me look better.
- ☐ I like to deceive others.
- ☐ I repeat sensational things I read on the internet.
- ☐ I repeat rumors that I hear about others.
- ☐ I speculate about others' motivations.
- ☐ I believe something to be true because I feel like it is.
- ☐ I think truth is defined by how I feel today.

How can you be a better lover of truth?

Chapter 13
Walking in Love

1. Do you find it easier to accept love when you feel you have done something to earn it? Do you believe that there are people who don't deserve to be loved? Have you ever felt as if you wasted your love on someone? Do people have limited opportunities to gain your love?

2. Read Luke 6:27-36. Who are we to love?

3. Look at the words on page 206. Which of these corrupting influences of the flesh are apparent in your relationships?

4. Read the questions on page 207 and right down any names of people that come to your mind. Read the guidelines for loving others in the Appendix (pages 239-241). How can you begin to love these people in the Spirit? (Ask the Lord to show you specific ways.)

5. Why is walking by the Spirit a team sport?

Begin learning to love in the Spirit by showing Christ-like love to everyone in your church body, especially toward the unlovable. Jot down one or two specific attitudes you can change your mind about (repent before the Lord).

Chapter 14

Walking with Spiritual Gifts

1. Why would you seek to have spiritual gifts?

- ☐ for personal gain
- ☐ for your own edification
- ☐ for the boosting of your value
- ☐ for the common good
- ☐ for being seen by others
- ☐ for acknowledgement
- ☐ for another's honor
- ☐ for praise
- ☐ for position
- ☐ for your own good
- ☐ for God to be magnified
- ☐ for your own satisfaction
- ☐ for your own righteousness
- ☐ for the growth and righteousness of others

2. Should you know your spiritual gift(s)? Why or why not?

3. Look at the spiritual gifts survey on pages 241-247, and the definitions on pages 218-222. Do you identify with any of the gifts? How can you improve the practical exercise of your gift? Be specific.

4. Do you ever think that because you don't have the spiritual gift that someone else has, you are less important in the church? Do you ever feel that you are not needed in the body or have nothing to contribute?

Read the four passages on spiritual gifts: 1 Corinthians 12:12-30; Romans 12:3-8; Ephesians 4:7-16; 1 Peter 4:7-11. What should your attitude be regarding your place in the body of Christ?

5. Ask the Spirit to show you how you should be exercising your spiritual gift(s). Jot down specific actions you can begin this week.

Chapter 15

Walking in Prayer

1. Are you ever distracted by the flesh when you pray? In what way?

2. What is the primary focus of your prayer life?

- ☐ what you have to say
- ☐ what God wants to say to you
- ☐ for God to change your plans
- ☐ to talk to God
- ☐ to listen to God
- ☐ to know God's will

3. Whose mind or thoughts are you expressing when you pray?

4. Read Ephesians 6:18. What do you think it means to pray in the Spirit?

5. Read Luke 18:1-8. Praying in the Spirit requires alertness and perseverance. Think of one or two specific ways you can practice praying in the Spirit this week.

6. What do praying and the coming of the Son of Man have in common?

7. According to Scripture, what should characterize your prayer life?

Conclusion

1. Is it God's goal to make your life easier? Why or why not?

2. What is God's purpose for your life? How can you begin to live by that purpose today?

3. Is the Spirit guiding you to do or change anything? Be specific.

About the Author

---◆---

A my Hernandez enjoys a delicious cup of quality coffee—just make sure it's dark roast and freshly ground. But even more than hot coffee, Amy cherishes investing her life, time, and energy into other people, helping them treasure a personal relationship with Jesus Christ.

While attending Emmaus Bible College in the 1980s (where she met her husband Joel), Amy recognized the need for Christians to serve whole-heartedly wherever the Lord led. With their yearning to proclaim Christ, the Lord led Joel and Amy to serve in California, Texas, and then eventually in Guanajuato, Mexico—where they helped teach and encourage believers and churches for eight years. In 2007, Joel, Amy, and their daughter Sarah, returned to the United States. Joel leads the Intercultural Studies Department at Emmaus Bible College in Dubuque, Iowa.

By being honest and exposing her struggles with the flesh, Amy has helped others let down their own masks. She has discovered that behind the perfect veneer reserved for public viewing, we all share similar stories of defeat—and desire to move beyond that defeat to obtain growth and victory.

Amy is passionate about speaking truth into the lives of younger women. This sometimes takes the form of one-on-one guidance. Other times, Amy helps lead Bible studies for groups of women in the church. Above all, Amy cherishes her favorite book—the Bible. She is eternally grateful for God's Word which is able to cut through even the toughest, most stubborn heart out there (including her own), and provide practical teaching, instruction, and hope for any who would turn and call on Jesus Christ.

Printed in the USA
CPSIA information can be obtained
at www.ICGtesting.com
JSHW011629270823
47206JS00004B/9

9 781593 872328